D0929947

WITHDRAWN

RHETORIC IN SOCIOLOGY

Sociological books do not consist of neutral sequences of arguments which can be exhaustively analysed in terms of logic and the rules of scientific evidence – in fact what professional conventions require them to present as evidence often has quite other functions, such as affecting the nature of the reader's personal responses to some dispute in progress. These books are processes of personal arguing, incorporating the preferences and perspectives of their authors and impinging on those of their readers. This is not to be deplored but to be welcomed, for reasonable arguing about events in society requires us to acknowledge those of its elements which are personal, moral and political, and to develop public criteria for assessing them in appropriate terms.

This book makes an original use of themes taken from the tradition of rhetorical argumentation, to show how sociologists argue in practice – as opposed to what sociological methodology would lead us to expect – and hence to contribute to the understanding of reasoned arguing in general. It briefly introduces the theory of rhetoric, which deals paradigmatically with the development, through social interaction, of reasonable opinions about human affairs. Then it explores what the author defines as textual uses of example, rhetorical induction and rhetorical deduction. Here it uncovers a characteristically sociological tension between relying on consensus with readers about that social conduct which can be expected and justified, and assaulting readers' preconceptions about what conduct is normal and acceptable – changing their modes of participating in social life.

Ricca Edmondson is now doing research work at the Max Planck Institut für Bildungsforschung, West Berlin. She took her BA degree at the University of Lancaster and her D Phil at Oxford. She has taught at the Free University, Berlin, and the University of Maryland in Europe.

RHETORIC IN SOCIOLOGY

Ricca Edmondson

Foreword by Anthony Heath

© Ricca Edmondson 1984
Foreword © Anthony Heath 1984

First published 1984 by
THE MACMILLAN PRESS LTD
London and Basingstoke
Companies and representatives
throughout the world

Printed in Hong Kong

British Library Cataloguing in Publication Data

Edmondson, Ricca
Rhetoric in sociology,
1. Rhetoric
I. Title
808   PN187

ISBN 0-333-34785-4

For Markus and Tom

Contents

Foreword

Anthony Heath

Rhetoric in Sociology is an original and important book which should change the way in which sociologists view their own work. It is quite different from what we usually think of as the philosophy of social science, and seems to me all the better for being so.

Like many sociologists I have always been somewhat impatient with the traditional philosophies of social science, which generally have rather little connection with sociology as it is actually practised. They tend to be largely prescriptive, telling sociologists what is to count as an acceptable explanation, but they do so from a position of almost total ignorance about the current content of sociological writing and research. If you consider two such contrasting philosophers as Winch and Nagel, you will find that they are none the less remarkably similar in their cursory reading and quotation of sociological texts. They refer mainly to the methodological writings of the founding fathers, and while I am an admirer, albeit a distant one, of Marx, Weber and Durkheim, I believe there was quite a gulf between what they practised and what they preached; and the contemporary practice of sociology has in any event moved on considerably since their day. Contemporary sociology is a serious intellectual activity in its own right and worthy of serious philosophical study.

And this is what Dr Edmondson gives us. She begins by making the deceptively simple, but fundamental, shift from classical methodology to contemporary practice. She bases her enquiry on the work of leading current sociologists – Blau and Duncan, Goldthorpe, Dore, Rex and Moore, Willis and Goffman – selecting their works on the basis of peer-group evaluation. And she concentrates throughout on describing the explanatory strategems which they actually employ rather than on prescribing *ex cathedra* what they ought to be doing.

This basic move leads Dr Edmondson to two discoveries. First, sociological arguments do not fit neatly into the formal canons of the philosophies of science or even the methodological prescriptions of Weber or Durkheim. The practice is rather different from the prescriptions, and although Dr Edmondson is too courteous to say it in so many words, so much the worse for the prescriptions. It seems to me that rules which people never follow, like laws which are more honoured in the breach than the observance, must inevitably fall into disrepute.

Second, Dr Edmondson rediscovers rhetoric. The sociological texts which she examines prove to abound with rhetorical devices. They turn out to be exercises in communication and persuasion, addressed to specific audiences and taking account of the audience's presumed attitudes, expectations, and personal positions, and they employ a wide range of rhetorical strategies which are necessary to make the writer's view accessible to the reader. Sociological texts are thus not to be regarded as formal deductive structures but rather as quasi-forensic documents set within a specific social context.

Again, Dr Edmondson argues that sociology is none the worse for this. True, rhetoric has long had a bad name in Western culture and has been regarded as a matter of stylistic embellishment which is at best merely decorative and at worst a dishonest attempt to manipulate the unsuspecting reader. But Dr Edmondson tries to rescue rhetoric from its bad reputation and return to an earlier tradition, Aristotelian in origin, which viewed it not as 'a technology of manipulation but an exploration of reasonable intersubjective communication in society'. In this sense, the techniques of rhetoric are used, indeed are essential, in order to enable the reader to grasp for himself or herself, to appreciate, the meaning of what is being said. Dr Edmondson's point is that the subject matter of sociology itself requires the use of such techniques. In the interpretive approach to sociological explanation, for example, it is not enough for the sociologist to understand the subject; the understanding must be communicated to the reader in such a way that he or she can perform essential parts of constructing the account which the author offers. And the reader's position as a member of a similar social world to those of the writer and the subject poses constraints and conditions on the form that that communication can take. Sociological explanation, therefore, cannot be divorced from sociological communication. They are inevitably linked together.

The great interest of *Rhetoric in Sociology* is in Dr Edmondson's demonstration of how this communication is actually carried out – of the explanatory-cum-communicative techniques which contemporary sociologists of all schools, not just the interpretive, use. The ideal type, for example, is a standard explanatory device in the sociologist's repertoire, much discussed by philosophers and methodologists, but Dr Edmondson shows that in practice sociologists make a great deal more use of related, but distinctly different, devices which she terms 'actual types' and 'epitomes'. In place of the formal deductive argument she shows that sociologists use the 'enthymeme', a method of 'reasonable inference' first described by Aristotle. Simultaneously she discusses the techniques of 'rhetorical induction'. And in place of formal models of rational action sociologists make much more use of commonsense notions of 'the ordinary person' and 'the reasonable person'. What all these techniques have in common is that they depend on particular taken-for-granted assumptions about the way in which people behave, assumptions which must be shared by both reader and writer if the explanatory argument is to convince. It is for this reason that sociological explanation must be seen as a social activity, not as an exclusively logical or statistical one.

Dr Edmondson's aim is not to reform the practice of sociology but to bring our preaching more into line with the practice. She would like to deflect us from ambitions to be natural scientists and to offer us a methodology which is more true to the nature of our own subject. She would, I am sure, like us to accept the epitome and enthymeme as legitimate and indeed essential tools of our trade. I find this a refreshing – and persuasive – change from our usual fare.

Jesus College, Oxford

Preface

I first came to sociology from philosophy, when I was confronted almost at once by two problems. First, I was unable to make much connection between sociological methodology and what seemed to me convincing and explanatory in sociological books. The aspects of sociological texts which struck me most seemed to have no counterparts in the theoretical accounts of what sociologists ought to do. Second, when I tried to write up some fieldwork of my own I found that I had accumulated a number of experiences which seemed to me important but which, according to these theoretical prescriptions, had no place in a sociological report. I became very puzzled about what it is that sociologists really do, and in order to find out I set to work to examine their actual practice as it is revealed in the texts they write.

In order to describe this practice here I have used concepts taken from the tradition of rhetoric – where 'rhetoric' means the study and exercise of arguing in such a way as to make what one says plausible and accessible to one's hearer, to bring it home to him or her – in a manner which enhances the hearer's ability to make what one says an independent part of his or her own perceptions and decisions. Since this is a conception of rhetoric which differs from everyday, more pejorative uses of the term, I explain its origin and functions in the Introduction and Chapter 1.

The remainder of the book shows what difference rhetorical notions make to our conception of what sociological writing is, and to methodological prescriptions about it; not least prescriptions about textual evidence, objectivity and understanding. In the end two things have interested me most: the integral and legitimate place of rhetoric in understanding and reasoning about events in the social world, and the implications this has for the roles of feeling, personal reaction, and moral and political judgement in sociology.

I should like to thank Alessandro Pizzorno for first suggesting that the textual phenomena I was talking about might be rhetorical ones; and for their advice and support since that time I should like to thank Angela Cunningham, John H. Goldthorpe, Anthony Heath, Christel Hopf, Klaus Jacobi, Russell Keat, John and Aveen Maguire, Markus Wörner, as well as my D Phil examiners, Kenneth MacDonald and Herminio Martins; and my editor, Anne-Lucie Norton.

For making it much easier and pleasanter to combine writing a book with family life I should like to thank Anke Bauer, Eileen Edmondson and Barbara Otto.

Any errors which this book may contain are almost certainly not the faults of the people mentioned above. I am relieved to be able to say that if my theories are correct, at least some of them may have been contributed by the reader.

R. E.

Acknowledgements

The quotations from John Rex and Robert Moore, *Race, Community and Conflict: A Study of Sparkbrook*, © Institute of Race Relations 1967, are reproduced by permission of Oxford University Press; those from Goldthorpe *et al.*, the *Affluent Worker* series, 1968–69, by permission of Cambridge University Press.

Introduction

Debates about the nature of social science and the explanations it provides focus exclusively on 'theories' and what these theories are *about*; they ignore the relationship between theories put forward by particular proponents and those to whom the theories are addressed.

Positivists have claimed that the logic of theory-testing and evidence is identical in the social and the natural sciences, but they ignore the way in which this logic comes to function from the reader's standpoint – the way in which the reader assimilates the meaning of a theory and becomes persuaded of its acceptability. Interpretivists have emphasised the need for sociologists to understand their subjects; they have failed to realise that the reader too must come to understand this understanding. Explanations are not only about something; they are *for someone*. This book explores some of the considerable implications of this fact.

This is not an enquiry which is intended to replace the standard methodological forms, but neither can it be kept strictly separate from them. This is partly because what is basic to sociological writing is an actual process of arguing, not the abstract argumentative forms filtered out from this process to which attention is usually directed. But I shall show too that reading sociological books as cases of arguing between people undermines assumptions which are customary and crucial in methodological debate.

Discussions of the problem of objectivity versus value-ladenness take it that values enter sociology at the level of choice of subject-matter, or in terms of specific concepts, claims or judgements, or even in terms of an author's selection of theoretical framework. But the approach to texts I shall take here shows that 'values' operate in a much more systematic and ineliminable manner than any of these discussions show – evaluative positions are properties of communicative processes as a whole.

Similarly, induction and deduction in sociology are characteristically argumentative processes; because of this they cannot be properly justified or understood in terms of 'pure' logic, but they become entirely comprehensible when the roles played in them by author and reader are taken into account. Citations of evidence in sociological texts do not in general serve the purpose of support for theories, abstractly conceived; their presence can more often be explained in terms of what the reader needs to experience in connection with the author or some particular stage in his arguing. Sociological understanding is not merely a process of entering into the position of the subject; it is a method of making his or her conduct assimilable by the reader.

What I have said implies that there is a striking contrast between the ways in which sociological arguing actually goes on and what it is *taken* to be like, not least by its authors. But I do not want to assert that this means that sociology is in some way not what it ought to be.

The deviations from conventional methodology which are examined in this book have a common character: they deal much more with personal events, attitudes or reactions than their authors' theoretical positions would justify. Because of this, though not only because of it, I claim that the sociological arguing I investigate takes place in terms of 'personal communication'. This type of communication is not necessarily irrational, unscientific or unduly biased. It is simply more closely connected with the personal existences of author, subjects and reader than most current assumptions about academic writing imply.

It is my view that this form of communication is highly appropriate to sociology, as the study of the social and political organisation of people. The analytical concepts introduced in this book can be used for examining and evaluating – often positively – what goes on in this type of communication. They should be used to replace those more abstract components of methodological theories which they contradict.

It is not surprising that positivist methodologies are lacking in responsiveness to a conception of communication which emphasises that it develops between *people*, but this unresponsiveness is pervasive in interpretivism too. It might have been expected that we could turn to Weber for a treatment of hermeneutic questions about people's reception of sociological texts. This expectation would be consonant with Weber's emphasis on understanding subjective social action, but it would none the less be disappointed. This seems to me connected with the philosophical anthropology underlying his views, and his distrust of the fluid and flexible aspects of human nature which are reflected in argumentative processes. Weber's ideal of interpersonal understanding would, he says, be attained if the other's motives were formulable in logical and mathematical terms;[1] his own recalls Jarvie's view of human beings as essentially 'trying, striving, attempting, aiming'[2] – just as the Protestant Ethic says that they ought. This means that he is guided by a notion of human activity which poses fewer communicative problems the more the sociologist can understand it.

This is consistent with Weber's siting of conduct whose univocal description would be difficult on the very borderline of the category of the meaningful.[3] It is consistent too with the inhospitality of his explanatory schemata towards activity which cannot easily be conceptualised in goal-directed terms.[4] For him the understanding which is characteristically to be reflected in sociological texts is that which arises when someone else 'tries to achieve certain ends by choosing appropriate means on the basis of the facts of the situation, as experience has accustomed us to interpret them'.[5] And Rex gives it as his opinion that Weber's 'most lasting contribution to sociology' was his elaboration of 'a systematic formal sociological language in terms of which comparisons could be made between one sociological system and another' so that concepts could be operationalised and tested.[6] That is, understanding is a matter between the sociologist and the subject, and theories are to be compared in terms of formal criteria. The sociologist's communication with the reader does not enter the question.

Even in that version of Weber's ideal type which explicitly concentrates on attributing subjective meaning to someone else,[7] his interest is restricted to the sociologist's recognition of a ' "typical" complex of meaning'.[8] He is not interested in the problems involved in getting the *reader* to recognise it. Textual items which in fact help here, such as quotations of subjects' utterances, should on Weber's view be displayed only if they possess the character of strict evidence. His own quotations play a different role – those from Benjamin Franklin in Chapter 2 of *The Protestant Ethic*, for instance,[9] show us what sort of documents have made an impression on the author, and what feelings he wants the reader to experience in connection with what they say. But this is only one of many cases in which sociologists' texts in practice diverge from their own methodological specifications.

For anyone hoping to turn from positivist to interpretive writers for some recognition of personal factors in arguing, it is instructive to find that Alfred Schutz, celebrated for perceiving a remarkably richly populated world of social action, commends a scientistic style for sociological writing. Schutz claims that for the sociologist the social world is 'not of practical but merely of cognitive interest'.[10] This claim is scarcely based on an exhaustive dichotomy, but Schutz infers from it that the enquiries of the social scientist need not differ greatly in style from those of the natural scientist. He in fact declares his own methodology compatible with that of the positivist writer Ernest Nagel.[11] Yet the greatest concession among prominent positivists to the question of taking the reader into account is contributed by Hempel – who simply mentions semi-justifiable types of incompleteness which occur when a hypothetico-deductive argument is stated 'informally'.[12]

The most obvious reason for this reluctance to allow the reader an influence on texts is the fear that it would threaten sociological objectivity, and this is a question with which I shall deal in the course of this book. It is worth noting here that this fear does not stem purely from methodological considerations, but is also associated with attitudes, or prejudices, arising from very ancient feelings about the nature of human beings and of language. These views also form appropriate accompaniments to the development of sociology as, like other university pursuits, a chiefly male profession.

First, there is a long history of distrusting the capacities of the malleable human being, formed by and dependent on so many social influences, to purvey correct and unbiased views without strong measures to fortify him and his language.[13] This distrust fits well with a conception of language such as that proposed by Locke and which retains much popularity today – namely the view that linguistic conventions are there to aid the smooth transference of ideas from mind to mind by diminishing the influence of language upon thought. Locke holds this to fail 'when any word does not excite in the hearer the same idea which it stands for in the mind of the speaker'.[14] These views of people and of language unite when, to combat the effects of human unreliability, it is proposed to purge away the results of transient feeling and impressions so that speech and truth coincide. Thus in Locke's time Bishop Sprat praised the 'primitive purity and shortness' of scientific language, in which 'men deliver'd so many *things* almost in an equal number of *words*.'[15]

The notion that utter plainness – whatever exactly this may mean – is an optimal communicational characteristic is one which might be supposed to lend itself to a pursuit developing its own *Fachsprache* within the confines of the predominantly 'male' cultural values of recent times. A stereotype of academic maleness in terms of avoiding emotion, imagination, changeableness and spontaneity is well expressible in this type of language. But taking this stereotype seriously seems to me liable to cause confusion between scientific impartiality and the attempt to create a style which disguises the fact that its author is a person at all (a confusion exemplified in some ethnomethodological texts[16]). As a matter of fact impartiality is a *personal* characteristic, not an abandonment of all standards and preferences but in some sense an achievement of balance between them.

Since this is so, it is not surprising that many sociologists in practice fail to suppress all signs of personal communication in what they write. Nor is it a cause for disapprobation before these personal elements have been assessed in terms which are appropriate to them and their contexts. In order to do this, I propose to use concepts derived mainly from a single source: that of the tradition of rhetoric.

1 THE RHETORICAL TRADITION

Here I take the rhetorical approach to language to concern argumentative procedures which are used in, and responsive to, specific communication situations, in order to make contentions suasive for their hearers or readers. I use the term 'suasion' to refer to the immediate aim of all arguing, and should account for its meaning in terms of a distinction in addition to that between merely conveying information with no additional interactive intentions at all, and saying something so as to get the other person to show some reaction or take up some course of action. In between these two there is communication in order that what is said should mean something to its recipient, that its significance should be appreciated, that it should come home to the other person.

Here I mean much less than what Habermas and other writers seem to mean by *Verständigung*.[17] I do not claim that arguing necessarily aims at agreement or community of purpose, but I do take arguers standardly to want the import of what they say to impinge on others, to be taken seriously by them. Rhetorical analysis – which this book tries both to explore and to test – shows that even the relatively modest aim of suasion involves interaction

on more levels than those which sociological methodology generally
anticipates; and on some which it proscribes.

In terms of the rhetorical tradition on which I am relying here
then, rhetorical (per)suasion does not entail arbitrary, insufficien
or morally dubious means of getting others to do or believe
something. It is concerned with discovering in a subject aspect
which aid one's interlocutor's grasp of it,[18] enabling this interlocu
tor to arrive at a convinced judgement of his or her own. Gadame:
says that rhetoric presents considerations which are *einleuchtend*:[1]
plausible in such a way as to illuminate the question for the hearer
It deals with some of the ways in which communication can be
made to matter to the person receiving it. This, presumably, is wha
people mean or ought to mean when they say that rhetoric i
concerned with how language 'becomes effective'.[20]

In ordinary interaction – and it will be seen that this applies to
sociology too – it is neither usual nor useful to frame one's remarks in
total disregard of the type of person one is addressing. A speaker or
writer cannot communicate normally if he is unresponsive to the
opportunities and limitations of the case he is dealing with and
the situation in which he is doing it. Aristotle, the author of one of
the oldest extant works on rhetoric, claims that 'it is . . . the hearer
that determines the speech's end and object;'[21] the hearer is also the
judge of what is said. Plato, though he is sometimes misrepresented a
an opponent of rhetoric in all its forms,[22] does not deny that righ
reasons can and should be expressed in a mode of speech apposite to
the person addressed.[23]

Aristotle heads a tradition in which rhetoric is not a technology of
manipulation but an exploration of reasonable intersubjective
communication in society.[24] The Roman, 'Ciceronian' stage of this
tradition (from about a century before to a century after the birth of
Christ) emphasises that rhetoric is a branch of politics, and relates i
chiefly to practical oratory. From this part of the tradition come the
argumentative 'figures' mentioned in Chapter 1 below, as well a:
the notion of alterations in words or expressions for the sake of
ornament. But both Cicero and Quintilian stress that the use of
rhetoric presupposes a knowledge of philosophy and of humar
nature, and properly functions as a civilising influence. If grammar
deals with *correct* speaking – and interpreting the poets – rhetori
deals with speaking *well*, in all senses of the word. Quintiliar
incorporates into his treatise on rhetoric a method for educating the
ideal speaker and citizen (c. 92 AD).[25]

After the Second Sophistic in Rome, which is usually considered a period of decay, the study of rhetoric passes to St Augustine (AD 354–430), who himself was educated in the Ciceronian tradition and who had an immense influence on the Middle Ages. In opposition to many Church Fathers, Augustine sees that it cannot be assumed that someone who perceives what is true will automatically be able to communicate it to others. For him, rhetoric is to be used to trigger off learning (about God) on the hearer's part. It is facilitated by a special relationship between speaker and hearer; not just one of well-disposedness, as Aristotle puts it, but one of love.[26]

The idea of rhetoric was kept alive by writers such as Boethius, Isidore of Seville, Alcuin, then Rabanus Maurus in the ninth century. Though Aristotle's *Rhetoric* was rediscovered in the thirteenth century, Ciceronian rhetoric was dominant in the Middle Ages, when the fields of grammar and rhetoric covered an enormous variety of linguistic enquiries, both analytical and preceptive. Two important medieval applications of rhetoric concerned the composition of letters to different people in different social positions, and preaching. The latter produced a welter of practical and theoretical research on the division of addresses into standardised arrangements of parts, and it also incorporated into the tradition some of the Hebrew experience of rhetoric as woven into the texture of communal life.[27]

Quintilian, as well as the *Rhetorica ad Herennium*[28] and previously lost works by Cicero, was rediscovered in the early fifteenth century. These works exercised a great influence on the Renaissance because of the synthesis they offered in contrast to the analytical divisions of the Middle Ages, and because of their perception of rhetoric as part of a coherent social system entailing a respect for civic life. At this period too there was an emphasis on the education of the good man, and the rhetorical speaker was perceived in his capacity as a morally involved agent.[29] This perception could of course be used in different ways; Erasmus saw rhetoric as a potential force for good in itself, Luther as a means to goodness inculcated by God.[30]

In the mid-sixteenth century, however, Petrus Ramus took up objections to the similarity which had grown up between the disciplines of rhetoric and logic, and initiated a widely accepted educational 'reform'. Logic was to be taught as dealing with the invention and arrangement of material, and rhetoric as concerned only with style and delivery.[31] This destroyed the crucial rhetorical insights into the connections between form and substance in communication, but at the time it was welcomed by people who had independently developed an overwhelming interest in style. Representative of the stylists is George Puttenham, writing in 1589, who treats rhetoric as *only* a matter of linguistic deviations from normality, for the sake of ornament.[32] This is an attitude which survives today in many quarters but which will not be adopted here.[33]

The original approach to rhetoric was continued in modernised form by writers such as Fénelon, and in eighteenth-century Scotland and nineteenth-century America,[34] but in general terms it faded from view in Europe during the eighteenth century – for reasons which are usually linked to the predominance of Cartesian rationalism.[35] The revival of rhetoric in the middle of this century has resulted in a variety of treatments, but new interest in the argumentative tradition outlined here was initiated chiefly by Perelman and Olbrechts-Tyteca (see below) in 1958.[36]

In sociology it tends to be assumed that the written texts produced in the discipline are affected chiefly by what the writer thinks about the subject. Rhetoric, as it is presented here, yields an analysis of communication in terms of the relations between writer, reader, situation and subject-matter – with many more allowances for the reader's role than conventional methodological discussion can provide. It is thus able to take account of the fact that readers of sociology have peculiarly intimate and engulfing connections with its subject-matter; in a sense its readers are reading about themselves, or at any rate about their own social worlds. This closeness means that suasion in sociological matters presents its own special problems, with which rhetoric is able to deal. It can take account, too, of the fact that authors are – for good or ill – exposed to pressures from their subjects, their readers, and the socio-political contexts in which they write; developing sociological argument is shaped by situational influences apart from the author's theoretical approach to his subject.

This is a concatenation of factors which has its own implications for sociological meaning and objectivity. It implies that if sociological texts are to mean anything to their readers – in any sense but one so narrow as to be self-defeating – they must be constructed and judged at least partly in the social, moral, political and emotional terms connected with suasiveness; even if these vary in relation to different situations and audiences. In terms of the rhetorical tradition, it is possible to respond to these textual phenomena with a notion of reasonableness and truth which is not based on an artificially cognitive conception of language.

2 RHETORIC AND REASONABLE DISCOURSE

The term 'rhetoric' is often understood in any of a variety of ways different from my use of it here; for example, to mean a use of language in the interests of manipulation and the acquisition of power, to mean excessively elaborate, verbosely ornamented language, or to mean jargon which grossly inflates the claims of some particular point of view – as in 'the rhetoric of the arms race'. Any of these usages can easily function as a corollary of the perennial assumption already mentioned, that anyone wishing to deal in true statements need take into account no other linguistic considerations than simplicity. Bishop Sprat, who in 1667 had praise only for language of 'mathematical plainness',[37] is joined in this assumption by writers as different from each other as Basil of Caesarea, who in the fourth century expressed his distaste for 'polishing periods',[38] and in our own time B. F. Skinner: 'humor, wit, style, the devices of poetry, and fragmentary recombinations and distortions of form all go unreinforced, if they are not actually punished, by the scientific community.'[39]

I query this notion that correct statements should be couched in forms purporting to indicate that all non-cognitive influences have been purged from them. Instead I shall urge that we use the rhetorical tradition to accept, rather than repudiate, the complexities of ordinary linguistic usage, so that criteria for reasonable discourse can be evolved on a realistic basis: one which presupposes that communicative phenomena which go beyond the strictly intellectual should be assessed in terms of their appropriateness, not automatically excoriated.

The notion of arguing is one which implies that arguers wish to be suasive in the sense supplied above, and *in so far* as 'humor, wit, style' and so forth can be used to this end, it is not obvious that they should be expunged from reasonable discourse. In so far as they form aids to suasion, excluding them serves the undesirable end of reducing the extent to which reasoned conclusions are effectively disseminated.

It might, of course, be claimed that this can be done in Skinnerian (or Hempelian) terms, remaining within purely intellectual parameters: for example, just by making what one says simpler or more complex. I do not believe that such moves are in fact at all likely to be adequate for achieving suasive communication, given the actual requirements of readers, and I think that this is shown in the textual analyses below.

I do not want to argue that sociological authors need be aware of rhetorical concepts when they write. It is possible to use 'the faculty of observing in any given case the available means of persuasion'[40] without conscious reflection and without any explicit knowledge that it exists. Adjusting reasoned talk to the general requirements of one's interlocutor's position is a routine social facility, though one which some people possess to a greater degree than others. It seems to me artificial and arbitrary to distrust it as necessarily inimical to considered discussion. Moreover, though the usefulness of rhetoric cannot *prima facie* be excluded from any type of discourse, its incorporation of interpersonal factors into reasoning seem likely to give it a central role in texts dealing with specifically social matters.

A further feature of sociological discussion makes a rhetorical mode appropriate to it: the fact that it is forced to deal reasonably with situations in which certainties are particularly difficult to come by. Aristotle himself points out that it is pre-eminently 'about our actions that we deliberate and enquire',[41] but that practical social action is not a subject to which fixed and necessary propositions are applicable. Solutions are not self-evident, and we have to decide between 'alternative possibilities'.[42] This is in the very nature of arguing, for people do not take the trouble to deliberate about matters which they hold to be quite certain and inevitable[43] (cf. the term 'incontrovertible'). So despite this lack of irrefragable evidence, decisions must be taken in and about the social world, and reason must be used to this end. Aristotle refers to 'the use of rational speech' in connection with rhetorical reasoning,[44] connecting the notion of reason with the use of rhetorical interchange in order to negotiate acceptable and usable opinions. This is what is meant by the claim that rhetoric takes place within the area of the probable. We base decisions about action not on what we know will happen, but on what can sensibly be anticipated – using what Cicero terms 'the ordinary beliefs of mankind'.[45]

This point of view implies that in the social sciences it is unwise to be too eager about importing natural-scientific methodologies wholesale, and it also requires a more flexible account of reasonableness than, say, the notion of strict means–ends rationality.[46] The widespread application of the latter idea to human affairs would require the isolation and comparison of alternative 'means' to be much easier than is actually the case – as Hempel, interestingly, points out.[47]

A notion of reasonableness which applied to the way in which discussions are normally carried out in the social world would incorporate different factors. H. W. Johnstone suggests that reasonable arguing is non-manipulative, bilateral, deliberative, reflexive, attentive to data;[48] others point to the ability to follow argumentative forms appropriate to the field at hand,[49] and the O.E.D. mentions attitudes such as moderation, and abstaining from excessive expectations. These interpretations of reasonableness are in principle wholly compatible with rhetorical discourse. The questions whether all sociological arguing *is* reasonable in this sense, and in what ways – acceptable or otherwise – rhetoric in fact contributes to sociological texts, cannot be answered *a priori*. They are matters for empirical investigation.

Here I have suggested that reasonable arguing need not be couched in language of a compulsively cognitive tenor, and that for reasons to function suasively in communication they must be framed so as to take some account of the hearer and his requirements. I have suggested too that the notion of reason embodied in discourse as the rhetorical tradition conceptualises it will be characterised by a flexibility appropriate for assessing human interaction. The earliest treatments of rhetoric deal with the oral discussion of public matters; *mutatis mutandis* this does not prejudice the hypothesis that present-day practices closely bound up with the public discussion of social considerations, not excluding practices such as the writing of sociology, may also be particularly apposite for the investigation of rhetorical phenomena, and for the generation of a rhetorical concept of truth-telling.

The following chapter explains working rhetorical ideas more fully, and may be read closely or fleetingly according to taste. After it the book develops a number of rhetorical conceptions, whose significance is shown in terms of their application to successive sociological texts. Their order is intended to augment clarity of exposition and also to make it easier for the reader to check the claims which are made for particular rhetorical constellations. It is a frequent fault of works on rhetoric that they select curtailed examples from scattered sources; given the ease with which it is possible to support almost any thesis if the net of evidence is spread widely enough, this is not in effect convincing. Also, my own emphasis is on rhetorical *processes*, so it is necessary to show what difference rhetorical factors make to much longer sections of texts.

As the Appendix explains, the first criterion used in choosing this particular selection of texts for analysis was that they seem to have as good claims as any to the status of authoritative, or at any rate acceptable texts in the discipline. This I hope supports the degree of generalisability which I claim for my conclusions.

Chapter 2 approaches the question of sociological arguing from example, examining *Race, Community and Conflict* by Rex and Moore, and *Learning to Labour* by Willis. Both their rhetorical characteristics and their places in public discourse ensure that these texts cannot be impersonal or value-free; they are 'addressed' to particular audiences for particular reasons. A new form of rhetorical arguing from example is isolated, and linked with the quality of readers' responses to texts, and with systematic divergences from methodological tenets connected with this. I suggest that the rhetorical examples discussed in this chapter are connected with what I term 'rhetorical induction', a specifically social and sociological form of anticipating what is liable to happen inside a given range of situations, and how to interpret it.

Before working on an expansion of this idea, in Chapter 3 I deal with a possible objection, to the effect that the findings of Chapter 2 can be expected to be associated with interpretive texts only. Taking the positivistically oriented *The American Occupational Structure*, by Blau and Duncan, and Woodward's *Industrial Organization: Theory and Practice*, I explore different types of mutual influence between author and reader. This has immense importance even in texts where we might least expect it. Suasive and personal elements are surprisingly strong in these books, and some of their evaluative and explanatory elements are found to depend on the reader's interventions.

Chapter 4 deals with the *Affluent Worker* trilogy by Goldthorpe *et al.*, and Dore's *British Factory – Japanese Factory*, which both illuminate modes of communication on several levels and registers at once. This chapter explores the questions of rhetorical meaning, and of sociological communication which conveys understanding of people not in terms of 'models' or actors or homunculi, but in terms of the more everyday rhetorical form which I term the 'epitome'. The notion of rhetorical induction is expanded and linked with a characteristically sociological tension between relying on consensus with the reader and forcing him or her to alter expectations about the social world.

Chapter 5 uses the same texts to show how the rhetorical features examined in preceding chapters culminate in the concept of the enthymeme, or rhetorical deduction, which is central to reasoned arguing about human behaviour. Two contrasting types of enthymeme are distinguished, and their uses in changing readers' opinions are discussed. Returning to the question of values in sociological texts, I emphasise that these do not presuppose the use of specifically evaluative *concepts*. Apart from the evaluative pheno- mena already mentioned, sociological authors invariably show 'communicative attitudes': rhetorical and explanatory patterns and preferences which cannot be expunged from texts.

In the Conclusion the place of rhetoric in sociology is brought into sharper definition, and I use works by Goffman – chiefly *Asylums* and *The Presentation of Self in Everyday Life* – to show that (evaluative) changes in readers' attitudes are integral to conceptual innovation in sociology and can be prerequisites of its explanatory structures. I discuss the contributions made by the rhetorical phenomena observed here to conveying 'understanding' in sociology, and consider how the claims to accuracy of rhetorical communication can be assessed with regard to sociological texts.

If these suggestions are accepted, the degrees of importance conventionally attributed in sociology to the exhibition of evidence for theories and to interpersonal arguing about society must be reversed.

1 Rhetoric and Sociology

The idea of rhetorical arguing as I am presenting it here – arguing which lays stress on what arises from suasiveness to the hearer – incorporates three assumptions which can be treated as especially relevant and congenial to sociology. First, it is taken for granted that in the realm of social action irrefragable solutions are not available for either practical or theoretical problems. Second, there is the claim that it is none the less possible to construct standards of what can reasonably be assumed, what the participants in a situation can be expected to perceive and do, and what sorts of opinion will function adequately for given purposes in given circumstances. Third, it is emphasised that these standards and expectations are evolved in active conversation between people.

Rhetorical analyses based on these three considerations are therefore compatible with an awareness of the provisory nature of our ideas about the social world (whether or not we care to believe that events in society are determined in principle). They are compatible too with realising the dependence of these ideas on the social structures within which they evolve. At the same time they avoid unnecessary concessions to subjectivity; the fact that we cannot say for certain what the outcome of a particular course of action will be by no means entails that we cannot argue sensibly about what alternatives to expect and what reactions to make to them.

In this chapter I shall deal first with the question what parts personal factors can properly play in arguing – in order to challenge the assumption that textual arguing in general and sociological arguing in particular should ideally be neutral and intellectualist, devoid of all factors connected with personal feeling or experience. Many of the concepts I use here are derived in some sense from Aristotle, but I make no claim to be putting forward an accurate summary of his views. I try instead to adapt and explicate some of them in the light of their appropriateness for contemporary theory.

Next I describe those rhetorical figures which I have found to be most useful in describing sociological texts; most of these are taken from contemporary reworkings of the Ciceronian tradition (see introduction above). Since arguing takes place between people, where sociological books are concerned one of these people will be the reader, and the third section of this chapter explains in what sense I conceive of him or her – so that in Chapter 2 I can go on to begin showing what differences the roles of the reader and of rhetorical forms make to our understanding of sociological texts.

PERSONAL ASPECTS OF ARGUMENTATION

The conception of communication which I should like to term 'personal' is one which takes account of the fact that it is produced by people who have, for better or worse, social, political, moral, emotional and other predilections and predispositions. Participants in communication vary in terms of social and linguistic conventions, emotional and intellectual experience, societal position and relative power. Given all this, I wish simply to suggest that it is more realistic to try to assess the appropriateness of these influences on what is said than to try or to pretend to remove them.

I have contended in the Introduction that an ideal of communication as purged of non-cognitive influences has come nowadays to be associated with 'masculinist'[1] personality traits such as lack of demonstrativeness or suppression of emotional responses; these are also approved in the characteristically male occupation of academic writing.[2] But a rhetorical view of communication takes account of, even welcomes, those of its components which are not exclusively intellectual. It can show that academic works in fact contain many more personal and non-'masculinist' features than has hitherto been thought desirable.

The personal elements of arguing are described in some detail by Aristotle, who divides the means of (per)suasion into three interacting functions: 'ethos', 'pathos' and 'logos'. The last of these components is the abstract, intellectual structure of the argument itself (see below); the first two are connected with the forms which arguments take on as they actually *occur* in human contexts. They deal too with an aspect of arguing neglected in most contemporary theory: reasons not just for relying on certain sorts of evidence or procedure, but for believing people. These personal components

have a dual character: they are phenomena analysed from observation of what in fact goes on in arguing (this is why they do not
have to be learned by their users, though no doubt their implemen-
tation can be improved by study), and they are in principle open to
justification. Not only *do* they form part of arguing; it is right that
they should.

In this book I shall not use the term 'ethos', which now has an
English meaning very different from its original one, but shall refer
to 'self-presentation'. I understand it as connected with both
general and specific grounds on which it may be sensible to take note
of what another person says. In its original formulation, it depends
on 'the personal character of the speaker' as it is revealed in what he
says.[3] Here the relevant qualities of character are divided into a
sound grasp of practical reasoning, a human (moral) fitness for
dealing with the matter under discussion, and well-disposedness
towards the audience.[4]

The first two of these characteristics in effect acknowledge the
socio-linguistic fact that arguing is usually perceived and understood as in some type of relationship with its propounder. Even in
artificially impersonal situations such as examination marking, the
recipient of an argument will try to form an impression of relevant
characteristics of the person who is advancing it, of his or her
capacities for soundness, insight, cogency and so forth.[5] In more
everyday situations, criteria of 'personal character' are often taken
to be indicated by secondary factors which can be described
sociologically – such as role, status or political allegiance. Argumentation does not take place in a social void, and, as Perelman and
Olbrechts-Tyteca write in *The New Rhetoric*, 'some quality is
necessary in order to speak and be listened to' at all.[6] One cannot
just advance on a group of strangers in the street and begin to
discourse on a topic with no relation to them; and the factors which
can bestow on one the right to be regarded as an interlocutor can be
described in social terms.

Thus, for example, deference shown to the claims of apparently
'competent experts'[7] in various fields (electricians or economic
planners) is based on the assumption that what is now termed the
social distribution of knowledge ensures that what they say is backed
by a sufficient scaffolding of reasons, even if these are unknown to
oneself. Given the constant reliance everyone is obliged to place on
the judgements of others, the notion of 'self-presentation' can be
used in support of the contention that 'one *ought* to grant' some

redence to 'whatever qualified men and women agree on, *unless* one has specific and stronger reasons to disbelieve'. [8] This claim does not recommend conformism; it merely reflects the fact that conventional criteria for credibility are often – emphatically not always – so reasonable that, when they are satisfied, the burden of proof is on the disbeliever.

These features of self-presentation, then, depend on the facts that arguments tend to be perceived as someone's arguments, and that the perceived moral, social and intellectual competence of their propounders yields additional reasons for or against taking notice of what is said. Especially when the subject of discussion is itself personal or social, it can be assumed that the speaker's personal or social qualities are counted as relevant to his or her arguments and contribute to an appraisal of the claims concerned.

The last component of self-presentation, well-intentionedness towards the hearer, acknowledges a different kind of phenomenon: that the relationship between speaker and addressed can help or hinder correct appreciation of what is being conveyed. This might be termed a psycho-epistemic point; it is also one of practical importance, for if a speaker is well disposed to the audience, they can feel safe in assuming that he or she will refrain from efforts detrimental to them.

It seems to me that we do in fact estimate arguments partly according to our views of the reliability, maturity and moral authority of those making them – qualities which we perceive through the medium of our relations with the speaker. Aristotle claims that the more uncertain the subject under discussion, the more influential the speaker's character is liable to be. 'We believe good men more fully and more readily than others,' and 'where exact certainty is impossible and opinions are divided' a speaker's personal qualities may be crucial in influencing a decision. [9] In practical terms it is indeed more sensible to allow the balance to be swung by a competent and well-disposed person than by an incompetent and ill-disposed one; hence, if speakers do actually possess these positive qualities, it is helpful to their hearers for them to show it.

The second of the three interacting means of persuasion being examined here is 'pathos', which I shall term 'sensitisation': 'putting the audience into a certain frame of mind'. [10] The point of this notion is *not* to excuse speakers for manipulating their hearers so as to dominate their judgements, nor for perverting their hearers' decisions through the arousal of inappropriate emotions.[11] Nor is either sensitisation or self-presentation particularly closely associated with the claim[12] that since auditors respond to what they hear in ways determined partly by their characters, and since these characters are not always strong or virtuous, a speaker may be obliged to adopt spurious tactics in order to commend himself or herself in their eyes. The concept of sensitisation, then, cannot be used to show that rhetorical communication is essentially a matter of exploiting positions of relative power.

I should claim that there are at least two sides to the functioning of sensitisation; both are displayed again and again in the sociological texts analysed below. First, there is the idea put forward both by Plato in the *Phaedrus*[13] and by Aristotle that anyone who wishes to communicate effectively must do more than argue logically; it is necessary to 'understand human character and goodness in their various forms' and 'understand the emotions'.[14] A speaker must take note of the fact that arguing takes place in a mode which is social and psychological as well as intellectual, and be able to function in this mode. The second aspect of sensitisation is, it seems to me, again a partly epistemic one. A particular frame of mind may be essential for the appropriate consideration of a particular argument: 'Our judgements when we are pleased and friendly are not the same as when we are pained and hostile.'[15] (Note that this does not claim that the former attitude is always the most apposite.)

This observation is connected with the very point of 'suasion'. Consider the case of someone who is indifferent to the claims of, say, socialism before becoming personally involved with people whose lives are spoilt by subjugation to particular social structures; or someone who is unimpressed by arguments for feminism before being denied a particular job on the grounds of her sex. In neither situation need it be the case that the people concerned are influenced *only* by political or personal experiences; but it may be that these experiences are necessary conditions – what I should term 'enabling experiences' which take particular forms for particular individuals – for *taking seriously* the arguments connected with them.

There are several possible reasons why this might be so. Different types of barrier can originate in a person's nature, socialisation or predicament to obstruct his or her appreciation of particular arguments – to make one 'see red' when a particular subject is mentioned, or else to 'leave one cold'. Political arguments are only the most obvious cases in which the opponents of a point of view can be perfectly familiar with its structure and contents without being able to adduce the faintest reason why anyone might wish to hold it. Thus for hearers in particular moods or with particular preconceptions, certain contentions are in an important sense *unintelligible*. It is not just support for but also *comprehension* of particular arguments which involves sympathy and experience as well as intellect. The function of sensitisation is to create conditions in which the hearer's personal faculties function to promote rather than to inhibit appreciation of what is being said – whether or not in the end he or she agrees with it.

These may seem to be routine implications of the work of intellectual historians where people who have lived in the past are concerned; it seems much more difficult for contemporary writers to admit the relevance of similar intermixtures of cognitive and non-cognitive compounds to arguing carried out in the present. But to assume that academic arguments are wholly cognitive in nature, even if others are not, would be to create a division which does not reflect the realities of the arguing in the sociological texts investigated below. (In so far as methodologists suppose that sociological work should take place on an exclusively cognitive plane, this fact requires some revision of their claims.)

Sensitisation, then, directly concerns the interconnections between cognitive and non-cognitive responses to arguing; it is that aspect of communication which deals with the hearer's or reader's reception of what is said, and treats this as performed by the person as a whole. Simply setting out a position is generally insufficient to impel its recipient to grasp it; so techniques of sensitisation are in principle capable of making arguments accessible to a far wider range of people than would otherwise be the case.

I have referred to 'logos' as the abstract structure of the argument itself. Here 'the argument' is not thought of in its addressed or adversarial senses, and focuses on the tenor or burden of what is said. By definition this concept is an abstraction; it does *not* signify an actual piece of communication expressed in purely cognitive terms. An argument in this sense does not occur by itself but is expressed *by* what is said; if self-presentation is the aspect of communication most concerned with the character of the speaker, and sensitisation most concerned with the hearer, logos is most concerned with the subject-matter of discussion. Its function is to prove some point – or at least to try or to appear to prove it, since it cannot be assumed in advance that all arguments are of necessity admissible and correct.[16]

Aristotelian rhetoric both describes and commends a form of arguing between people in situations where it would be inapposite to pretend to incontrovertible conclusions. This form of argumentation aims to advance reasonable accounts of events which at the same time allow the hearer a degree of personal insight into the situation.

Such a concern for the hearer is marked in the case of the 'enthymeme', an inference which encapsulates the way in which self-presentation, sensitisation and abstract argument are blended in everyday deductions.[17] I shall take an enthymeme to be an inference whose communicative effectiveness depends partly on the hearer's conception of the speaker's qualifications for making his or her remarks; whose form is adjusted to its hearer's presumed capacities for response; and which is based not on some genuinely universal empirical generalisation but on an assumption about what is probably the case or can reasonably be expected. This type of assumption (technically known as a topos) is a generalisation with an everyday standard of rigour, not purporting to hold for every single example possible, but applicable to most cases, sound enough to ratify the arguments it generates.[18]

The topos seems to me important not only because of its role in argumentation but because of its role in our perception and experience of social life. Topoi form the backcloth, so to speak, which gives general meaning to social happenings. (The genre of the detective story deals with what might happen if topoi were *not* reliable: if some of the central assumptions which make up the basis of daily life were confounded.)

Thus the concept of the enthymeme shows how logical and non-logical components can be intertwined in reasoned inference, and that of the topos recognises that many or most of the generalisations we need in everyday life are provisory; that this state of affairs is (at least for the foreseeable future) inescapable; and that it does not imply that everyday generalisations cannot be reliable enough to give rise to reasoned discussion.

The account of sociological arguing in subsequent chapters will include an exploration of the role it gives to enthymematical inferences based on topoi – and to altering and rearranging the topoi current among the people who read it. The roles of self-presentation and sensitisation in sociological arguing and explaining show that, in the personal communication which they involve, there is more to be found in what sociologists write than their methodological precepts would imply. Even in texts whose style would lead us to expect it least, sociological writing takes the form of dialogues between reader and author which are forceful enough to involve considerable mutual influence and adaptation.

Thus the effective contents of sociological texts are determined less than at first sight appears by their subject-matter in the strict sense, and more by the personal figures of reader and author – who cannot avoid the fact that they are involved in a process of communication which is not only intellectual but emotional, moral and political as well. The accumulated experience in describing communicative patterns which is provided by the rhetorical tradition makes it an appropriate source of instruments with which to analyse these interlocking strands – and it shows that rhetorical projects are essential components of sociological explanations as such.

2 RHETORICAL FIGURES IN ARGUING

Building on this approach to communication, I want to combine it with some figures deriving from the more pragmatic Ciceronian tradition. Many of these figures have been revised by Perelman and Olbrechts-Tyteca in their *New Rhetoric*,[19] as well as by other writers chiefly in the USA or on the continent of Europe. Versions of these figures, which I have sometimes adapted in the light of sociologists' uses of them, can be used to enable us to detect the imports of passages which are not specifically inferential in function.

In this section I shall introduce figures which in my experience are prominent in texts such as those I shall deal with. Their presence in sociological books is far from suggesting the deliberate employment of strategy by their authors; indeed, many of these figures have become so routinised in textual communication that their very perception is difficult. This fact itself, however, allows them to exert an influence which is in many ways wider than that of their exotic cognates in more elaborately literary texts.

The authors of *The New Rhetoric* contrast argumentation with the mere construction of a logical chain in which variables are 'strictly equivalent', so that 'A plus B' has exactly the same import as 'B plus A'.[20] In arguing, on the other hand, the figure of order (1) shows that 'the place allotted' to elements 'alters their significance.'[21]

Particular arrangements of the components in the early stages of
text can open or close possibilities for introducing later ones, or can
influence readers' likely reactions – which themselves affect the
author's range of manoeuvre. 'In argumentation, a change of order
is hardly ever a simple permutation.'[22]

Thus, a sociological author who begins his or her investigations of
deviance with detailed examinations of the deprived backgrounds
of its subjects will, all other things being equal, find it difficult to put
forward a non-environmentalist explanation of their actions. His or
her arguing is ruled by communicational conventions, even if these
are not consciously recognised by either author or reader. For
example, placing an item first or last in a series tends to function as
signifying that it is to be considered as in some sense more important
than the rest. I should deny that the influence of order here is just a
communicational 'effect'. As will be shown below, rhetorical order
has conventional implications which affect the *meaning* of an
argument itself.

Arguments are evolved and experienced in terms of positions held
by different speakers rather than in terms of facts which are directly
apprehended; people arguing about the state of the economy, for
example, are forced to appeal to views, theories and assumptions to
counter the views, theories and assumptions of the other side. If
utterly certain facts and interpretations were available and
everyone were able to perceive them as such, there would *be* no
argument. This accounts for the preoccupation within the
Ciceronian tradition with working out the optimum order for
presenting the parts of an argument – beginning from some position
which the audience is also able to accept, one may adopt a procedure
such as adding new points in ascending order of acceptability so as
to establish a pattern which hearers can find convincing.[23] There
are obvious possibilities for manipulation in this; it is none the less
true that as a rule there is little point in beginning a discourse with
remarks which one's interlocutor is sure to find incredible or
repugnant.

It is also usually the case that a speaker or writer has more views
on a subject than can be advanced all at once. Some criterion is
necessary for choosing where to begin, and like other authors in the
Ciceronian tradition Perelman and Olbrechts-Tyteca dwell on the
necessity for a speaker to attach importance to the hearer's 'mental
cooperation', to find arguments capable of 'acting on' his views, to
'show some concern for him, and be interested in his state of mind'.[2]

Though they express such points pragmatically, it is possible to associate them with the notion of sensitisation so as to explore the contribution made by the reader's or hearer's influence in arguing. If, in order to communicate a case about a given subject, an author has first to adapt it for other people's comprehension, the end result does not contain only what he or she had intended to say. It is a product of the interaction, actual or hypothesised, between the author and the audience.

Concern with an audience's reactions is the origin of Perelman's and Olbrechts-Tyteca's interest in the figure of presence (2), which means making a textual item stand out far enough from its context for the reader to become especially aware of it, and so as to make him or her inclined actively to take it into account. They remark that presence 'acts directly on our sensibility',[25] but again I should claim that this figure plays a large part in making an argument *intelligible* to a hearer. It is possible to understand an argument in a superficial sense without allowing it to make a difference to one's views – even if it is incompatible with them. Similarly, it is possible to know that a state of affairs exists without taking any genuine notice of it; being sensitive to its existence is part of finding it intelligible. By marking the salient points of arguments and mapping out their patterns of priority, the figure of presence militates against the production of distorted or diluted versions in the minds of hearers.

In this connection it is interesting to find that authors of sociological works often give presence to features incompatible with the priorities stressed by the methodologies they claim to uphold. Like patterns of order, patterns of presence may be evidence that authors' real views can differ from those which they picture themselves as holding.

There are other rhetorical figures whose uses can have methodological implications. One of these is emphasis (3), a term I shall use in its everyday sense[26] and which can be treated as an extreme but localised form of presence. Patterns of emphasis can draw attention to authorial attitudes which are not formulated in other ways; in particular, they allow writers to communicate value-judgements without doing so openly or even consciously. To continue the example from the sociology of deviance: in emphasising the deprived backgrounds of offenders at the expense of, for example, procedures of rational decision, texts may be (and often are) interpreted as offering excuses for the conduct of their subjects. In order to detect patterns of emphasis, the reader can ask what implications a text would have had if its stresses had been placed on different components.

This also applies to the figure of repetition (4), which has attitude-enhancing properties quite apart from its mnemonic value to both author and reader. These properties seem to me to arise because in making sense of a rhetorical pattern, so that what the author has written is transformed from a *mere* pattern into an intelligible text, the reader absorbs (often unstated) reasons why some items deserve repetition rather than others. Thus he or she may take over the attitudes which form the backgrounds to these reasons.

The figure of amplification (5) shows a further feature of rhetorical communication which distinguishes it from the abstract structures which academic texts are often taken to be. I shall treat this figure as the elaboration of a theme, in which intellectual capacities are not the only ones involved. For example, Worsley's elaboration of the theme of colonial brutality in his book *The Trumpet Shall Sound* functions not only to explicate an historical point but also to show its significance to the reader, to get him or her to work through a development at a gradual pace which allows the formation of moral and emotional impressions about it. The reader is encouraged by this to extrapolate from his or her own experience to supplement the work of grasping the evolution of a situation; the resulting 'vicarious' experience gives the author's amplified accounts added social and political significance.

Uses of amplification in promoting understanding of sociological arguments are thus largely, but not exclusively, connected with sensitisation. The frequency with which this figure occurs in sociological texts is itself an argument against over-intellectualising our views of their contents. Moreover, rhetorical figures such as order and amplification – or what I should call 'negative amplification', systematically *refraining* from amplifying certain themes – can be used as instruments with which to explain phenomena such as the uneasy feeling which some readers experience on reading 'positivist' works. It is possible to use rhetorical means of blocking various political or humanitarian interests without ever stating views with this tendency.

Further rhetorical uses of factors which are not strictly or exclusively cognitive are exemplified by the occurrence in sociological texts of figures such as metaphor or hypotyposis (6),[27] giving a description so vivid that the reader envisages the event as happening before his or her very eyes. (*The Trumpet Shall Sound* is replete with examples, as its Melanesian millenarians sing and feast and paddle their canoes, as is – in a different way – *The Power Elite* by C. Wright Mills.) I take it that identifying such figures will vary between different groups of readers, since what induces images of great clarity in some readers may have less effect on others, and since the literary conventions affecting responses to descriptions vary according to different cultures and periods.

Current academic convention militates against uses of hypotyposis which appear fanciful, and metaphor (7) may be most influential on a grand-scale conceptual level. Here I shall not stress the traditional fine distinctions between different types of metaphor,[28] and in the cases of both metaphor and hypotyposis I shall concentrate on their contributions to arguing and to the activity which readers are prepared to invest in handling a text.

Sociologists' uses of example (8), too, are often chiefly rhetorical in function. This is not generally acknowledged, since authors overtly connect examples with the provision of evidence. But when a sociological statement concerns a large social group, the three or four cases which most texts can provide in fact have no strict probative value for the reader. This does not mean that they are not argumentatively significant, and there are two rhetorical uses of example which are especially interesting.

First, readers can use examples as tests of whether the author has the ability to sustain a coherent thesis; whether, that is, the examples really appear to exemplify what the author says they do. This is in effect a test of the author's self-presentation. If he or she passes, it is this evidence of competence which persuades the reader that the text should be believed, rather than the direct evidence of the examples themselves.

Second, examples can equip readers with insights into the ways in which particular features of a situation can be interpreted as signs or symptoms of larger states of affairs. This yields a new version of the example, which I shall examine at length below: what I term the 'actual type' and its role in sociological arguing.

The notion of humour (9) will be used here in a broad sense, to include many related techniques such as ridicule, sarcasm and irony. This and the argument from authority (10) are cases which show how rhetorical usages can lend themselves to misconstruction which causes them to fall into disrepute. Ridicule is commonly associated with arguing *ad personam* in an attempt to score off an opponent by making him or her seem foolish. Arguing from authority, though no one can help using it, is still associated with a slavish adoption of other people's ideas. As generalisations, these are misconceived – although most figures *can* be misused in the ways envisaged in the popular views of them. Techniques of humour, I should claim, are in fact most often used in sociology for removing blocks to comprehension, making it possible to perceive an argument within a framework which a reader's prejudices or loyalties might otherwise have led him or her to reject. They can hold a reader's attention while allowing him or her to change some point of view, or set up a relationship such that this can occur. Thus humour can facilitate the formation of essential parts of the background against which the reasoning in an argument must be understood.

This may be said of arguing from authority too. It is generally acknowledged that no investigator can prove all even of his or her central assumptions alone,[29] and that writers are both entitled and forced to rely on the work of other members of the scientific community. Citing such a member (referring to Marx and Engels rather than to Weber, say, or vice versa) can stand for a whole train of unstated arguments in the author's own text, locating him or her in an intellectual tradition and showing the reader in what light to interpret what is said. Furthermore, the *reader's* need to be able to rely on more than what a single text can prove means that authors must show that they themselves are reliable members of the academic world; their self-presentation must show the reader that it is safe to accept *them* as authorities.

The last figure to be used extensively below is that of reticence (11). I shall take its definition from Perelman and Olbrechts-Tyteca, who term it a figure which 'makes it possible to evoke an idea, while leaving its development to the reader'.[30] But though these authors are concerned with its literary uses in connection with rhyme and alliteration, I shall claim that its argumentative functions are more important.

It frequently happens that an author refrains from pointing up conclusions which he or she leaves the *reader* to draw, or understates even points which are crucial for a thesis. It seems to me that this is explicable in terms which apply to most of the figures described here, and to rhetorical communication in general. Arguments have most opportunity of impinging on their audience – achieving suasion, in my terms – when this audience can be brought to make active efforts in the course of assimilating them. Rhetorical analysis assumes that an audience's participation in making arguments intelligible is characteristically *active*. Even in academic texts, therefore, the reader can be expected to participate in constructing their sense.

3 RHETORIC AND THE READER

The view of the reader's role presupposed by the 'active' approach to it taken by the rhetorical tradition is one which neither regards the reader as subservient to the demands of a text, nor sees the text as a neutral carrier of symbols with which the reader can do as he or she likes. It is still the case that the history of rhetoric yields no developed theory to provide a detailed account of the reader's work, so the approach I shall take to it here will necessarily be pragmatic. I shall try to infer the influence of the reader from a use of textual evidence which does not attribute permanent dominance to either reader or author, and which takes into account the fact that reading is less a matter of construing individual sentences than a set of longer-term reactions to interrelated sections of text.

My approach to rhetorical communication here is applied to a specialised form of writing – that to be found in mid-twentieth-century sociological books – and thus it involves some presuppositions which need explaining. First, all that I say about audiences refers equally, unless it is explicitly stated otherwise, to both hearers and readers; the two terms are used interchangeably here. This is because I have taken from a tradition which dealt originally with hearers only that which I take to be applicable to readers as well. It is not intended to indicate that the functions of reader and hearer are identical in all types of communication, for this is clearly not true.

Moreover, in envisaging my reader as a reader of books I am omitting certain comparisons. It may be that authors of books need to make efforts to secure the reader's interest and cooperation which authors of academic articles, for example, are spared. The institution of the learned journal may perform the social task of preselecting smallish groups of readers who are prepared to devote effort to understanding given sorts of topic, and this may have considerable effect on the types of language which academic articles display.[31]

It is also the case that the individual rhetorical usages to which I

draw attention below are often of a sort to be characterised a
defensible, justifiable or essential. It might be objected that thi
leaves out a degree of academic chicanery to which attention ough
to be drawn. It is true that where there is chicanery, it ought to be
exposed; still, this is a different task from mine. I am anxious to
explore the notion of rhetorical communication as forming an
integral part of the meaning of a sociological text. The attempt to
show that sociological communication cannot be achieved without
rhetorical uses, and that rhetoric is concerned in the first place with
conveying meaning suasively, is an operation which would only be
confused by performing it in parallel with one of an opposite
impetus.

The claim that rhetoric should be seen in terms of the light it casts
on meaningful communication is one which I am making side by
side with the awareness that communication takes place in forms
which are socially influenced. We might well anticipate, for
example, that sociological schools can be identified by characteristic
patterns of rhetorical expression. It might be possible to claim that
the influence of a particular 'paradigm', in the sense used by Kuhn
to mean an exemplary case dominating a whole set of scientific
procedures,[32] directly affects the language of work it generates –
and this for social as well as methodological reasons, for reasons
explicable in terms of authors' interaction with particular reader-
ships. Rhetorical analysis might also be used to identify the effects of
even more explicitly extra-scientific social pressures from readers, or
potential readers, on what authors write.

But such investigations can only be carried out *after* more general,
and fundamental, questions have been dealt with. They are
investigations which *presuppose* answers to questions about what is
valid and what is invalid in rhetorical communication, what can be
attributed to 'mere' social pressure and what is intrinsic to
rhetorical interaction, which rhetorical features are peculiar to
given schools and which arise *whatever* view of social science one
takes to be correct.

In order to approach such questions I take rhetorical communication to take place according to rules and patterns of which the
user need be no more conscious than he or she is of the rules of
grammar. This makes it possible to discover rhetorical usages in
texts without having to attribute to their writers intentions which
aim at planned effects. (This applies far more closely to the types of
figure exemplified in the previous section than to the more elaborate

onstructions of poetry or the more deliberate ones of propaganda.)
Thus when I refer here to a particular author I am not making
hypotheses about his or her thoughts as an empirical individual; I
am referring to the author's persona, to the author only as he or she
s revealed in the text.

This is not to claim that authors' intentions are never relevant to
he meaning of a text; in one sense, interpreting a text does mean
searching for the author's probable intentions at the time he or she
wrote it. But other senses of 'interpretation' are just as admissible for
different purposes. In one such sense, interpretation means using the
text for what later audiences, or the interpreter, wish to extract from
t for ends of their own (somewhat as I have done with Aristotle);
this entails no commitment to any view about whether the later
reading coincides with what may be conjectured to have been the
author's.

But the sense in which the texts below will be examined is a third
one: it concerns what a text can reasonably be *taken* to mean, in view
of the conventions current in the circles providing the types of
audience to which it is directed.[33] The fact that I deal with
contemporary texts makes it a little easier to offer opinions on what
audience reactions to them might be, but this is not to claim that
recourse to public views and conventions always produces a single
and irrefutable reading. Nor does this procedure overrule the
author's views altogether. He or she may be taken to share most of
the audience's conventions with regard to meaning; the author is
also regarded by them as some sort of authority on his or her own
text. Even so, interpreting in the light of what a text publicly counts
as saying does allow for occasions on which the final arbiter of
meaning is the reader.

This third sense is probably that in which most readers treat what
they read when, like readers of sociology, they are more interested in
the subject-matter of a book than in the minutiae of text interpretation or of the author's minute-by-minute intentions. And in cases
where author and reader come from the same culture and period,
and are not divided by radical ideological differences, linguistic
conventions might be taken to ensure that readers' and authors'
meanings do not wholly diverge. None the less, this leaves
considerable room for disagreement on matters of moment even
apart from questions associated with 'personal communication'.
Consider a text such as Kuhn's *The Structure of Scientific Revolutions*.
After the intense critical investigation which this work has received,

it is still not possible to claim that there is an agreed version of its implications, nor even an agreed version of what the author means by his key terms.[34] This is some indication that textual interpretation is a practical problem in academic discussion.

Though it is plausible to hold that readers make a difference to what a text is taken to mean, then, it is by no means clear just how this happens or to what extent. This is not to say that authors compose their texts taking absolutely no cognisance of the fact that they are to be read. On occasions such as supervisions of dissertations, or informal readings of chapters taken from projected books, authors collect opinions on passages which need more emphasis, should be omitted, could be made more striking or concise or placed elsewhere. In effect these are largely lessons in rhetorical composition. But they tend instead to be connected by their participants with an invariant and impersonal – that is, audience-independent – notion of intelligibility.

Peter Achinstein, who is less unobservant than most writers of the connection between a text and its readers, remarks rightly that philosophers who concentrate on the logical at the expense of the pragmatic sides of explanation produce inaccurate accounts of it.[35] But for him these pragmatic sides chiefly involve presenting remarks 'in a sufficiently clear, simple and organized manner' for comprehensibility.[36] Achinstein connects this notion of comprehensibility with appropriateness to the situation of the interlocutor – but only in the very general sense in which observations intended for university students will explain nothing to schoolchildren. In fact there is a great deal more variation than this implies in what makes it *possible* for one person even to *perceive* a remark as clear and well ordered, and impossible for another to do so. In this book, rhetorical concepts will be used to contribute to the question how readers of sociology are *brought* to use what they read so that it becomes intelligible to them.

For this reason I shall not accept the contrast sometimes made between 'expository' and 'persuasive' texts, where the latter term is the only one linked with rhetorical communication.[37] Such a contrast is used to suggest that expository texts are concerned with getting people to understand something, while rhetorical ones try to get them to do something – possibly by not impeccable means. One of the many objections which can be made to this dichotomy is that getting people to understand things itself presupposes getting them to perform activities of various sorts. This does not imply that the

hetorical usages authors employ are always *optimal* for getting
eaders to do whatever is necessary to achieve understanding of
vhat they read. Assessments of this sort would require empirical
nvestigations going beyond the scope of this work.

In trying to show how rhetorical suasion is part of explaining, and
what role the reader can play in this, this book will not be examining
especially rhetorical passages in explanatory texts. Rather, it deals
with rhetorical aspects of texts whose chief function is to convey
sociological accounts of what happens in society, and which –
unintentionally but inevitably – use rhetorical processes in doing so.

2 Qualitative Sociology and Arguing from Example

This chapter begins an examination of the form of rhetorical reasoning known as arguing from example, suggesting that sociological examples have a special relationship to what I shall term rhetorical induction. Examples play a central part in a form of generalising which does not only guide readers' interpretations of situations they judge comparable with those the author investigates; it also directs reactions in and evaluations of them.

I have claimed that rhetorical features need not be treated as in principle inimical to reasoned dialogue, nor as easily separable from it, and that they can be expected in cases of suasive communication – from however intellectual a standpoint this communication may be conceived. In qualitative sociology, which aims among other things at showing what particular social situations are like (investigating their quality), the provision of examples is essential: without examples, the reader cannot form an adequate idea of what the author is talking about. But in the texts examined in this chapter, examples do not function in a straightforward fashion as evidence for more general propositions. They function rhetorically, in ways which are characteristic of qualitative writing.

The books examined here are *Race, Community and Conflict* (1967), by Rex and Moore, and *Learning to Labour* (1977), by Paul Willis. The former deals with the decline of an inner-city area in Birmingham and the racial patterns and problems associated with this decline. It consciously keeps in mind 'the conclusions reached by sociological theory' and tries to 'bring these conclusions to life' (p. xiii) 'in terms of the sociology of the industrial city' (p. xiv). Willis's book is concerned with a group of disaffected working-class 'lads' at school in the same large conurbation. He wishes to account for their group culture in terms of a partial understanding of the

32

workings of the capitalist class structure, and to show how this understanding works, paradoxically, to impel the 'lads' to embrace the deadening and oppressive forms of manual labour they eventually take up.

I shall look first at the overall sociological enterprises engaged in by Willis and, chiefly, by Rex and Moore. In their Introduction the latter try to affect the quality of what readers derive from the text by arguing with them directly, in defence of taking a sociological approach to Birmingham's problems at all. Here passages with conventional textual functions also display rhetorical uses of order, presence, hypertyposis and emphasis. The functions of these figures in activating what the authors say – and the fact that they are by no means confined to the Introduction – underline the fact that it is necessary for a book to be effectively suasive in order to make a point clear *to* anyone. Its rhetorical components may be the ones which bestow on a work the status of an explanation.

In section 2 I shall look at the rhetorical ordering of both *Race, Community and Conflict* and *Learning to Labour*. The figure of order demonstrates that the rhetorical effects of a text cannot properly be perceived in terms of statically envisaged concepts and sentences, but derive from the ways in which whole passages interact with each other. In these two texts, order affects the actual meaning of what is conveyed, in ways which include preventing both from being 'value free'.

In section 3 I turn to two different uses of example which raise problems which I try to deal with fully in the subsequent section. In the first type of case we find untypical examples occupying places of textual prominence which from a methodological point of view we should not expect. In the second, we find uses of example *not* contributing to configurations which from a methodological point of view we *should* expect. In both cases, authors may take themselves to be conforming to methodological conventions about the production of sociological texts when they are in reality satisfying needs connected with communicating with their readers, and to some extent imposed by those readers.

In the last section, I shall examine the contributions of both texts to what I call 'rhetorical induction', and shall then assimilate many of their methodologically puzzling uses of example to a special form of the argument from sign, which I shall call the 'actual type'. This has a special place in the personal communication between author and reader: authors are prepared to run considerable communi-

cative risks in order that their readers should achieve the insight
which actual types can convey. In investigating arguing from
example, we shall see that qualitative sociology *prescribes* operation:
to which rhetoric is essential.

1 ARGUING AND EXPLANATORY EFFECTIVENESS

There is a startling difference in style between the introduction
which set the tones of the two texts to be examined here. This
difference can be explained, no doubt, partly in terms of the dates a
which they were written – Rex's and Moore's is ten years earlier -
but largely in terms of the compositions of their appropriate
audiences. Rex and Moore claim to be addressing the world at large
as well as their own colleagues; Willis, as will be seen below
perceives problems in communicating what he has to say, and he
tells us that the laymen to whom he has shown his text – its subjects -
claim not to be able to understand it (pp. 195ff.).

Thus Willis provides a statistical account of the composition of
'Hammertown' in the assumption that his readers will know why
it is significant to do so, and some of his central assumptions are
expressed in neo-Marxist terms, neither standardly everyday nor
standardly academic. Labour, for example, is 'the dialectic of the sel
to the self through the concrete world' (p. 2). In contrast, Rex and
Moore try to explain why they have taken a sociological approach
to their subject at all. This does not mean that Willis is any les
concerned to make an impact on his readers (see below); but Rex'
and Moore's introductory remarks furnish a particularly un
ambiguous case of authorial attempts to provoke active understanding
ing of and reaction to their work. It is clear that it is their 'hearer
who 'determines the speech's end and object' [1] in the sense that thei
explanation is patently *addressed*.

Though its aim is not merely to remove what Jarvie term
'psychological puzzlement', [2] its criteria are not simply forma
either. They are criteria which depend on the reader's responses
and show that it is Rex's and Moore's whole text, rather than
particularly persuasive parts of it, which must be regarded a
'addressed' to the person from whom these responses are expected

Rex and Moore are writing 'both as sociologists and as citizens'
'This book arose out of our concern with the immediate and
practical problems of life in Birmingham in 1963' (p. xiii). This

concern is twofold: with the degeneration of Sparkbrook, a once ' "respectable" ' area, into a 'twilight zone', and with deteriorating race relations in the city. There are at least four respects in which such a concern dictates aspects of Rex's and Moore's relations with their readers. First, they wish them to take action about the problems they analyse. This presupposes that something should provoke readers to *wish* to take such action, and there is recurrent textual evidence to show that the authors try to provoke them in this way. Second, though they wish to give a causal account of Sparkbrook's troubles, in the nature of the case this account must not seem so deterministic as to inhibit intervention. This is a matter to which Rex and Moore address themselves directly.

Third, to the extent that as sociologists they are in a position to discover information accessible only through methods such as large-scale investigations which are unavailable to the layman, part of their task is to make this information accessible and credible to readers.[3] Fourth, though, Rex and Moore admit that the account they provide is 'not easy to grasp'. 'The man in the street', they say, 'is easily convinced by an entirely different diagnosis of the problems of the city' (p. 265). (Willis, who contrasts 'explanations-in-use' with 'proper social explanations' (p. 62), is thoroughly aware of a similar problem.) It is thus impossible that Rex and Moore should be indifferent to what the reader makes of the text; without their intervention it may be misconstrued altogether.

In *Race, Community and Conflict* the Introduction (written mainly by Rex) supplies an opening sentence which gives a prominent ordering to the practical urgency of the book's subject-matter: the racial problems in question are 'of immense practical political importance'. Birmingham's reactions to them 'will have consequences not merely nationally but internationally' (p. 1). Later, the reader is warned that 'the long-term destiny' of a city which responds ineptly to these problems 'is some sort of urban riot' (p. 9; no doubt this assertion seemed less probable to its readers at the time it was written than it does fifteen years later).

Rex sets against this the claim that it is possible to plan rationally towards a more desirable solution, 'knowing full well what obstacles lie in the way' (p. 5). The closing sentences of the chapter – also prominent in terms of order – draw attention to the authors' hopes for 'rational control' of the situation (p. 18). In terms of the figure of reticence, the contrast between 'confronted', 'perplexed', 'riot' and 'realistically' and 'rational', commends the authors' own approach.

This, of course, augments their self-presentation. I shall not comment in detail on this here, but it is worth noting that their commitment to their argument requires them to use terms which also enhance their own appearance of worthiness to argue – so close is the perceived connection between argument and propounder.

This makes it clear that Rex wishes to act on the reader's sensibilities, on his or her social and political concern, but he does not wish only to do this; if the introduction does not culminate in the reader's preparedness to attend to the book's arguing all the way through, he or she will not know what action to take up.

Here Rex addresses himself to the reader who needs to be convinced that specifically sociological methods are relevant to the matter at hand. He shows an almost classical adherence to an argumentative strategy traditionally prescribed by rhetoricians,[4] directing his arguing at a reader who is taken to prefer a different approach from his own – that of history or psychology – and agreeing that each has much to commend it; but he goes on to stress that exclusive adherence to either would have consequences which the same reader is assumed to judge undesirable. Rex claims that the historian is unable to expose 'general processes' and 'explanatory laws' in social situations (pp. 1–2), while psychological analyses of Birmingham's racial problems would have to deal with hypothesised 'innate and universal tendencies' and 'personality disturbance' (p. 2).

The unacceptability of a purely psychological approach is highlighted by Rex's association of it with 'demonology': he undertakes to show instead that 'that which possessed' those people whom he has observed 'acting in contradiction of their own ideals and sometimes of their own interests' was not 'some evil demon' but 'the social system of which they were part' (p. 3).

Rex's writing here can be used to form an account of what is meant by 'addressed': he does not construct his text according to purely formal criteria, nor in a fashion derived exclusively from considering what he is writing *about*. He tries to arouse the *reader's* interest in Sparkbrook, to convince the *reader* that the situation ought to be changed, to persuade the *reader* that sociological explanation is the tool with which to begin doing this. Since he needs to preserve this involvement on the reader's part for the whole text, not just for its introduction, he begins to prepare the way for the sort of explanation he and Moore intend to give.

Claiming that 'the determinants of an on-going social system are to be found in the . . . interests of the typical actors in the system' (p. 4), Rex points out that people with common interests form groups and that it is 'out of the clash of interests, the conflicts and the truces between these groups that Birmingham society emerges' (p. 6).

Some such groups have abandoned Sparkbrook already; many of its lower middle-class inhabitants have become able to 'forsake the centre of the city' for a suburban lifestyle in imitation of the upper middle class (p. 8). Their 'deserted homes' pass to 'a motley population' which consists of 'the city's social rejects' as well as 'newcomers' who need to substitute 'some sort of colony structure' of their own for the 'defensive communal institutions' available to the indigenous working class (pp. 8–9). This group is 'at the back of a queue' (p. 9) for a style of living found desirable by the population as a whole.

Here Rex is very cautious. As will become clear, he is anxious that the immigrant group should not be blamed for what is happening in Sparkbrook, and just here he tries to block the reader from blaming anyone at all. 'People who had not in the past shown racial prejudice,' he states (p. 12), 'began to do so in a new social situation.'

What we have to do is not merely to classify behaviour as prejudiced but to understand the part which customs, beliefs, norms and expectations play in a larger social structure . . . Once we understand urban society as a structure of social interaction and conflict, prejudiced behaviour may be shown to fit naturally into or even to be required by that structure . . . [and] to follow as a logical consequence, given the beliefs which are held (p. 13).

Sociology, Rex implies, has moral as well as explanatory advantages: it precludes castigation which is unnecessary and (by the figure of reticence) unjust.

Rex turns his attention to the plight of immigrants in general, as a prelude to dealing with a group more difficult to protect from condemnation – the apparently rapacious lodging-house landlords. He emphasises the extent to which the immigrant is a victim of circumstances, not simply an intruder – his earlier reference to 'deserted homes' has prepared the way for this, with its implication that lower middle-class residents have left Sparkbrook voluntarily; they have not been pushed out by a wave of invaders. Rex deals with 'the immigrant' in visual terms:

> we *see* the immigrant, not simply as moving from one culture to another, but as being *cut off* from his native culture and *groping* for some kinds of cultural and social *signposts* in a colony structure which belongs neither to his homeland nor to the society of his hosts (p. 14; my emphases).

This use of hypotyposis – description whose vividness brings the reader to envisage something as before his very eyes – precedes a reference to the immigrant's 'extreme' situation (p. 14); 'cut off' is repeated, and 'extreme' differentially repeated as 'minimum situation'. The immigrant's primary community is described as preventing him from 'falling into a state of complete demoralization and anomie' (p. 15). But within this community there are social functions to be fulfilled, even if they cannot be fulfilled ideally and are carried out 'by a particular ethnic group' in ways which are 'morally dubious in the eyes of the host society' (pp. 16–17). Rex refers first to the Jews in medieval Europe – a group which the reader himself may be expected not to wish to see blamed – before stating that in a situation like this 'a pariah group of lodging-house landlords drawn from a particular group is always a likely possibility' (p. 17). The emergence of such a group, it is implied, is almost a natural phenomenon.

These tactics do function so as to direct the manner of the reader's response to the landlords; but this, to which I shall recur in the next section, is not merely a gratuitous intervention on the author's part. It is necessary to the correct reception of his explanation, for Rex does not believe that the emergence of the landlords is wholly a matter of individual responsibility.

Nor is this introduction a part of Rex's and Moore's book which is *more* 'addressed' than others. Their introduction initiates a set of positions which are sustained throughout their text, and its rhetorical form is one which attempts to ensure that the reader places those emphases on different components of their account which are required for him or her to grasp it as an explanation at all.

2 RHETORICAL ORDER AND VALUE JUDGEMENTS

For Rex and Moore, to explain something sociologically entails seeing it from 'the perspective of the interconnectedness of the social structure' (p. 7). The concept of perspective itself implies indicating relative magnitudes or significances, seeing items from one spot rather than another. It is not possible to use perspective in a text in this way – still less to change it, if the reader is taken to start from a vantage point which does not coincide with the author's – without employing rhetorical techniques. At the least, devices of order and relative emphasis must be used. And as they occur in real communication situations, these devices are not value-neutral. The items with which sociological accounts are intended to deal are necessarily ones to which social and ethical meanings are already attached – just because they are events in society – whatever the author may write. And since he or she is forced to deal with them in some order, it is impossible to avoid either changing or accepting the evaluations with which these events are equipped.

Neither Rex and Moore nor Willis attempt to avoid this situation; it is difficult to see how they could, and since the authors of both books write as if they are contending with prejudices against their subjects on their readers' parts, it is difficult to see why they should.

Rex and Moore approach the question of the landlords of overcrowded immigrant lodging-houses in Chapter 5, written chiefly by Moore. The authors have ordered their description of the shifting populations of Birmingham as a whole, the city's housing situation, three different areas of Sparkbrook and its English and foreign inhabitants *before* they embark on Chapter 5. In the absence of strong and stated reasons to the contrary, this order itself implies that the landlords' activities are at least to be understood in a manner which takes account of the influence of their situations.

During the foregoing chapters other arguments (see below) have given presence not to the landlords as responsible individuals but to the social pressures leading to multi-occupation. The landlords' personal characteristics have been relegated to the background by the simple device of excluding them from mention, and even the title of Chapter 5, 'The Lodging-House', indicates that its focus is rather upon a situation than upon individuals. To have named it 'The Landlords' would have had very different moral implications.

This effect recurs in the internal order of the chapter itself, where

concentrating on the interconnectedness of the social structure has
the usual effect of perspective, both literal and figurative: it draws
attention to what might have been missed from a different
viewpoint and alters perception of relative importance. (These
effects are comparable with those of metaphor.)

The chapter begins by rehearsing the reasoning of an immigrant
who wishes to buy a house in which to live, at the same time as
saving for his return home and housing any of his dependants who
might need assistance (p. 133). Thus presence is given to a motive
which is blameless in terms of society at large and possibly in terms
of the hypothetical reader's values too. (Merely to have altered the
order of the chapter by starting with a record of exorbitant rents
charged would have placed a different complexion on the landlords'
acts.)

Moore continues, 'none of it works out quite like this' (p. 133) –
this everyday phraseology is, by reticence, an appeal to the reader's
own experience of things which do not go right – for mortgage
companies will not lend to people they see as bad risk clients buying
bad risk property, and the landlords are forced to take up expensive
private loans. If they try to maintain the ageing houses which are all
that they can afford, they find it costly; and their social conventions
prohibit them from asking rent from a very wide range of people to
whom they have obligations. Hence the fact that the landlords ask
high rent from the people from whom they are able to ask it at all no
longer seems surprising. And the linguistic conventions attached to
exhibiting first an intention and then the outside pressures which
transform its results mean that Moore's account *counts* as an excuse
for what the landlords eventually do.

The order of *Race, Community and Conflict* as a whole is an
important constituent of its 'addressed' character as a non-neutral
intervention in a discourse which had already begun before the
authors arrived on the scene. The book is not arranged as a
collection of pieces of evidence from which a conclusion is finally
deduced; its formal argument is stated in its first chapter, and
further chapters do not merely produce extra evidence for this
argument. They control the way in which it is understood. An early
statement of the book's explanation is given as early as p. 20, where
Rex states that it is incorrect to suppose that immigrants have
exacerbated the Birmingham housing situation by the sheer fact of
their numbers. Rather, segregation has 'compelled coloured people
to live in certain typical conditions' and has itself contributed to

'racial ill-feeling' (p. 20). But the author himself points out that simply to state such an argument is not enough: 'in order to understand it we must begin with an analysis of Birmingham's housing problem' (ibid.).

The analysis offered begins by anticipating the argument of Chapter 5, and ends with what – given the rhetorical situation within which the authors are writing – is in effect an accusation of the City Council. Rex attributes immigrants' difficulties in finding council accommodation in part to unadmitted discrimination by officials (p. 27), and points out that it is the 'lodging-houses in the so-called twilight zones of the city' which cater for those for whom the council has 'refused to accept responsibility' (p. 24). There is an immense demand from people 'at the back of the housing queue' (pp. 30–1), but since house owners have no long-term interest in expensive fabric maintenance, buildings are 'bound to deteriorate very rapidly' (p. 31). Older residents leave these areas, partly 'in panic', fearing 'a decline in house prices', and partly because they can get good prices 'for houses which [are] not much use to them'; multi-occupation snowballs (p. 31). City officials deplore this, but offer no alternatives, and a 'pariah group' of landlords is blamed in terms of both left- and right-wing ideologies for stopping a gap in the system of each (pp. 40–1).

It may not be that Rex deliberately intends to find a door at which to lay blame for this situation; but in the type of discourse in which he is participating it is inevitable that other people will wish to do so, and indeed he mentions that mistaken attempts in this direction have already been made. Then he writes,

> In these circumstances 'stopping the cancer from spreading' becomes, consciously or unconsciously, a policy of creating ghetto areas for immigrants. This, we believe, is where Birmingham's housing, planning and public health policies have led (p. 41).

Formally, Rex is adducing a social cause for a set of developments; in terms of the public discourse in whose context his book is to be read, and despite his own expressed wish to avoid moral condemnation, he is accusing the City Council of playing a prime part in exacerbating racism.

Despite their practice, Rex and Moore show uncertainty about sociologists' right in their professional capacity to interfere with their readers' attitudes and perceptions as they do. (In my view such fears are ungrounded; it is more important to reflect on the manner and content of impingement on readers than to regret its existence.) Their book has two last chapters, in so far as 'practical men-of-affairs' (p. 1) may be expected to skip the general sociological reflections in Chapter 12, and to clinch the authors' arguments each of their final chapters ends with a plea for action. But Rex and Moore, in making these pleas, try to separate their personal hopes from their views as sociologists. They stress 'the built-in reasons in the structure of our society which will make increasing racial tension likely', and add, 'it is because we, as individuals rather than as sociologists, wish to see it arrested that we have written this book' (p. 271). Again,

> If we succeed in drawing the attention of British planners to the importance of understanding the zone of transition within the context of the sociology of the city, we shall have accomplished one of our main aims in writing this book (p. 285).

It would be unreasonable to suppose that an author's main aim in composing a text should not affect its contents (whatever methodology might dictate), and as we have seen, the 'addressed' nature of Rex's and Moore's work gives it rhetorical components which make a separation between aims and execution impossible.

The most striking feature of the order of Paul Willis's book is that it enables the reader to evolve a certain personal response to its subjects *before* the author advances a detailed sociological account of their situation. The response which the first part of the book is clearly intended to evoke is one of sympathy; sympathy not just in the sense of particular feelings towards Willis's subjects, but also in the sense of a preparedness to consider their points of view and to refrain from the dismissive evaluations of their conduct which are usual (the book makes clear) from people outside their own class and group. In his introduction the author refers briefly to the 'tragedy' and 'contradiction' of the boys' plight. Their 'self-damnation' to lives in deadening occupations which, on the face of it, it is hard to imagine anyone deliberately choosing, derives from a partial understanding of the nature of the class structure and their own fates within it (p. 3).

Willis does not dwell on the usual social perceptions of the 'lads' in his study – the aggressive and villainous hooligans of popular imagination – but stresses the experience as of 'true learning, ffirmation, appropriation, and . . . resistance' bound up in their conduct (ibid.). Part I of his book is chiefly devoted to showing the reader what it is *like* to be one of this group, and it *opens* with a quotation whose effect is to put the boys' behaviour in school in a new light. Discussing teachers, a 'lad' called Joey says,

(. . .) they're able to punish us. They're bigger than us, they stand for a bigger establishment than we do, like, we're just little and they stand for bigger things, and you try to get your own back. It's, uh, resenting authority I suppose (p.11).

Further quotations show that the 'lads' are able to be more penetrating about reasons for behaviour than are their teachers; Joey remarks that sudden demands by staff for the removal of jewellery in class are made as 'a sort of show like' (p. 11). On p. 18 we see the headmaster reacting literally to teasing which is in effect a game about authority relations:

Spike And we went in, I says 'We warn't smoking', he says (. . .) and he went really mad. I thought he was going to punch me or summat.

Spanksy 'Call me a liar', 'I'm not a liar', 'Get back then', and we admitted it in the end; we was smoking (. . .) He was having a fit, he says 'Callin' me a liar'. We said we warn't smoking, tried to stick to it, but Simmondsy was having a fit.

Spike He'd actually seen us light up.

Willis also uses the device of humour to deflect the reader's disapprobation:

Bill . . . We was going to the ten pin bowling, you know, up by the Brompton Road, there was an 'ouse there for sale. We took the 'For Sale' sign out of the one, put it in the next door, then we took the milk carrier from the one, put it next door (. . .) we took a sort of window box on legs from the porch and stuck that next door. We swapped stacks of things.

Spanksy And dustbins! [Laughter] . . . every night, go in to one garden, tek a dwarf out, and in the end there was a dwarf, a sundial, a bridge, a dwarf fishing, all in this one garden, and there's a big sundial up the road. He got one end of it, I got the other, and carried it all the way and put it in (. . .) (p. 31).

The fact that Willis arranges the more sympathetic and the more innocuous sides of the lads' life-style first can also be seen from the order of the subsections in his second chapter. They *end* with 'Sexism' and 'Racism'; they are arranged, that is, in order of least likelihood to alienate the reader.

There are several reasons for which this presentation of his subjects is important to Willis's argumentative strategy (independently of whether one considers the evaluative overtones of his ordering correct in themselves). First, the author is entering a realm of public discourse in which his subjects are already generally regarded with considerable disfavour. If he is to make the reader open to an understanding of the lads' perceptions and experience, Willis must do something to remove the blocks to comprehension which such negative attitudes are likely to cause. He remarks on p. vii that the 'practitioners' in his audience are likely to concentrate on Part I of his book; this part is where he can make an intervention into the practical attitudes governing the debate to which he is contributing.

Second, Willis's sociological explanation requires the reader to accept a class analysis of relations in society; and yet he is writing for an audience which – as his own views would lead us to expect – is largely middle class, and hence an audience in which preferences for some other type of explanation of social action are likely to preponderate. If the reader can evolve a sympathetic receptiveness to his subjects, this attitude may extend to his explanatory framework, at least as far as this one case is concerned. At any rate, it is important for Willis's argument that his audience abandon any (class-based) notion of the lads' conduct which presents it as merely irresponsible.

Third, a different ordering of descriptive components would have had different evaluative overtones. If Willis had begun with the lads' sexism and racism, he could too easily have appeared simply to condemn them. He is forced to choose between rival evaluations, not between some evaluation and none.

If this is so, it seems that the Weberian view that value-judgements should not be added to sociological texts is beside the point. It is more urgent to consider how we should react to those that are there already. Equally, it is unnecessary to argue that sociological work *ought* to be evaluatively committed; it already is. Russell Keat argues that while it seems unnecessary to ban all evaluative commitment from sociological texts, value-freedom can still be attained in the following way:

I suggest that, for any concept that appears to express or presuppose a particular normative attitude, it is always possible to replace it by one that does not do this. In other words, in any situation where the statements of a social theory seem objectionable on normative grounds, from a particular moral or political standpoint, it is possible to reconstruct them in a way that removes the normatively problematic element, and thus enables their truth or falsity to be assessed by non-normatively dependent criteria of validity.[5]

But, at the very least, all books must arrange their contents in some order, and all must include some and exclude others; and the conventions of discourse are such that this is enough to convey a normative position. So no amount of attention to concepts alone will remove the difficulty. Indeed, nothing will – except working out a position which reveals that it is not a difficulty at all.

3 EXAMPLES AND TYPICALITY

One of the most prominent, and enjoyable, features of both Rex's and Moore's and Paul Willis's texts is the wealth of example they contain; but I want to suggest that the use of example in qualitative sociology poses problems which its methodology does not answer. According to that methodology, examples are supposed to be related to generalisations in terms of typicality – in terms, that is, of representativeness. Here I shall examine some cases of exceptionally telling but highly unrepresentative uses of example in both texts (which theoretically we ought not to expect) and I shall point to the absence of some representative constellations which we should expect. I believe that giving significance to unrepresentative examples is a practice not unrepresentative of qualitative sociology in general – so that Paul Willis is right to claim that 'the ethnographic account' deals with 'activity, creativity and human agency' 'without always knowing how' (p. 3). By referring to authors' rhetorical needs in communicating with particular readers, we can explain how.

Rex's and Moore's first chapter opens with a reference to 'the way in which racial problems dominated public discussion' in Birmingham in the 1960s, contrasting this with the 'radical and egalitarian tradition' of the city (p. 19). By the figure of reticence, this can be construed as a reproach; it is followed by a long extract from a letter to the *Birmingham Evening Mail*. This is introduced, by differential repetition of the previous contrast, as a document which 'smacked more of the Deep South in the United States or settle Africa than of the City of Reform' (ibid.), and in it one Councillo Collett writes as follows:

> How much longer have we Englishmen to tolerate the over propaganda urging us to love the coloured immigrant who come in peace and humility and ends by being the arrogant boss . . . On Monday a T.V. programme showed how a coloured man suffered when he came to live amongst us. He was expected to do the menial jobs and why shouldn't he? Few if any are capable o doing a skilled job and they could, of course, return home. But do they? Not on your life! Whether they be intellectual or not, they stay on, hoping to wear us down with the old theme 'love thy neighbour' . . . (p. 19).

According to Rex, the main author of this chapter, 'the fact that such sentiments could be expressed at all' is evidence of 'widespread disquiet amongst Birmingham people' about the 50 000 and more black immigrants among them (pp. 19–20). But he also expressly states that he does not believe Collett's views to be typical of Birmingham's inhabitants (p. 19); and strictly speaking, one untypical letter in a newspaper is evidence of little more than the editor's willingness, for whatever reasons, to print it. I do not wish to dissent from Rex's claim that there was disquiet, but since this letter is not in the ordinary sense evidence for such a claim, it is worth asking what purpose its very prominent inclusion in Chapter 1 does serve.

It is possible to draw conclusions from what Rex says about the audience he regards himself as addressing. These conclusions yield at least four communicative reasons for the citation of Collett's letter. All these fall under the general heading of sensitising the reader, and the differences between them demonstrate the width of the range of purposes for which sensitisation may be important in arguing.

We have seen from his Introduction that Rex takes the reader to concur with him in treating expressions such as 'rational control' (p. 18) as terms of commendation, in contrast to the notions of perplexity and confusion. He also assumes that the reader does not wish to have to believe his or her fellow-men to be moved by innate impulses to racism, while he or she does hope that a real desire to explain what is happening in a situation may lead to its amelioration. Given Rex's terms of reference, it is clear that the 'rational' improvements which he wishes the reader to accept will involve some degree of reformation to the social structure. Taken literally, this does not commit Rex very far; in terms of the conventions of political discourse, it indicates that he is addressing an approximately liberal reader.

Given the difficulty Rex attributes to his own explanation, it follows that he expects his reader to be an educated person, and in the nature of contemporary socialisation processes this educated, liberal reader will probably be in some sense of the term middle class. For such a reader, the incoherence and aggression in Councillor Collett's letter may be expected to underline the frailness of its arguments. The first function can be performed much more effectively by the rhetorical means of exhibiting an example and allowing the reader to react to it than by stating at great length the reasons for which racism is reprehensible.

This first function overlaps with a second: if the reader is reminded now that he or she finds racism repellent, he or she can elaborate Rex's own arguments against such an attitude for him. This encourages a division of labour with the reader which in fact allows Rex to preserve some of the conventions of lack of involvement which pertain to sociological writing. The reader can amplify political positions which the writer need only indicate.

If it is assumed that Rex is addressing a liberal reader, it follows that this reader is likely to disapprove of racism, but there are many gradations of opinion within this general position. A third function of Councillor Collett's letter is to enable Rex to reach as wide a spectrum as possible of readers within this broadly defined group, and to make them more receptive to his representations of the urgency of Birmingham's plight. Rex wishes to speak 'not merely to an academic audience, but to the widest possible audience of citizens and practical men-of-affairs' (p. 1). Among those of his readers whose predispositions allow them to be sensitive to his views there may well be those who believe racism to be bad, who are prepared to accept Rex's arguments that it can be combatted by social change, but who are uncertain about the extent of its actual influence in contemporary Britain. In order to sympathise with Rex's arguments it is necessary to agree with him on all three of these preliminary points; so to reach his 'widest possible audience' he must convince readers of the last one too. Collett's letter is not an *argument* for the prevalence of racism; but by its vividness, by its forceful and extreme character it makes such a notion present to the reader. If the reader cannot easily dismiss it from his or her mind, he or she can less easily evade the force of those arguments on the subject which are already familiar. The letter may offer an 'enabling experience' needed for accepting arguments about the distribution of racism.

There is one prejudice attributable to Rex's hypothetical reader in particular which would predispose him or her against the authors' arguments, and attacking this prejudice is a fourth function of Collett's letter in this text. From the fact that Rex *calls on* Birmingham's 'radical and egalitarian' tradition (p. 19), it can be inferred that he takes the reader to respect it; but if the reader really does, he or she may be reluctant to admit that this tradition is in danger among responsible public bodies such as that of which Councillor Collett is a member. But acceptance of Rex's and Moore's explanation for the developments in Sparkbrook depends on the reader's capacity to overcome his or her reluctance, since they trace much of the blame for the situation to the council. The exhibition of Collett's letter functions to combat, by the figure of reticence, any of the reader's prejudices which might lead him or her to reject explanations attributing morally repugnant conduct to people in authority.

The functions which I have attributed to Collett's letter emphasise the importance to this text, too, of processes of thought which are sparked off by it rather than explicitly stated – of arguments which occur off the printed page. In this case these arguments are chiefly concerned with sensitising the reader, but though they involve strong implicit appeals to moral and political beliefs they cannot be described as purely 'emotional'. Displaying the case of Councillor Collett might, among other things, be termed giving counter-evidence for an hypothesis ascribed to the reader – to the effect that responsible persons can be assumed to hold unprejudiced views.

It seems to me that it is highly doubtful whether the multifarious purposes of this passage could as well be served by any method more explicit than the one Rex uses. Certainly, if he had displayed all the reasoning I have just given, it is most unlikely that the same communicative result would have been achieved. It appears that effective communication often requires that the *reader* perform the activities of drawing conclusions and pointing up contrasts, without excessive instruction from the author. There may be a limit to what it is possible to state directly without destroying one's own message.

This last point applies with especial force to *Learning to Labour*. It is essential to Willis's personal, political and sociological enterprises that he convey to the reader the fact that 'the lads' are active, alert and alive. What they say, feel and do is

> not simply . . . a set of transferred internal structures (as in the usual notions of socialisation) nor . . . the passive result of the action of dominant ideology downwards (as in certain kinds of marxism), but at least in part . . . the product of collective human praxis (p. 4).

It is profoundly unlikely that Willis could *convey* his point by a succession of theoretical statements of this sort – especially given the image of 'the lads' which the reader is likely to have already. What he does, and what qualitative sociology instructs him to do, is to *show* the lads being humorous, rebellious, reflective, ingenious and so forth. As in the case of Councillor Collett, this does not form an explicit refutation of the sociological views Willis opposes; but from a rhetorical point of view it is more effective.

The 'lad' who makes the strongest impression in this direction is Joey, whom Willis cites frequently. Speaking of a more conformist acquaintance, Joe says

> I mean look at Tom Bradley, have you ever noticed him. I've always looked at him and I've thought, Well . . . we've been through all life's pleasures and all its fucking displeasures, we've been drinking, we've been fighting, we've known frustration, sex, fucking hatred, love and all this lark. He's never been with a woman, he's never been in a pub. We don't know it, we assume it – I dare say he'd come and tell us if he had – but he's never been with a woman, he's never been drinking, I've never known him in a fight. He's not known so many of the emotions as we've had to experience, and he's got it all to come yet (p. 16).

Though Willis remarks on Joe's 'considerable insight and expressive power' he stresses that he is *not* typical of the lads he is dealing with (p. 16). Willis adds that Joey is none the less 'representative', but he means by this only that he is working-class,

unqualified, identified as a troublemaker, and from a 'fightin
family' (p. 16) where the father is a foundryman; the qualities fc
which he quotes Joey are not representative. There is a problen
here: it must be important to qualitative sociology that autho
should produce telling examples, but how are these related t
generalisations if the features for which they are chosen are nc
representative? By the standards of the natural sciences, it is as
someone claimed to have made a discovery about the amount c
interferon needed to cure cancer in his or her patients, but exhibite
in support of this claim a patient who had reacted differently fron
all the others.

But I suggest that we should not regard quotations such as thos
from Joey and Councillor Collett in the light of evidence as it is use
in the natural sciences, and that the question whether they ar
literally typical in the statistical sense does not arise. (The same ma
be said of the quotations my own text supplies from those of othe
people.) If instead we regard such citations as rhetorical devices fc
enabling and encouraging readers to perceive the force of genera
remarks, we can expect examples to exhibit particularly concen
trated cases of what happens generally but, perhaps, less remark
ably. Joey can make apparent the creativeness, perceptiveness an
energy which Willis attributes to all the lads, but which he woul
find difficult to exhibit on the printed page, where not all that goe
on during long processes of interaction can be directly reproduced

Forceful examples compensate the reader for his or her narrowe
experience of the field than the author's, and they circumvent som
special limitations to textual communication. This does not mak
them immune to criticism. It can be asked, first, if such devices ar
acceptable according to stated standards, which may be moral o
political; second, whether they are misleading or not – whether it i
clear to what general remarks they point; third, whether thes
general remarks are true, and what roles they play in the discourse
of which they are part.

In view of Rex's and Moore's and Willis's responsiveness to th
rhetorical needs of communicating with readers, it is perhaps not a
surprising as at first it seems that some methodologically com
mended forms are missing from these texts. Rex and Moore assum
that 'an on-going social system' can be understood by reference t
the 'typical actors' in it (p. 4), and they intend to apply the tenets o
Rex's *Key Problems in Sociological Theory* (1961) in their joint wor
(1967, p. xiii). In the earlier book, Rex's definition of a socia

relationship seems to indicate what attributes should be included in models of social beings. If A is to be said to have a social relationship with B, he writes (1961, p. 53), the author's model must include A's purposes or interests, and A's expectations of B's behaviour; B's purposes and A's knowledge of them; the norms A knows B to accept, and B's desire to win and keep A's approval. But in *Race, Community and Conflict* the notion of typical, hypothetical actor-models is used only in the Introduction, and the list of attributes for it is virtually ignored. (For Willis the question seems not to arise; he has observed relatively small groups and does not try to construct amalgam figures.) When Rex and Moore refer to 'the immigrant' or 'the landlord' they do not specify such terms in any way which distinguishes them from ordinary language usages. Nor do they differentiate between these and average types, as advised on p. 15 of *Key Problems*. They do provide a good deal of information about specific individuals, and do not indicate which should be included or excluded for the purposes of any model-building that might be required.

If we were to regard works such as *Key Problems in Sociological Theory* as manuals of instruction for textual composition, the authors' writing in *Race, Community and Conflict* might be considered culpably inconsistent. If we do not so regard them, we can make more sense of authors' actual practice, and it is possible to alleviate the concern of those who, like Paul Feyerabend (1975, *passim*), fear that methodological restrictions will inhibit research practice: writers are capable of ignoring such restrictions in the execution of their work, however they may characterise such work afterwards. No doubt methodological texts provide useful blueprints to direct the attention of sociological investigators; but if Rex and Moore do not use rigidly constructed models of typical agents, it is because they do not *need* them to convey the idea of Birmingham's inhabitants as groups with various views of each other's behaviour, attempting to defend their interests.

It is true that this idea must be distilled from the pages of *Race, Community and Conflict*, and is not stated schematically; but if it is true that the reader *needs* a certain amount of work to do in comprehending a text, this may not be a disadvantage. Moreover, there appears to be a psychological and communicative opposition between interpretive sociology and a consistent use of formal models of agents such as those outlined by these authors or by, for example, Alfred Schutz.[6] It seems more appropriate to qualitative sociology

to write about 'social agents' in a way which makes clear that they
are people, not models or other artificial constructs. I shall return to
this question in Chapter 4 below.

Here I have concluded that formal models are excluded from
qualitative texts because they do not communicate in a way
appropriate to the genre, and that untypical examples are included
because they do. In the next section I shall examine the question
whether what examples convey so aptly is necessarily connected
with sensitising the reader only, or whether they can convey
specifically sociological content in their own right.

4 ACTUAL TYPES AND RHETORICAL INDUCTION

In this section I shall continue to deal with the sociological use of
example – central to qualitative texts but by no means confined to
them – a sociological book[7] wholly devoid of examples is barely
imaginable. I shall continue to concentrate on examples and
illustrations selected without reference to statistical typicality
although my claim is that the rhetorical functions they perform are
attributable also to examples which are selected according to
natural-scientific standards of representativeness (certainly the
smaller class in sociology).

These examples, I believe, function rhetorically as signs: signs a
symptoms of states of affairs, signs as encapsulating states of affairs in
some way which enables the reader to interpret future situations
and only very rarely necessary signs of states of affairs. When such
signs form parts of sociological texts I shall call them 'actual types'.
In the previous section I related examples to the reader's grasp of
general remarks, implicit or explicit in a text. I should like to
interpret 'general remarks' not as strictly universal generalisations
but in terms of 'rhetorical induction' – a characteristically socio
logical form of generalisation, which it is one of the tasks of actual
types to convey.

First I should like to point to the dominant position which
examples take in Rex's and Moore's and in Willis's work. At least
half of Part i of Willis's text is taken up by quotations from his
subjects. In Chapters 2 to 10 of *Race, Community and Conflict* example
preponderate in all writing not given up to analyses of tables. On
p. 90 the authors record the importance they attribute to 'qualitat
ive material'; they term it, conventionally, 'impressionistic descrip

ion' (p. 57) and say that it is intended for readers unfamiliar with
the social relations and the "feel" of Sparkbrook' (p. 56). The first
concentrated block of examples occurs in Chapter 2 of Rex's and
Moore's work, which Moore inaugurates with an account of what
Sparkbrook 1' is like (thus bestowing presence on his description).
He mentions 'large, three-storey brick buildings, at one time richly
ornamented and porched', where 'headmistresses, doctors, businessmen and, at one time, the Town Clerk of Birmingham' used to
live (p. 43). He goes on,

> The daughter of the Lloyd's last head gardener still lives in a
> cottage in the Park and clearly remembers the big dinner parties
> at the house at the turn of the century, when the coaches stood
> from the house door to the Park gates (ibid.).

Some of this atmosphere remains:

> In summer the streets are green and leafy, and the houses stand
> back from the pavements; but the ornate facades are crumbling,
> the paint peeling, and in many blocks the front gardens are
> beaten into flat areas of hard earth, littered with broken bricks
> and glass, children's bicycles and dolls' prams battered beyond
> repair. Unfamiliar cooking smells and loud music issue from the
> windows and the street litter bins overflow with refuse (pp. 43–4).

Moore repeats this contrast, again emphasising it by punctuation:
Forty years ago people put on their best suits to cross the Stratford
Road into this area. Now they avoid coming over unless it is
absolutely essential' (p. 44). In the artisans' cottages of 'Sparkbrook
2',

> Women can be seen popping in and out of their neighbours'
> houses, and in the warm evenings people sit on their front steps
> and call across the road to one another. The figure of Mum,
> wearing an apron, arms folded, yelling up the road to her
> children, is a familiar sight (pp. 44–5).

The fact that the reader has a role in interpreting and making use
of such observations, as well as the fact that these observations must
refer outside themselves to more than they literally state, are
indicated by these examples: there would be little point in referring

to dolls' prams or to women wearing aprons in the street if this were *all* that were being said.

Moore states that such passages as these examine 'the historical differences in the three zones of Sparkbrook and the immediate visual variables in housing' (p. 47). The term 'variables' functions rhetorically to fit what he has written into a linguistic register associated with science; but it is most unlikely that he has counted the broken dolls' prams in front gardens and mentioned them here because there are more of them than, say, broken roller skates. And there are almost certainly more torn newspapers – which are not mentioned here at all – in these gardens than either.

Moore says too that the details he provides give 'a hint' about social structures and life-styles (p. 47) which cannot be conveyed by 'figures' (p. 56). But it is left to the reader to work out what exactly it is that is being indicated. In Chapter 3 Moore observes that he has 'looked at the changing social patterns' in the different zones of Sparkbrook 'as seen by a number of inhabitants, both young and old', as well as at 'the family lives they live, and the way in which they see the present situation' (p. 72). What he has *written* consists of ten or eleven direct quotations, embedded in general remarks and covering only fourteen pages; he explicitly denies that the respondents he quotes 'represent all Sparkbrook' or, on the other hand, that he has conveyed the type of information encompassed by large-scale surveys (pp. 72–3). Thus there seems to be some tension between this account of what he puts onto the page and his own summary of what he communicates by doing so.

This tension is not immediately resolved by Moore's uses of the terms 'typical' and 'representative' in a manner which exactly parallels Willis's applications of them to Joey (see preceding section). In the course of Chapter 3, Moore describes a Miss A. as 'typical' of a response to Sparkbrook's problems which involves 'an element of fantasy and constant references to the "good old days" when all the big houses were nicely kept, the area inhabited by respectable people and the streets safe at night' (p. 60). But he adds various personal details which appear to be those for which he has chosen to mention Miss A. rather than anyone else in the group to which she belongs: she ' "keeps herself to herself" ', devoting her time to 'her aged and infirm father' and 'keeping the large house in spotlessly good order and working for her parish church' (p. 61). The latter are presumably not typical details in a statistical sense, and Moore goes on to describe a Mrs T. whom he conjectures to be ntypical of the English residents'. None the less he states twice that he 'represents' an activism among those English who wish to stay in parkbrook to fight its ' "social disease" ' (pp. 61–2).

It seems to me that there are some ordinary language usages and some traditional rhetorical ones which cast light on these authors' procedure. In the first place, 'typical' may be used of features which need not themselves occur frequently but are either symbolic of or attributable to some state of affairs which is considered fundamental to a particular situation – as when people cry out in a quarrel, 'That's just typical of you!' (Taking the car out and crashing it may not happen often, but carelessness and inconsiderateness might.[8]) When whatever is termed 'typical' is *attributable* to the more general feature, there is an obvious parallel with the notion of sign as symptom.

A typical feature which is symbolic, rather than symptomatic, of some general condition may be accounted for as a case which so tellingly encapsulates some state of affairs that it teaches us about what to expect in the future. (In a traditional example, the wisdom and justice of Socrates give us a special insight into the connection between these two characteristics, and allow us to respond to them so that we know what qualities and behaviour to expect of a genuinely wise man when next we meet one.[9]) In either of these cases, it is plausible to suppose that authors might cite examples not typical in the statistical sense but still call them 'representative'.

Hence it is possible to set out some common attributes of the examples we are examining here. First, they are details or quotations from real cases; this fact alone would distinguish them from 'ideal types', whose components are not intended to represent real events, and I propose calling them 'actual types'. Second, they need not be statistically typical of the situations in which they occur in the sense of having been chosen from many similar items, just because they are similar. Instead, they are related as symptoms or signs to more general states of affairs.

Third, it appears that 'actual types' rely to a considerable extent on associations which the reader already has; thus the references made by actual types will be partly conventional, given a context of social meanings common to author and reader. Thus the language attributed to Miss A. above – she ' "keeps herself to herself" ' – has definite implications about her social status and life-style. These implications are definite in the sense that for anyone familiar with the English cultural background they are fairly difficult to mistake;

none the less, they may be symptomatic of a certain attitude to life but they do not allow the reader to deduce with *certainty* that the speaker has this attitude. (It is possible to use Miss A.'s expression ironically or sarcastically.) Necessary signs are those which do permit certain inferences – as Koplick's spots allow us to infer with certainty that whoever has them has measles – and it seems probable that such signs are rare in the social world. Where necessity is unobtainable, it is to be expected that sociologists should deal partly in conventional associations, since it cannot be a matter of indifference to them whether they are understood.

But, fourth, actual types do not communicate in an *exhaustively* conventional way; they frequently rely on the reader to take active steps to combine associations in a creative manner. The notion that creative activity of some sort is required in reading novels has been emphasised by, for example, Lubbock (1921) and Iser (1972) – though it would be a mistake to assume that an active, creative role is required only of the reader of non-natural scientific literature. But presumably different sorts of activity are required according to different types of text, and it seems characteristic of qualitative sociology that it treads a balance between the conventional and the creative. Thus the comprehensibility of an actual type for a given reader forms a partial test both of the extent to which social meanings really are shared by author and reader, and of the extent to which the reader is willing to exert himself or herself with regard to the text.

Since actual types are much more dependent than routine and univocal terminology on the reader's active participation in making sense of the text, their use entails more risk that the reader will not take the author's point. It is therefore interesting that authors are willing to take this risk so often, and I suggest that there are three main reasons for this.

First, actual types form a singularly economical way of conveying what a place or a person is like. Inferences from sign are much more common in daily life than is usually recognised; the work of Goffman (see below) consists partly in pointing out to us the signs we use, but do not always notice using, in forming judgements about each other. So-called 'atmosphere' can be conveyed textually by assembling details which the reader is accustomed to treat as signs in everyday life, or which have acquired a literary reputation as signs, from which the reader can infer to a number of states of affairs not explicitly mentioned. It would normally be impossibly cumbersome to enumerate these states of affairs in literal terms; and it seems too that readers prefer to work out the implications of signs on their own, each extrapolating from those details which particularly interest him or her.

Second, the use of actual types provides a method of altering the reader's attitudes – as we have seen that sociological authors may wish to do – without provoking his or her irritation by too forthright an assault. Thus Rex and Moore attempt to dismantle prejudices against the type of person to be found living in overcrowded 'slum' conditions:

> The rooms are all in bad condition. J.'s room could only be called a cubicle. She has divided it into two with a partition. On the 'living room' side she has managed to fit three wooden chairs, a chest of drawers and a paraffin stove. However, J. is a very cheerful person and she talked about her activities in the local Methodist Church, of which she is an active member, and discussed moral questions, especially the problem of young West Indians going astray in England. (p. 102)

Thus although actual types are *dependent* on the reader's associations they may also function to *change* them, as this excerpt does by connecting the idea of slum habitation with those of cheerfulness under adversity, parish work and intelligent moral concern. In the previous section we have seen Willis using actual types to connect the notion of extreme uncooperativeness at school with humour, ingeniousness and a spirited resentment of oppression.

A third reason for the use of actual types is a linguistic one, and can be deduced from remarks about language which are made by Willis. I have already remarked that Willis's own language differs somewhat from that of what he terms 'mainstream sociology' (p. 183); he is prepared to refer to 'the axis' in which teachers' superiority is held as being 'partially dislodged' (p. 72) or to use expressions such as 'The logic of a living' (p. 121). This, it seems to me, is because he wishes to avoid 'mechanistic undialectical notion(s)' (p. 59) which reify concepts such as intelligence (ibid.) or ' "parental attitude" ' (p. 73). Willis points out that cultural phenomena become distorted by being stated in terms which are of necessity artificially well defined. In order to be comprehensible sociologists posit 'clean and coherent insight(s)' (p. 121), when what they are referring to may not be 'in any one person's head' at all

(p. 124). Thus Willis is opposed to concepts which reduce the 'tension and uncertainty' (p. 183) of people's active adoption of cultural forms of thinking, feeling and behaving, and is anxious to show his subjects as 'recognisably human' (p. 172), with all the ambiguities this involves.

Here there are two ways in which the use of actual types solves problems which are inherent in Willis's aims. There is, first, the problem of translation. The 'lads' speak a language whose structure and whose terms frequently incorporate their own particular social experience and their attitudes to it. In so far as it does this their language conveys different meanings from the conventional ones – as calling them 'the lads' shows; the term 'schoolboys' would be ridiculous. Thus, for example, the term 'pisstakes' has a different meaning from that of the term 'joke', and Willis uses both in the same sentence to show that he means both (p. 55). Actual types allow the reader a relatively undistorted access to the 'lads'' remarks but – secondly – without merely presenting them exactly as they see themselves.

Incidentally, Willis's actual types are not just quotations in the sense of being simply straightforward written reproductions of what his subjects say. (Hess-Lüttich points out that such written reproductions cannot be straightforward.[10]) They use what I should term 'gestural recording'. Enough of the speaker's *behaviour* is indicated (by devices such as including slang terms with strong connotations in terms of life-style and conduct) for the reader to *visualise* the speaker. (This forms a type of hypotyposis.) But not enough of the original verbal productions are included to confuse or estrange the reader.[11]

Willis is clear that he perceives factors in their situation which his subjects cannot (see his last chapter), and the setting he provides for his quotations as well as his selection of them allows him to give presence to his subjects' agency *and* comment sociologically upon it. Clusters of actual types can convey general comments without reifying them in the way Willis wishes to avoid.

This effect occurs partly because actual types do appeal to the reader's sensibility as well as his or her intellect, and partially compensate for the divorce of sociological details from the social and emotional contexts in which they originally occur. Actual types are addressed to the reader as a whole person, so that he or she is able to grasp what the author says in a peculiarly personal mode. In so far as the reader expands by his or her own efforts on what the author actually writes, the persuasive power of what is written is increased – without making it necessary for the author to destroy his or her message by labouring it. For Rex, actual types have the added advantage of overcoming the limitations imposed by his own Weberian methodology, according to which it should be impossible to account sociologically for irrational conduct. Some of the racist reactions his and Moore's work describes (see pp. 201–2) are decidedly irrational, but the reader is not left with the impression that they are mysterious.

To explain this fact I should like to return to the criteria I proposed in the last section for evaluating what I now call actual types: in terms of their acceptability in moral, emotional or political senses – which allows for criticising, say, 'little Nell'-type illustrations for emotional manipulation; in terms of their clarity or fruitfulness in pointing to what the author wishes to say; and in terms of the truthfulness of this general point and its place in the discourse of which it is part. What, though, is meant by 'general point'?

The general remarks which actual types convey can be described, I should like to claim, in terms of what I call 'rhetorical induction'. They do not only give 'insights' into social situations – valuable though this is in itself – but also convey characteristically sociological generalisations. The examples in Rex's and Moore's and Willis's texts function as signs for states of affairs which are general in the sense that we can reasonably expect them to pertain in comparable circumstances. They do not, and cannot, entail hard-and-fast laws about social situations, but they teach us how to react in similar circumstances. Rhetorical induction, in the highly adapted account I am offering of it here, does not argue from a few cases to the next one (as is done by that version of arguing from example which is termed 'arguing by analogy' in traditional texts[12]). It argues from a selection of cases to what we are to expect in the foreseeable future.

This account of the general reference of actual types is able to explain the prominence of these figures in sociological texts. When Rex and Moore present the reader with the case of 'J.' in her tiny cubicle talking about morality, they mean him or her to generalise so as to *expect* positive qualities such as moral seriousness – rather than negative qualities – from (black) people in similar circumstances. On a larger scale, rhetorical induction is not performed by actual types only. Rex and Moore, writing in 1965, do not mean that neglected inner-city areas and neglected race relations are likely to lead to riots in Birmingham alone. Their work allows us to form similar expectations for London or Liverpool.

   Willis makes his licence to rhetorical induction even clearer: 'It is no accident that different groups in different schools . . . come up with similar insights, even though they are the products of separate efforts, and thus combine to make distinctive class bonds' (p. 121). Willis rightly avoids claiming that there is a law which ensures that boys in the lads' position will produce similar views on their situation; but he tells us that we can expect it. Thus rhetorical induction provides a more realistic and practical predictive format for sociology than would appeals to lawlike generalisations which the discipline is in no position to offer.

5 SUMMARY

In this chapter, beginning from an examination of the 'addressed' character of the sociological explanations dealt with here, I went on to claim that both their basic rhetorical structures and their places in segments of public discourse ensure that such explanations cannot be value-free. Even such simple figures as that of order inevitably convey evaluative judgements when the components they involve are imbued with social meaning independently of what the author writes about them; this follows from the conventions of linguistic communication itself. And given that the social context of sociological discussion also confers an additional evaluative role on what sociologists write, no amount of concentration on the evaluative implications of isolated concepts can save the notion of value-freedom – which therefore needs replacing by different criteria of professional responsibility.

   In the second half of the chapter I began a discussion of the use of example in sociology, here qualitative sociology. The main problem addressed was that of the functioning of the descriptive details required in qualitative work, given that they are not usually statistically typical and are often expressly exceptional. I claimed that these details are based on the everyday form of reasoning from signs, terming signs as they are used in sociological texts 'actual types' and setting out the conditions which seem – judging from the practice of Rex and Moore and of Willis – to be attached to their use.

   Not only do actual types permit a particularly personal and active apprehension by the reader of what the author has to say; they convey generalisations taking the form of what I term rhetorical induction. Here sociologists do not attempt to predict using lawlike generalisations, but tell the reader what, in comparable circumstances, he or she can reasonably expect – and how he or she should *take* the states of affairs concerned. This is a potentially far-reaching intervention into the reader's social world (I return to it in Chapter 4) – though it is also interesting that most sociological writers leave it to the reader to judge exactly which situations *are* comparable with those expressly examined. Rhetorical induction is a form of generalisation characteristic of the basic rhetorical assumption that reasonable views and decisions can be attained through interaction, even in the absence of complete certainty, and it is also characteristic of sociological texts.

3 'Scientific Social Theory' as Suasive Dialogue

The preceding chapter concentrates on interpretive texts, and before I go on to extend its results I should like to deal with a possible objection, to the following effect: rhetorical phenomena may well occur in books which deliberately stress subjective meaning, but in more positivist, 'scientific' works they are likely to be absent.

In order to remove this objection I shall look at two books which might seem eminently likely to present arguments in purely informational terms – establishing facts, making logical inferences from them, and using language with no place for the variety of functions and interpretive demands to be found in 'personal communication'. These texts are *The American Occupational Structure* by Blau and Duncan, and Woodward's *Industrial Organization: Theory and Practice* – which I shall show to be replete with features which disappoint expectations that they might form neutral, unrhetorical and unpersuasive examples of scientific impersonality.

These are features which allow us to examine patterns of influence and opportunity which author and reader afford *each other* in sociological texts. They underline the inappropriateness of the notion of one-way domination as far as standard cases of rhetorical interaction are concerned; they show too that rhetorical usages are typically not separate from but parts of ordinary communication – hence endemic to sociological writing.

Blau and Duncan, who see 'the purpose of scientific enquiry' as 'to establish, and then to explain, general relationships between variables' (p. 8), set out to examine the 'dynamics' of the occupational structure in the United States (p. 1). They analyse questionnaire data taken from some 20 700 people in 1962, in an attempt to find factors responsible for occupational mobility – which they understand as the relation between social or career origins and occupational destinations. Occupational status is conceived in their work as the outcome of a 'lifelong process' in which ascribed positions at birth combine with intervening circumstances and early attainments to 'determine the level of ultimate achievement' (p. 21). Thus their central path-analysis model is intended to measure the relative influences of various factors at once on occupational attainment, and to discover how they modify or reinforce each other. Their final chapter includes speculations on general causes and effects of occupational mobility in contemporary industrial society.

Both Blau's and Duncan's concern with 'advancing scientific social theory on the basis of systematic research' (p. viii) and the sheer bulk of their data lead them to transpose their basic concepts into quantified form, and their text consists largely of statistical manipulations of this data, and accounts of their results. Hence it might seem that their book has as good chances as any sociological text of consisting of language which is explicable in terms of information-giving and neutrality. It does indeed supply a lot of information; but this does not entail that this function should be seen as expunging, or even as dominating, the rest. Its style is frequently plain, but this does not prohibit it from rhetorical effect.

Joan Woodward's work is mainly concerned with formal structures of management in 100 firms in south-east Essex, starting in 1954; she makes additional case-studies of three and follow-up investigations into seven more. She focuses on the relations between these structures and technological conditions, and she too is anxious to evolve techniques 'to describe systematically, and evaluate quantitatively, complex and intricate' situations (p. 248). Woodward sees her research as 'a step forward' in 'the determination of conditions under which behaviour becomes standardized and predictable' in organisations (p. 209).

Her style is less technically complex than Blau's and Duncan's, and in this sense nearer to standard English and that of the majority of sociologists. Yet rhetorical figures are central both to Woodward's communicative strategies and to Blau's and Duncan's; this enables us to look in detail at the ways in which such figures contribute to argumentative dialogues, affected by and dependent on readers' reactions to the text.

In the first part of this chapter I shall deal with three different types of case in which exertion of influence over the reader might be attributed to Blau's and Duncan's work. Beginning with ar unusually pronounced effort by these authors to convince the reade of the correctness of a particular socio-political analysis, I shall show that if the authors' hypotheses about the beliefs of their audience are correct, if they are to communicate with this audience at all the have no alternative to expressing themselves so forcefully.

Then I shall show that other ways in which Blau and Duncan car be taken as defending given political views originate with the *reade* and not (necessarily) with the authors at all. Lastly I shall examine some methodologically quite impeccable remarks by the author and show that these *do* in fact tend to exert an influence over the person reading them. These three cases will elaborate the account so far given of self-presentation and sensitisation in suasive com munication, and the sense in which the term 'influence' should be understood here.

The second part of this chapter is concerned with the fact tha though Blau's and Duncan's text contains comparatively little evidence about its individual subjects, the figure of the *reader* is much more apparent in it than we might expect. This clarifies the nature of the personal communication characteristic of these authors: thei uses of metaphor, their suggestions of plausible histories to accom pany statistical findings, and their frequent exhortations to the reader all involve attempts to spur him or her into *activity* This fact stresses the dialogic nature of these authors' argumen tation.

Turning to *Industrial Organization: Theory and Practice*, we shall find that this phenomenon of the active involvement of the reader in the text reappears. First, I shall examine the argumentative structure o Woodward's book, which takes the form of 'prolepsis': she states a case, only to refute it herself. I shall argue that this strategy make clear part of the nature of suasion, and shall account for it as a method of allowing the reader to *experience* the significance of wha the author is saying, rather than grasping it only in the abstract Second, I shall connect the reader's activity with the question of the meaning of a text (which I pursue in Chapter 4 below). If we take into account what a reader may bring to a work, we can see that effective explanations may extend off its pages altogether, and that their statuses as explanations may depend largely on the reader This impact of the reader on textual meaning has its own implications for the question of sociological objectivity.

INFLUENCING THE READER?

Chapter 6 of *The American Occupational Structure*, chiefly the responsibility of Blau, contains what we might at first sight describe as an energetic rhetorical assault on the reader's socio-political views. This assault concerns Blau's assertion that racism is not in decline in the United States. In a most un-positivistic manner, Blau combines his findings on this matter with an attempt to stimulate his reader's perceptions and conscience. His style in doing so makes it clear that this attack is reserved for a particular type of reader: one who disapproves of racism but who believes that in contemporary society, especially in its upper echelons, it is being stamped out – a reader, therefore, who is likely to show some resistance to Blau's assertions that this is by no means the case (and who, interestingly, strongly resembles the reader envisaged by Rex and Moore, possibly also by Willis).

The author's procedure in this chapter can be explained in terms of his choice of audience, and is to this extent forced upon him; and we shall see that this choice of audience is itself, in realistic terms, hardly a free one. Thus it is that the exercise of influence in this chapter can be credited in large part to its communication-situation.

The chapter starts brusquely: 'Equality of opportunity is an ideal in the United States, not an accomplished fact' (p. 207). By the figure of reticence (leaving unstated what may none the less be inferred) this constitutes an offer to expose inequality in America; but the pages immediately following it allay any fears which such an offer might be supposed to arouse that the chapter will launch a radical attack on the American social system. Combining effectiveness with tact, Blau actually denies the existence of some forms of discrimination before concluding on p. 256 that 'Discrimination in education against Negroes has not really declined in the United States; it has merely moved to a more advanced level.'

Formally, this is *merely* a conclusion from data. In effect, again by the figure of reticence, it attacks the liberal assumption that the position of black people is continually, even if slowly, improving. It is followed by a further implicit attack on the notion that such beneficial changes as black people have experienced have sprung from social enlightenment: 'As eight years of schooling have become a bare minimum necessary for the most menial jobs, restrictions against Negroes on this level have subsided' (ibid.). Blau repeats his

initial claim in different terms: 'Simultaneously . . . the handicaps
Negroes suffer when continuing their education on higher levels
have become more severe' (ibid.).

These and several similar sentences show that a figure as simple as
that of repetition can transform statements not in themselves
'biased', and which occupy ordinary methodological status in terms
of rendering data intelligible, into a *series* of which the reader can
only make sense by interpolating a political direction into it.

Blau does not proceed by these means only, dealing also more
directly with 'the complacent belief' that the position of black
people is 'gradually improving' within 'a democratic society that
prides itself on the educational opportunities it offers to all its
citizens' (p. 227). Blau is attacking complacency, which the reader
may be assumed to disfavour, on behalf of principles with which
most people might be hoped to agree. He continues visibly to bear
his reader in mind, considering social myths connected with racism
and offering rebuttals to the objections to his claims which such
myths might be expected to produce.

> Moreover, whereas educated persons are generally considered to
> be more enlightened and, specifically, to be less prejudiced
> against Negroes and other minorities than less educated ones, the
> data show that in actuality there is more discrimination against
> Negroes in highly than in less educated groups. It can hardly be a
> pattern of prejudice unique to the uneducated laborers and
> operatives that forces enlightened employers to discriminate
> against hiring Negroes on these levels, as is sometimes alleged, for
> there is even more discrimination on higher levels. Another
> anomaly implicit in these findings is that although it is the
> uneducated Negro who is the main object of the prejudiced
> stereotype, the educated one being often explicitly exempted
> from it, it is the better educated Negro who in practice suffers
> most from discrimination (pp. 239–40).

Besides discussing possible explanations for disadvantages suffered by black people, Blau is attacking the educated white's
treatment of them and attempting to dismantle the hypocrisy which
allows it. But he is writing *for* an educated audience, which, on his
own hypothesis, he must expect to be largely white – hence,
prejudiced. It seems, furthermore, that he *must* address this
audience. He can write either for people who already agree with

im – in which there would perhaps be little point – or for people who do not. The latter group may be divided into those who, whether they believe that it is in decline or not, approve of racism, and will thus be unmoved by Blau's results; and those who do not so approve, but are and possibly prefer to be unaware of racism's extent. The rhetorical onslaught in this chapter, which I should summarise under the heading of sensitisation, appears to be directed towards enabling these readers to overcome their reluctance sufficiently to give fair consideration to Blau's claims about the facts of racial inequality – whether or not they are prepared to go as far as the political 'helping hand' (p. 425) which he recommends. Given the views which his data themselves encourage Blau to ascribe to his readers, if he wishes to communicate with them at all, attention to sensitisation will be essential.

Turning to the second case of 'influence' to be dealt with here, we can distinguish between examples – such as the above – where there is textual evidence that an author hopes to make a specific impact on the reader, and examples in which such impacts derive from factors external to the text.[1] This case is an example of the second kind, and consists simply in Blau's and Duncan's general conclusion (Chapter 12 and *passim*) that the occupational structure in America has not grown more rigid in recent years. The rhetorical force of this claim consists not in any special linguistic form which it may happen to use but in its place in a particular communication-situation.

At the time when Blau's and Duncan's book was written, both conservative and left-wing writers were affirming for different reasons that the American occupational structure had remained static, or had even grown more rigid, in the course of this century.[2] In the context of such a debate, to claim that this was not so *counted* as a defence of the structure, quite independently of whether the author of such a claim intended it to be. (By contrast, in Britain at the same time this would not have been the case. Given several post-war measures designed to increase social mobility, assertions that mobility had not declined would have been insufficient to defend the occupational structure and might well have counted as an attack on it.) This is possibly the most significant rhetorical impact of this text; but its force derives from the book's place in a particular piece of public discourse.

Third, Blau's and Duncan's Introduction provides a con-veniently concentrated source of remarks which, though method-ologically unexceptionable, build up the authors' self-presentation and thus provide their audience with additional reasons for believing what it reads. Also, they point out that differences in 'Orders of significance and priority emphasis' mean that what seems interesting from one point of view 'seems trivial from another' (p. ix; cf. pp. 135, 202). Nor do quantitative data always yield unarguable accounts of the ' "facts" of the case' (p. viii). It follows from these somewhat Weberian observations that it is necessary for the authors to *motivate* the reader to follow the implications of their 'point of view'.

Hence many of the passages in this Introduction have dual functions. In discussing the relation of their work to stratification theory, for example, the authors are not only telling the reader what place their work has in relation to other studies – in what context to understand it; they are also demonstrating their own awareness of theoretical and analytical problems. They stress too the 'essential' task of understanding the occupational structure if one wishes to understand modern society (p. 7). This is no doubt the case, and cannot be cavilled at; but in presenting themselves as experts on such a topic – as they must – the authors enhance their self-presentation. It is important that they should; the reader needs a reason for devoting time and trouble to working through a comparatively complicated text.

It is possible to perceive many of the traditional components of self-presentation in Blau's and Duncan's Introduction. Not unnaturally, they emphasise the ways in which their book improves on previous work, stressing its extremely large sample and its uses of complex statistical techniques in relation to analytical enquiries which are more differentiated than those in other studies (p. 8). This is a normal professional justification for the authors' proceedings; in the context of social conventions such that statistical comprehensiveness counts as a respectable path to understanding human affairs, this justification is also an indication of the authors' fitness and competence in the area they have elected to discuss.

Whether in fact they succeed in showing not just cleverness but 'practical wisdom' with regard to human affairs is a matter for the reader to decide at the end of their text. But it should be noted that in different social groups quite different factors are likely to be taken as indications of such wisdom. In so far as interpretive sociologists do not take mathematical competence to be a sign of common sense and thus do not see it as directly relevant to competent judgements about society, this may be a greater gap between them and writers such as Blau and Duncan than the one resulting from their more formal disagreements.

Blau and Duncan are also frank in admitting the drawbacks of their work; here and elsewhere they express reservations about particular uses of statistics (cf. pp. 115, 135, 145, 151, 169) and regret their lack of attitudinal data (p. 21). Such remarks may also be interpreted rhetorically by the reader as signs: signs that the authors' intellectual horizons are not narrowly confined by the bounds of their own work. Given the cultural conventions within which Blau and Duncan are writing, a readiness for self-deprecation may be seen as a sign of trustworthiness – and it may furnish further components of self-presentation – indications of good moral character and a concern for an open and honest relationship with the reader.[3] This yields what would, according to a widespread misunderstanding of the nature of rhetoric, seem to be a paradox: the more frankly and competently and the less 'rhetorically' the authors write, the more rhetorically effective they are, the more the reader is likely to be affected in their favour.

In this section I have examined cases of textual influence which, because books are subject to the necessity of communicating with their readers, are justifiable or inevitable or both. These cases of influence do not reveal the reader as subject to unfair bludgeoning; either they function to make arguments accessible to more people than would otherwise have taken note of them, or they are created by the ways in which audiences use the texts they read. (Blau's and Duncan's Introduction may be interpreted in both these ways.) It is for this reason that I use the word 'influence', which I understand in a morally neutral fashion, rather than associating rhetorical effects with the word 'power', which seems more likely to be construed as having negative connotations.

But none of this should be taken to imply that rhetorical influence is immune to criticism. For example, there is in Blau's and Duncan's text a defence of the American social system which is more deliberate than the one examined above, and to which many readers might wish to object.[4] Blau claims that

Objective criteria of evaluation that are universally accepted increasingly pervade all spheres of life and displace particularistic standards of diverse ingroups, intuitive judgements, and humanistic values not susceptible to empirical verification . . . The attenuation of particularistic ties of ingroup solidarity, in turn,

frees men to apply universalistic considerations of efficiency and
achievement to ever-widening areas of their lives.

Heightened universalism has profound implications for the
stratification system. The achieved status of a man, what he has
accomplished in terms of some objective criteria, becomes more
important than his ascribed status, who he is in the sense of what
family he comes from (pp. 429–30).

It would not be an objection against this passage to point out that
it functions rhetorically. It would be an objection to assert that it is
not true, or that the social and political judgements it embodies
are – for social and political reasons – incorrect.

2 RELATIONSHIPS WITH ACTIVE READERS

In this book I am claiming that sociological texts should be seen not
as abstract presentations of arguments, but as examples of the
activity of arguing. Arguing must take place between at least two
people, and hence this section is organised around the figure of the
reader, who is both implicitly and explicitly prominent in Blau's
and Duncan's text. The postulation of a 'relationship' between this
reader and the authors can be justified in terms of the mutuality of
the impacts between them, and the communication which takes
place within this relationship can be termed 'personal'. That is, the
authors take into account the reader's feelings, preferences, and
patterns of interest and activity, and they are affected by them in
what they write.[5]

In considering the reader's role in this relationship, we can
distinguish between reactions to the text expected by the author
from *hypothetical* readers, and real activities which actual readers
contribute to the work. Authors' views of their hypothetical readers
can be expected to have been influenced by their acquaintance with
colleagues who are potential members of their audiences – in the
case of Blau and Duncan, not a 'universal' audience but one made
up of sociologists and other specialists.[6] The conventions of written
academic argument also contribute to the figure of the hypothetical
reader by prescribing limitations to what may be demanded of an
audience.[7]

Here I do not want to speculate about details of the empirical
historical processes by which given texts have been composed; when

I refer to a hypothetical reader as he or she appears to an author, I am referring to what it is reasonable to assume about this anticipated reader so as to make sense of the text. But it will also be possible to point to places in texts whose imports can be affected by the activities of 'actual' readers, whether envisaged by the author or not. Hence the dialogue between author and reader has a break in it: the author is directly influenced by what he or she expects of the hypothetical reader, but it is the text which is affected by the interventions of the actual reader.

The nature of Blau's and Duncan's relations with their audience are subject to what will convince their hypothetical readership. We have seen that they take trouble to establish themselves as reliable witnesses, and it would reduce the plausibility of their arguing if they appeared merely to conjure up evidence or conclusions. It is also a corollary of the social relationship offered by these authors' self-presentation that they should be seen to communicate with the reader on relatively equal terms.[8] Thus Blau and Duncan do not confine themselves to trying to make their text easier for the reader; they make repeated attempts to *involve* him (sic) in their calculations. 'The reader should evaluate the comparisons for himself' (p. 126); 'It is not easy to read a table of this type quickly, but an extra minute is worth the trouble' (p. 304).[9] On p. 197, the reader is urged to 'make a guess' about relations between mobility from father's occupation to own first job, and from the latter to the respondent's subsequent job. This yields a humorous case of prolepsis:

> It could be reasoned that a man who demonstrated his mobility drive by achieving upward mobility from his origin level to his first job will further express that drive by strong intragenerational mobility. Conversely, a man who has already started to 'skid' when he takes his first job may persist in the habit, undergoing still further downward mobility . . . (p. 197).

But 'This fine example of deductive reasoning comes to grief' (p. 197): the correlation between early and late downward movement is negative. This ironic procedure drives home an argument by provoking the actual reader to work through alternatives and reject them, and Blau and Duncan occasionally use the figure of humour elsewhere to the same end.[10]

The more complex a chapter, the more energetic are the authors'

encouragements to readers' participation;[11] this shows awareness o
the fact that if readers are not active in attempting to master the
text, they are liable not to understand it, and its arguments will seen
to them neither memorable nor credible. But there are two furthe
reasons for which Blau and Duncan need to establish a relationship
with an active reader. They are engaged on a proselytising
enterprise with regard to their own branch of enquiry, offering base
for future research to potential colleagues (pp. 113, 358).[12] The
hope too that readers will react to their work outside the academi
sphere.

Blau and Duncan consider their research relevant to 'formulating
appropriate action programs and clarifying partisan controversy
(p. 1). Though they see their role as 'settling some matters of fact'
not resolving 'conflicts over policy' (p. 442), they do not take
'technological' attitude to value debates in the sense of seeking
means to ends which they perceive as undisputed or as no
concerning themselves; nor do they refrain from taking up mora
stances about what ought to be felt and done.[13] It is significant o
the importance they attribute to this that they both begin and end
their text by stressing its imports for social practice.

The fact that the hypothetical reader has influenced the com
position of their text is admitted by Blau and Duncan. On p. 1 the
imply that they have felt this influence recurrently, discussing 'wha
demands to place on the reader' in constructing their text. On pp
115–16, Duncan invites the reader to 'share' 'dilemmas' faced by
the authors: if they were to account for their methods fully enough
for thorough evaluation by statisticians, other readers would suffe
under a text 'burdened with methodological digressions' and
'intolerably abstract' (p. 20). Refraining from this means asking the
reader 'to take some things on faith'.[14]

I suggest that it is partly pressure deriving from knowledge
of readers' probable explanatory preferences which impels the
authors, especially Blau, to construct invocations of persona
attitudes to account for statistical patterns – despite their lack o
anything resembling information about such views and feelings. H
speculates, for example, that

> The skidder from a white-collar home, unfamiliar with the
> working class and possibly threatened by the prospect o
> becoming part of it, appears to be willing to pay the price of the
> lesser income offered by the lowest nonmanual occupations t
> preserve the cherished symbol of the white collar. (p. 42)

To explain the success of youngest children's careers as compared with those of their middle siblings, Blau suggests that a youngest child may derive 'special benefits' from being 'the beloved "Benjamin" of his family' (p. 308); this actually uses a symbolic term to explain a statistical relation. On p. 314 Blau proffers a similar reason for which the advantages of being an older son decline as family size increases, devising a scenario composed of imaginary individuals:

> Contributing to the achievements of younger siblings becomes a substitute for the older son's own success. If there are several older siblings, they may join in helping to support a younger one in a large family and derive satisfaction from his success, which demonstrates to the world that 'We Browns can be somebody too' . . .

The same applies to 'speculations' by Blau to the effect that unsuccessful men compensate for their lack of achievement by having large families over whom to exercise authority (p. 428) and to a connection by Duncan between the downwardly mobile lower middle classes and authoritarianism (p. 158).

Whatever the correctness of such suggestions may be, it seems likely that Blau and Duncan are right in their general assumption that readers need to connect the text's statistics about behaviour with some conception of the personal attitudes informing that behaviour; conjectures about attitudes may enhance the *intelligibility* of the text for the common reader. This would support the Weberian view that a sociological work ought to show how social phenomena work out in terms of the lives of individuals as well as on a larger scale – though it does not prejudge the issue of methodological individualism. (Even if Durkheim is right in taking individuals' actions to form a social 'compound' different from the sum of its separate parts, there is still a need to show the connections between this compound and people's everyday behaviour.)

A need on readers' parts for information about people's attitudes would also imply that works intended for a wide audience are to some extent predetermined as to content. Authors of works on the scale of Blau's and Duncan's, if they are not either to remain limited to a very specialised readership indeed or to produce merely *ad hoc* explanations, might be well advised when planning their research to respond to their audience's need for data about attitudes.

Blau's and Duncan's uses of metaphor, which play a large part in their text – their central mathematical model can be seen as a metaphor for sets of changes in people's lives – can also be associated with their readers' needs. Here I do not want to discuss the nature of metaphor itself, simply to point out that many of its uses by Blau and Duncan fall into the category of 'personal communication': they take special account of the person reading the text and how he or she can be expected to use it.[15]

Not all the metaphors in the text fall into this class; many are conventional metaphors – such as 'mobility' to 'destinations' within the 'stratification system' – which issue from the need to conceptualise data which, because of its scale, cannot literally be visualised.[16] They can be contrasted with the 'physical analogy' which Blau introduces on pp. 70–1 to 'help the reader not familiar' with the Guttman-Lingoes solution for plotting distances between respondents' fathers' starting occupations and their own in 1962. The analogy takes pictorial form: the reader is asked to imagine seventeen objects on a table, each tied by wires to each of the others and moved about until all the wires are taut. The hypothetical reader is apparently seen by these authors as requiring concrete images in order to acquire a clear grasp of statistical abstractions.

Duncan attacks metaphors which mislead the reader, such as those involving '"bio-social"' or '"psycho-social" mechanisms' (p. 369), and those which are over-simple, such as seeing social mobility in terms of 'what can be expected on the simple metaphor of a social elevator going up and down' (p. 117). He wants to 'complicate the pattern of movement' by introducing '"channels" of mobility' traversing horizontal planes (p. 117). This language is important for the paths along which a reader's thoughts are likely to be led, what he or she will consider next or not. As Mary Hesse points out,[17] metaphors function by highlighting particular similarities and disregarding particular differences; this leads in turn to concentration on various further factors and to the neglect of others. The heterogeneity of the above example's components, where the metaphor is exceedingly mixed, makes clear that Duncan's aim in employing it is not to construct a theoretical model for purposes of research; rather, usefully to direct his reader's thoughts.

On occasion these authors seem to carry too far their concern to use metaphors which enhance the reader's ability to make active use of data. Blau's and Duncan's work attempts to mediate between a vast number of statistical subtleties and a hypothetical reader who, they feel, is best addressed in fairly striking terms. This leads to the formation of metaphors which describe human affairs in a very impersonal fashion – thus offending against others of their readers' (legitimate) requirements.

On p. 66 Blau explicates some effects of the entry of farm workers, or farm workers' sons, into industrial occupations at a point low on the social scale:

> What seems to happen is . . . that the pressure of displaced manpower at the bottom and the vacuum created by new opportunities at the top creates a chain reaction of short-distance movements throughout the occupational structure.

On p. 243 he claims that 'Migration provides a social mechanism for adjusting the geographical distribution of manpower to the geographical distribution of opportunities' – although this 'flow' does not take place 'with the ease of water' (p. 244). What is objectionable here is not the mere fact that the reader has been considered and addressed rhetorically; Blau's metaphors must be criticised in terms which are partly personal and political. They highlight what can be grasped in simple terms, at the expense of people's experiences. Especially when carried over into practical politics, this has disadvantages which seem to me to outweigh the positive effects of their congeniality to the person who merely has to read them.

3 SUASION AND EXPERIENCE IN ARGUING

Blau's and Duncan's communication involves mutual influences between author and reader, affecting both presentation and contents. It shows respect for what the reader is likely to do with the text and what he or she is presumed to enjoy, to prefer and to need in terms of explanation; it is adapted to his or her feelings, especially in so far as they are expected to stand in the way of a grasp of what the authors have to say.

This contributes to an account of the word 'personal' as I want to apply it to the communication in these texts. The word 'impersonal' is often used to mean, or at least to imply, 'lacking feeling'; so 'personal' might be supposed to connote an excess of it – or else what Parkin calls an author 'spouting his own tedious opinions on this or that'.[18] This is not what I want to convey, for there is no need to assume that recognising the role of personal factors in texts will automatically produce an avalanche of abuses. Nor is it helpful to an understanding of academic texts to consider them 'cognitive' as opposed to 'emotional' – though no doubt their blends of intellect and feeling are in some ways different from those concerned in writing and reading other kinds of text.

The argumentative structure of Woodward's *Industrial Organization: Theory and Practice* illustrates some of these points; it shows that the opportunity to become convinced of a particular point of view involves *experiences*, over and above merely acting as the 'receiver' of arguments.

The most effective rhetorical feature of Woodward's text in this respect is its order, whose function is to allow the reader to undergo experiences which – distributed over a much longer period of time – convinced the author of her conclusion. Of course this is an attempt to persuade the reader too, but it would be over-hasty to disparage all such attempts *per se*. Kemp, for instance, examines scientists' uses of ' "tactics of criticism, persuasion, and justification" ', setting them in the context of an unscrupulous contest for rewards between members of an élite.[19] But it would be attributing an excessive degree of naivety to the reader to take for granted that every kind of persuasive remark is liable to sway and deceive him or her.

Forceful presentation does not of itself constitute coercion of the reader, and it follows from the fact that an author is prepared to undertake the arduous enterprise of writing a book that he or she will want to present its case in the best light. Colleagues in the scientific community can be relied upon to examine the work from a different standpoint.[20] In Woodward's case, there are reasons external to the text for assuming that without a persuasive approach her arguments might have been ignored. After the publication of her first report as a DSIR pamphlet in 1958, her work was acrimoniously rejected in several quarters.[21]

Its order means that Woodward's whole book forms an extended version of the technique of prolepsis we have seen used by Blau. She guides her hypothetical reader in one direction – after which she shows this direction to have been mistaken, and then takes steps to strengthen the reader's adherence to her final position. The 'research report' form in which she chooses to present her views is particularly well suited for such a re-enactment of her own thought processes; the impression of contemporaneousness it gives to each stage of her arguing helps to keep the reader's viewpoint in step with hers.

There are four stages in the process by which Woodward's order akes on its characteristic form. In the first, Woodward describes the tart of her research in 1953, when she had hoped to discover to vhat extent 100 industrial firms in Essex could be said to apply the heories of management organisation then current, and to see if any uch application could be 'linked' (p. 4) with management behaviour or business success. At this stage in her text she applies no lirect criticism to this 'narrowly conceived', 'problem-centred' approach (p. 5).

Rather, at the end of Chapter 2 the author simply states that 'No relationship of any kind' could be found between business success and attempts to apply theory, or between organisational and any other characteristics of firms (p. 34); she points to the 'disconcerting' nature of this result (ibid.). This is a use of litotes – refraining from a forcefulness of expression which might normally have been expected. Thus the reader too is left with the problem of what faults to attribute to Woodward's early approach, and how to repair them. The solution to this problem is *acted through* in the course of the next three chapters, which form the second stage of her argument.

Woodward's reader has retraced the author's surprise and puzzlement about her problems' intractability; his or her attention is now directed towards a possible solution, whose attractions grow throughout the third chapter of the text. This chapter shows the researchers casting about for more fruitful methods of responding to their data, and it recalls that whereas 'classical' management theory was developed 'independently of technical considerations' (p. 35), sociologists have since assumed that technological circumstances in a 'social system' form 'a major variable in the determination of its structure and behaviour' (p. 36).

These remarks prepare the reader for the view which Woodward comes to oppose to classical theory, and they are coupled with an appeal to the authority of Weber and Veblen, which establishes a respectable parentage for her view. The chapter thus has some of the reassuring characteristics connected with self-presentation which are usually found in introductions; and it is an introduction to the author's own approach. She goes on to assert that it 'soon became obvious' that firms' goals and manufacturing policies could be correlated with their manufacturing processes (p. 37). This is emphasised by repetition, and Chapter 4 stresses that 'for the first time in the analysis patterns became discernible' (p. 50). That is, 'firms with similar production systems appeared to have similar organization structures' (ibid.).

After the difficulties through which Woodward's reader has followed her, it may be something of a relief to reach the firm ground of a definite result; and this result is strongly emphasised and consolidated by a differential repetition of the point involved on pp. 50–1. Chapter 5 extends this, suggesting 'that one particular form of organization was most appropriate to each system of production' (p. 71). Woodward uses this – her central thesis – for two purposes. She infers that a single administrative system might be 'linked with' success in one production system but with failure in another; and she uses her thesis to explain and berate the failings of classical theory, which she attributes to undue concentration on large-batch production. This last point shows that some rhetorical features of texts can only be identified from the vantage point of the work as a whole, for Woodward's initial failure to criticise classical theory is now revealed as a case of reticence.

The third stage in her argument is made up of four chapters dealing with aspects of case-studies of three companies, and two chapters about follow-up investigations and the problems involved in analysing technical change. These chapters' chief rhetorical function is to consolidate the author's new position and to convey to the reader a feeling of secure familiarity with it. Internal features of the ordering of this argumentative stage underline the persuasive nature of Woodward's strategy.

First, she places her severest criticisms of the misleading effects of classical theory at the end of Chapter 8, on pp. 123–4; that is, *after* she has demonstrated the advantages of her own position at some length. Second, she arranges her own weaker arguments relatively late in this section of her work; what seems liable to arouse opposition is introduced from the author's strongest position.

In Chapter 9 her researchers are reported to have found that with regard to planning and control functions of organisation 'A link between organization and technology was not always apparent' (p. 154), except at the extremes of the technological scale. Woodward's suggestion to deal with this threat to her own viewpoint seems a little *ad hoc*: she says that perhaps 'situational demands impose themselves more rigidly and obviously at the extreme than in the middle of the scale' (p. 155). Now the text gives us no reason to suppose that this reflection occurred to the author at a later date than the more obviously positive findings set out in chapters preceding this one.

But its ordering at as late a stage as possible in the case-studies report means that Woodward's defence of this weak point gains in conviction from the weight of foregoing considerations. It avoids instilling insecurity about the thesis as a whole, and can be treated as an anomaly to be accounted for in factors compatible with the author's own view.

This shows how the arguments which an author feels entitled to advance can be influenced by their position in a communicational structure, and by the author's expectations about the hypothetical reader's attitude to each stage of the text. This is shown too by two arguments in Chapter 10, introduced by a further case of prolepsis. The reader has been informed that surprisingly little resistance to technological change could be found among either managers or operators' in the firms studied (p. 48). Now, though, it seems that even where the situation was well handled' 'the introduction of change was not as smooth sailing as the research workers had predicted' (p. 192). Woodward's arguments in this connection differ in terms of methodological thoroughness (whether or not in correctness) from those intended to carry conviction at an earlier stage of her book. She simply mentions Dubin's opinion that decisions tend to take longer in fact than a formal view of them would suggest (p. 192), and she illustrates this by a reference to a bottle-neck problem in one firm:

> It was interesting to observe how the fixing of the date for the meeting became an end in itself, and when everyone involved had been successfully accommodated, there was almost as much satisfaction as there would have been if an immediate solution to the problem had been found. Everyone felt that something had been done, and relieved of responsibility. The problem was therefore forgotten . . . (p. 193).

As far as actual arguments are concerned, the author has cited a generalisation made by someone else, and an impressionistic description of a single case; but this case is one which stimulates the reader's imagination and possibly appeals to his or her own experience. It is the reader here who takes over the function of equipping Woodward's argument with a conviction which she herself does not directly furnish.

It is the *overall* plausibility of her thesis by this stage which allows Woodward to assume that comparatively weak arguments will be extended and buttressed by the reader, and her follow-up studies provide an optimistic setting for this assumption. They confirm many of the researchers' predictions, and in Chapter 11 Woodward says that their outcome was 'extremely satisfactory', confirming her 'main thesis' (p. 209).

This leads to the fourth stage of Woodward's argument, her theoretical final chapter, which retraces her own chronological approach. She might have adopted some other arrangement for this discussion of theoretical points – for example, a systematic account or an attack on texts opposed to her own position; but the arrangement she does choose provides a retrospect on management studies which simultaneously re-emphasises the errors of past approaches and underlines the progressiveness Woodward attributes to her own view. This may be hoped to augment both the probability and the strength of the reader's acceptance of what she has written.

All this is not to claim that Woodward's readers can be expected to accept her arguments purely and solely because of the feelings and experiences which arise as part of reading it. It does show that feelings and experiences do arise as part of understanding an intellectual argument, and that they are encouraged by the author – because, I should claim, they can help the reader to give serious and thorough attention to what the author has to say. It would be artificial to suppose that the reading even of such a specialised text as Woodward's is an exclusively 'cognitive' process. As the editors of the 1980 second edition of her text write (p. xiii), 'this is a book where to know its main thesis is no substitute for reading the book itself.'

4 READERS' INTERVENTIONS IN ARGUING

Having looked at some ways in which expectations of a hypothetical reader may influence the composition of a text, I shall now examine some contributions which an actual reader might make to the argumentative dialogue arising from Woodward's work. On occasion, such interventions on the reader's part may be decisive for the meaning of the text.

It is well known in sociology that people in the social world rely extensively on 'taken-for-granted' items which allow them to make sense of each other's utterances and behaviour; this applies too to

he way in which readers make sense of sociologists' texts. Here I
hould like to draw attention to the fact that many of the taken-for-
granted items used in reading are of a nature which is neither purely
inguistic nor purely social, but an inextricable blend of the two.
Even a straightforward statement such as 'The advisory nature of
he specialist role was emphasized only when a mechanism was
required through which conflict could be resolved' (Woodward,
p. 19) takes for granted an ability to visualise industrial relationships, as well as knowledge of the meanings of the words involved.
The reader must be able to imagine what sorts of mechanism are
being indicated if he or she is to understand the sentence.

There are also occasions when the reader has a certain amount of
choice about the taken-for-granted components he or she uses in
reading a text, and where this choice transforms what the text
conveys. A series of overtly descriptive statements by Woodward on
p. 139 can be made to form an explanation if the reader is willing to
read particular assumptions about behaviour into the text.

Here Woodward states that in a certain firm making special
products tailored to individual requirements, development and
production engineers cooperate closely; the developers sometimes
come onto the shop floor and become involved in problems that are
not their own immediate responsibilities. 'In these circumstances',
the author says, 'friction' is 'almost inevitable'. If it seems clear to
the reader *why* this is so, it is because his or her taken-for-granted
knowledge transforms what is literally a narrative into an intelligible explanation. [22] This implies that the methodological distinction between description and explanation should be understood as
partly reader-dependent, and must take into account passages'
communicational contents.

The knowledge which a reader brings to a text in completing such
transformations may be derived from elsewhere in the same work
(so that what functions as background information for one passage
may be removed by the reader to the foreground of another) or it
may come from outside it, or both. In any of these cases, the effective
components of an explanation will extend off the pages of the text
altogether. In such cases the level of the reader's activity will be
relatively high; and though there may be implicit or explicit
indications in the text what direction this activity should take, they
may still allow the reader a considerable range of discretion.

In the following passage, reflection along lines which Woodward
may be taken to indicate but does not expound in detail not only

make the text more comprehensible, it alters the passage's forma status. She notes on p. 63

> how the role and functions of the draughtsmen differed from one production system to another. In unit and small batch produc tion the draughtsman was a bridge between the developmen function and the production function; a main channel both o communication and control. In large batch and mass productior he no longer filled this dominant role; he was merely one of a number of intermediaries who had some part to play in bridging the gap between the design of a product and its manufacture.

Woodward does not spell out precisely *how* the role of the draughtsman is affected by being a member of a small-scale system or a large one. Strictly speaking, the reader may not be obliged to infer more than the following correlation from the text:

1st role (correlated with Small Batch) – X (a 'bridge');
2nd role (correlated with Large Batch) – Y (not as X).

Yet the author's metaphorical language, her mention of a 'bridge' between two functions and of a 'main channel' for communication and control, carries an indication that there is something for which the metaphor stands. The conventional nature of her metaphors itself implies that they indicate fairly clearly for what sorts of item they can be taken to stand; the standardness of the associations they prompt mean that outright guesswork is not necessary.

A degree of reflection which may be too slight for the reader even to notice shows that a draughtsman in a small group who knows a lot about the matter in hand, who may have had some part in modifying an original plan (this can be inferred from elsewhere in the text), will be a convenient person for production workers to consult about the intentions of the designer; the draughtsman is more closely in touch with the latter than they are. As someone to whom people can turn for information and advice, the draughts-man acquires relatively high status.

By contrast, in more standardised operations where the designer's instructions are correspondingly clearer and less varying, there will be less need for conference and modification, so that the activities of the draughtsman will no longer be such as to attract the same degree of respect. Without the addition of these details, Woodward's passage merely provides *correlations*; with them, it forms a partly elliptical *explanation* of the draughtsman's changing status. Thus the degree to which a work, or part of a work, counts as furnishing explanations can depend at least partly on the degree to which the actual reader takes an active approach to the text.

In this example, incidentally, the extra explanatory detail provided by the reader is of a more 'interpretive' type than is characteristic of Woodward's written text as a whole. But like Blau and Duncan, she sometimes seems drawn to respond to or speculate about individuals' attitudes and behaviour in a way her methodology neither requires nor justifies. She refers to an 'ethos' (p. 133), an 'atmosphere' (p. 136), or an 'impression' (p. 159) in the factories she visits; she illustrates general points with remarks quoted from her subjects (e.g. pp. 22, 113–14, 130–1, 162–3, 226), refers to habits of dressing among workers of different status (p. 229), and describes telling details: one manager's organisation chart was over 20 feet long, another's was bound into a book 'the size and weight of a family Bible', and a third displayed one chart on his wall and another in his desk, showing 'how it would be if he could ignore the idiosyncracies and weaknesses of his present managers' (p. 12). These are in fact 'actual types'; it seems that even for positivist sociologists, interpretive interpolations about people are hard to resist.

5 SUMMARY

The two texts examined here are argumentative dialogues with their readers, not non-committal iterations of formal arguments. Their rhetorical features are not separable from some more 'ordinary' type of language; they may accompany or form parts of methodologically conventional textual items, but they may also derive from the reader's intervention or the social context in which the text is read; they are not wholly under the author's control.

The American Occupational Structure and *Industrial Organization: Theory and Practice* supply evidence for postulating a textual *relationship* between author and reader even in 'positivist' writing. While the author is concerned to bring home to the reader the import of textual arguments, the 'hypothetical' reader also influences the author. The author adjusts the text to the 'personal' preferences, interests and needs which can be attributed to the reader; the selection, contents and strength of arguments are also affected by what the reader can be taken to accept at different stages of the text. The 'actual' reader plays a role which is complementary to the author's; he or she can augment the text's intelligibility and even transform its methodological status. Hence the author has good reason to establish a collegial relationship with the reader; it is less disinterested than a matter of self-interest that he or she should conform to the personal and social conventions of the audience.

Thus even sociological texts which might have been expected to be conducted on strictly formal lines can be shown to function in a strongly rhetorical manner. This is by no means confined to texts of an 'interpretive' nature – though it is interesting that both Blau and Duncan and Woodward give evidence that, contrary to their methodological convictions, they feel a need to show how social processes are related to the lives and experience of individual people.

The personal and rhetorical forms of their communication cannot be taken as a source of accusation against either Woodward or Blau and Duncan. All are writing from positions in which they are frequently forced to express themselves persuasively; and their suasive tactics tend to function to make arguments more accessible to readers and to provide them with *experiences* relevant to achieving an understanding of the text. *When* their rhetorical usages are open to criticism, it is not for being rhetorical but for being rhetorical in what a critic would have to claim to be the wrong way; not for being personal or political but for being personal or political in a manner open to attack. This suggests that, to replace an unrealistic ideal of 'objectivity' for sociological texts, professional standards of truthfulness and responsibility would need to incorporate admissible grounds for criticising sociological procedures on a variety of personal and non-personal dimensions.

4 Meaning, People and Rhetorical Induction

The rhetorical texture of sociological communication shows that making sense of what is written about happenings in society involves interdependence between author and reader at many different levels. The argumentative nature of authors' projects by no means entails a one-way assault on readers' sensibilities, nor are these projects made up of series of mechanistic impacts on the reader. They involve processes endemic to conveying meaning and under- standing in the course of social interaction.

In this chapter I shall begin by examining some systematic effects which rhetorical aspects of communication have on the meaning of discourse – effects which it is difficult to notice if we think of meaning as attaching primarily to concepts or propositions. These effects show that the notion of meaning is a graduated concept, which can be extended from literal meaning over implication and presup- position to public associations which have to be actively manipu- lated by the reader. Here I shall deal with this only as it affects the sociological texts in our sample, particularly their evaluative implications.

In Chapter 2 I concluded that 'models of typical actors' had no dominant role in either Rex's and Moore's or Willis's books; here I shall use the notions both of actual type and of associative meaning to show that such models may be replaced by a more natural and everyday form of showing how subjects are to be understood. This I shall term the 'epitome'.

In this part of the chapter I shall concentrate chiefly on the *Affluent Worker* series, by Goldthorpe *et al.* (1968–9). This text is comparable with *Race, Community and Conflict* in that it exemplifies the 'action frame of reference' (1968 I, p. 184), though it has a different subject-matter and style and is less openly persuasive in a political sense.

Goldthorpe *et al.* deal with the 'attitudes and behaviour' c
workers in Luton who are well paid in comparison with manua
workers in general; they convey an image of 'an' affluent worke
which is composed in large part of actual types and of rhetorica
inductions based on breakdowns of interview results. In explainin;
the combination of such techniques to form an 'epitome' I sha]
draw attention to the functioning of actual types as signs twic
removed: in their original settings the signs involved will generall
have been taken by the *subjects* of the text to indicate somethin;
different from what the author uses them to mean. The notion of th·
epitome also underlines a point common to the rhetorical observa
tions in this book: the term 'cognitive' is most useful as a
abstraction, and cannot usually be predicated of continuou
activities in real discourse.

In the next part of the chapter I shall look at Dore's *Britis.
Factory – Japanese Factory*, and examine first its uses of rhetorica
induction to educate the reader in types of expectation he or sh·
could reasonably form in unfamiliar circumstances, and its associ
ation of these expectations with operations in terms of self
presentation and sensitisation. Although this book relies heavily o
actual types, it deals rather with varieties of situation than with
varieties of person, so that the author tries to avoid accentuatin;
single epitomes of 'the' British or Japanese worker – though h
occasionally resorts to 'stories' instead. Dore's explanations in term
of rhetorical deduction, with those of *The Affluent Worker*, will b·
dealt with in the next chapter. Both they and his rhetorica
inductions share a fundamental rhetorical purpose: to conve
understanding about given social situations at the same time a
dislodging the reader's personal views about the inevitability of th·
social arrangements in the society he or she knows.

1 VALUES AND RHETORICAL MEANING

In this discussion of rhetorical meaning I want first to investigate ;
case in which the text by Goldthorpe *et al.* can be shown to convey ;
particular (evaluative) meaning which is vital to its general aims
though it does this in a manner which ensues from rhetorica
characteristics of the work overall. Then I shall discuss the rol·
played in conveying meaning by public associations and b
rhetorical figures, and the evaluations they can communicate.

The 'primary aim' of the first volume of the *Affluent Worker* trilogy is 'descriptive': 'to give some account of' the attitudes and behaviour of a sample of relatively well-off workers 'in the context of their industrial employment'. The authors wish too 'to examine how the attitudes and behaviour in question can best be explained and understood' (I, p. 1). Two other aims are less obtrusive, and can be used to illustrate a distinction I should like to make between rhetorical strategy and rhetorical meaning.

First, the book is part of a project designed to test empirically

the widely accepted thesis of working-class *embourgeoisement*: the thesis that, as manual workers and their families achieve relatively high incomes and living standards, they assume a way of life which is more characteristically 'middle class' and become in fact progressively assimilated into middle-class society (I, p. 1).

In fact, though they do not state it baldly, the authors intend to reject this 'widely accepted' opinion and replace it by their own account of workers' 'markedly instrumental' orientations to work (ibid.).

Although, as they state, this volume is only indirectly concerned with the *embourgeoisement* question, it is none the less important to the authors' argumentative goal. This is most apparent from the fact that the order in which the trilogy presents its contents firmly establishes the authors' own picture of the affluent worker before the image of the worker attached to the *embourgeoisement* thesis can attain any prominence.

This is a matter of strategy not in the sense of being necessarily deliberate, nor in a pejorative sense – the authors are forced to present their arguments in some order, and nothing obliges them to choose one disadvantageous to themselves. It is simply an arrangement which heightens the accessibility to the reader of the authors' point of view. Far from being methodologically suspect, on a view of scientific progress in which it is assumed that theories are advanced in the anticipation that their audience will try to disprove them, it is reasonable that they should not be presented in a weakened state; otherwise more theories than necessary might be discarded.

But Goldthorpe *et al.* have a second unstated aim in this volume: to portray their subjects without either presenting them in a prejudicial light or reinforcing any negative attitudes about them

which readers might have. I shall show that this is not just an
evaluative accretion on their explanatory project, but that it is
inevitable in terms of the *meaning* of what they write that they
communicate a defence of the affluent worker.

In this work Goldthorpe *et al.* are joining in a discourse in which
various pictures of the affluent worker as a person are already
current. They supply some textual evidence to show what they take
these conceptions to be, and to show that they find them factually as
well as morally unacceptable. At the beginning of their first volume,
the authors avoid encouraging these views by giving them presence,
using only a footnote to reject 'the idea that many factory workers
are simply "happy robots"' (i, p. 16). Later, especially in volume
iii, they argue against the contention that workers enjoy or ' "good-
humouredly tolerate"' tedious jobs (iii, p. 63), and against
purportedly left-wing visions of ' "stunted mass-produced
. . . slaves"' (iii, p. 184). In volume i, Chapter 2, Goldthorpe *et al.*
move counter to these positions, first by implication and then
directly; both moves take place in terms of what I shall call
rhetorical meaning.

The first group of affluent workers brought to the reader's
attention in i, Chapter 2 are setters, relatively highly skilled and
distinguished by their 'very high' level of job satisfaction compared
with the rest (i, p. 12). They say, for example,

> 'As a setter you have to use your mind more and it [the job] is
> more responsible. You feel as if you *are* somebody.'
> 'Being a setter draws more skill out of you. There's nothing to it
> being an operator. [As a setter] you have to use your brains more;
> there are little snags to get round' (i, p. 13).

The original speakers, of course, are simply giving their own
views of their situations; but by virtue of being quoted their remarks
are given a more general status. Goldthorpe *et al.* reinforce this
impression, saying that the most important reasons for setters' job
satisfaction concerned 'the actual nature of the job itself – the
greater opportunity it gave for using skills and for acting autonomously, and the greater variety and interest in work-tasks which it
afforded' (i, p. 13).

In the context of the discourse about what affluent workers in
general are like, this implicitly attacks the assumption that it is
reasonable to expect them to be content with unchallenging work,

and to judge them according to standards different from those reserved for, say, more educated people. By leaving this an implication, the authors can reach their 'widest possible audience'. Those who share their own views of the workers are strengthened in their beliefs; those affected by the misconceptions in question find them countered in a manner which does not oblige them to admit to having entertained opinions which, when made explicit, might appear unflattering to their holders as well as to their subjects.

In any case, Goldthorpe *et al.* have not yet had time to present enough material for a concerted attack on attitudes contemptuous of their subjects without abandoning their own straightforward style and constructing a series of theoretical arguments – arguments which would distract them from their main project, which would be required against a portion of their readership only, and which need not be expected to seem particularly convincing to that portion.

Hence what Goldthorpe *et al.* write is affected not only by the mixed views attributable to their hypothetical readers but by their rhetorical situation as a whole – notably the fact that they are as yet only at the start of their argument. These constraints on the author's arguing are not complete enough to show their writing as wholly subject to determining forces (*pace* Bitzer[1]), but they do illustrate the key role which implication can play in a rhetorical situation where an author is writing under pressure of conflicting demands.

Implication is not the only type of inference which is possible about what a text can be taken to mean although it does not say so in so many words. At one end of the scale is literal meaning and at the other there is non-standard, voluntary, possibly eccentric interpolation into a text by an individual reader; between these there is a widely scattered set of inferences about what a text might be taken to say. These are differentiable in terms of conventionality. Terms such as presupposing and entailing[2] yield non-literal meanings which are comparatively rigid in scope; implication (in its common, not its logical sense) does not, for what a text is taken to imply depends among other things on how much of its context the reader is willing to take into account. Not only more but different kinds of things are implied if a text is, say, read as intimately related to its social and economic context rather than as isolated and self-enclosed.[3]

It is a familiar notion that the boundaries of what a text communicates are not obvious or fixed; and I should claim that many *associations* are conventionalised enough to be counted as part of what a text can be legitimately taken to mean – even if they do not all convey exactly the same things to the same people (so that textual meaning must be admitted to fluctuate in relation to its audience's activity).

We saw above that Moore introduces his account of life in Sparkbrook by actual types showing architectural details. I argued that such details, when they are provided with textual status, are commonly enough associated with more general conditions of living to count as signs communicating reflections on them; this claim is borne out by the fact that Dore begins *British Factory – Japanese Factory* in just the same way (pp. 21–4). Dore is aware of the associational meaning of what he reports; this is indicated by his mention of the 'jumble of tangled girders' in part of the Hitachi factory, which, he says, until its unregretted disintegration in 1968, formed an 'ambiguous memorial' of wartime and reconstruction (p. 22). Using, and allowing the reader to use, public associations with particular types of detail is a compact and accessible method of conveying what it is *like* to be in a place. Admittedly it is not precise; but judging from the practice of sociological authors, precision is not *always* their first priority, and there may be good reasons why this is so. Precision may on occasion be unnecessary as well as constricting.

In principle it is possible to distinguish between associations according to the distribution of knowledge and interests within a culture, and to class them in terms of progressively more limited ownership. 'Standard' associations would be those conventionalised for a whole cultural area (however defined), to which an author and his or her intended audience would normally belong. 'Group' associations would be those current among some sub-group of language-users in a culture – the group of sociologists, or the group of liberal readers, for example, and to which the author might or might not belong. Many other divisions are possible; but these two are enough to show that while not all readers need be expected to make the same inferences from a text, there is still a considerable difference between associations which depend solely on an individual's mood, disposition or personal experience and what I am prepared to call 'associational meaning'.

Associational meaning is not utterly stable, but then it is already agreed that there are not rigid limits to what a text (or any piece of discourse) can be taken to convey; and there are types of association which function with enough regularity for it to be the case that to ignore them would be to ignore a large part of what a text is treated as meaning by its readers.

The rhetorical manipulation of associations, as in actual types and elsewhere, is only a part of rhetorical meaning as a whole, since rhetorical figures such as order and presence also have semantic implications. All these phenomena are in evidence in the way Goldthorpe *et al.* continue to deal with the affluent worker in I, Chapter 2 of their work.

In this chapter, the authors have a major rhetorical problem to overcome. It is central to their explanatory project, to their opposition to the *embourgeoisement* thesis, and to their characterisation of new 'instrumental' attitudes to work that they have found that their subjects view their employment simply as providing financial means to their own ends. But to choose one's job from overwhelmingly financial motives, however frequent it may be in practice, is not approved in terms of conventionally accepted values. To give unqualified presence to this aspect of the workers' attitudes and behaviour would therefore *count* as disparaging them, and as we have seen, Goldthorpe *et al.* are anxious not to do this.

Instead they choose an alternative path which begins by examining workers' attitudes towards their work itself. After the setters (see above), the authors go on to deal with the assemblers, citing answers to the questions whether and why they would prefer different work – maintenance, for example. 'It's a better grade of job. There's more scope to use your initiative. There are different jobs every day. It's not so repetitive, not so boring, as assembly work' (I, p. 16).

Comments such as this presuppose that the respondents who make them – and, by implication, the group they are used in the text to represent – are by no means incapable of valuing other aspects of employment than money. They are followed by an amplified account of the 'clear sense of deprivation' (I, p. 16), the experience of 'monotony' (I, p. 18) and of 'the unfulfilling nature of the worktasks they were required to perform' (I, p. 19) evinced by the workers. Presence is given not to financial choices at all but to subjects' frustrated feelings and intelligence.

Then, by implication and association, moral components are added to the authors' report again by means of quotations cited from the men themselves. Various respondents suggest improvements for their work-situation which indicate an eagerness for responsibility, or which imply that the changes they envisage would benefit the whole work community rather than just themselves:

> 'One change I'd like to make? The supervision without a doubt. They're an inept crowd. And you can't offer an opinion of your own. In your apprenticeship, you're taught to be independent – how to design your own work. Here . . . they won't accept that anyone on the floor is capable of that. They've no faith in the chaps under them (I, p. 20).

> 'I'd like to see them get rid of the idea that if Harry organised it like that forty years ago, *you've* got to now. I like to use my own initiative' (I, p. 21).

> 'Every man should move down a job occasionally, then you'd know every job really well. You could have a move every fortnight or week' (I, p. 23).

In addition to what these remarks imply about the speakers and, by extension, about the group which they are being quoted to represent, there are generally positive *associations* with desires for independence and the exercise of initiative, and advocacy of faith in personnel, which extend the impressions created here some way beyond the literal bounds of what is said. These associations contribute to the sub-textual theme of emphasising the workers' positive qualities, a theme uniting the 'significantly different' attitudes (I, p. 10) examined in this chapter. It is only at this point (I, p. 28) that Goldthorpe *et al.* go on to their subjects' reasons for keeping uncongenial jobs: 'Money and again money – nothing else!'

Had this reason been presented earlier, the 'standard' impression would have been that this is a mercenary group of men. Just as a mercenary person is said to 'put money first', if a description of someone mentions his or her desire for money before any other characteristics, its order *means* that this person is mercenary. As Goldthorpe *et al.* in fact present their argument, its order shows their subjects as men with ordinarily unobjectionable motivations; it sets these motivations in a moral perspective quite different from that which would be implied by giving a position of textual dominance to a simple urge for cash.

If the authors left the issue here without further comment, though, they would imply a mystery about the workers' choice: if they would really prefer different jobs, and are not wholly driven by

reed, why are they still in their present work? Mysteriousness of this
sort would be good neither for the authors' self-presentation nor for
their explanation, and Goldthorpe *et al.* take immediate steps to
avoid it.

Investigating the men's 'decision . . . to give more weight to the
instrumental at the expense of the *expressive* aspects of work' (I, p. 33),
the authors show that though their subjects have resolved the
'dilemma' between rewarding jobs and well-paid ones in favour of
the latter, 'the decision' has 'often not been an easy one' (I, p. 34).
The remarks quoted to illustrate this show how the speakers made
their choices; they also give rise to associations which yield glimpses
of repondents' personal characteristics which not only reinforce the
impression of them endorsed by the authors but also anticipate and
begin to deal with a further problem in the authors' rhetorical
situation.

Goldthorpe *et al.* cannot usefully present themselves as offering a
tautological account of their subjects' attitudes: instrumentalism is
preferring work with better pay to work with intrinsic rewards; the
workers show this preference; so they have instrumental attitudes.
Instead, the question 'what *meaning* work has' for the sample (I,
p. 36) must be answered not just by naming a common decision
taken by its members but by showing that this decision is part of a
constellation of attitudes or a syndrome which they share. But at this
early stage of the authors' rhetorical enterprise it is in the nature of
the case impracticable for them to marshall enough evidence to do
this – the evidence is what makes up the rest of the book. So they
quote workers' comments whose associations suggest first that there
are personal attitudes involved here to be dealt with, and second that
these involve family and extra-work interests:

'When I came out of the R.A.F. the wife wanted income rather
than an interesting job for me. I was pushed into the highest-paid
work – which in Luton means Vauxhall' (I, p. 34).

'I liked being a waiter. It's a single man's job, of course – you've
got to go with the crowd to make money. It was clean and I didn't
mind the hours. Meeting people – that was the great thing' (I,
p. 34).

'I liked it at the tobacco company best. Being smaller, it was one
big family – in a big company you're just a part. There was less
money there, though' (I, p. 36).

Taken together, these quotations' ordering in the text and their associations make a crucial contribution to the meaning of what is written in this chapter. They have been preceded by accounts – also communicated partly in terms of rhetorical meaning – of subjects' reactions to work which make known their admirable or at any rate wholly normal characteristics. Then their choice of highly paid but uninteresting work is mentioned – fairly briefly. More presence is given to authorial assurances and quotations which demonstrate that this choice has been a difficult one. This standardly *means* that the men *cannot* be summed up in terms of a desire for cash, together with a low capacity for taking an interest in work anyway.

This rhetorical meaning contributes to the evaluative project of the trilogy; in the context of the discourse of which it is part, it *defends* the affluent workers. Moreover, it does so in a manner which intimately relates this defence to the authors' explanatory task; it indicates what sorts of questions there are to be asked about the affluent workers, and indicates in which directions their answers can be found. Lastly, the authors' procedure in this part of their text gives us some information about the questions sociologists try to answer when they wish to communicate an understanding of their subjects: what aspects of their characters come first? How are we to take them?

2 THE 'EPITOME' OF THE AFFLUENT WORKER

Goldthorpe *et al.* say that their 'ultimate aim' is that of 'forming some idea of the *total* life-situations and life-styles' of their respondents (III, p. 31). They also describe themselves – and must, to avoid tautology – as communicating an 'orientation to work' with an 'associated syndrome of attitudes and behaviour' (I, p. 146). This makes a great deal for the authors to convey and the reader to understand. How do they do it, and should we try to apply natural scientific standards of objectivity and exactitude to the results?

Goldthorpe *et al.* refer continually to 'the' affluent worker, and state a number of factors which obtain of all their respondents: for example, they are all between 21 and 46 years old, live in Luton, are married and earn at least a stated weekly sum (I, pp. 2–4). These facts by no means summarise the workers' 'life-situations and life-styles'; they are merely common to them all. To describe their subjects the authors do not limit themselves to any discrete set of variables, as they would have to if following Schutz's instructions for 'homunculus';[4] and at the end of I, Chapter 2 they *contrast* the discussion of their subjects in the body of the chapter with an "ideal-type" form' of 'three contrasting orientations to work' (I, p. 38) on pp. 38–41.

I shall argue that Goldthorpe *et al.* convey their account of the affluent worker's life-situation in a manner very common among sociologists who are dealing with a group of people too large for individual treatment, but discrete enough to share significant personal characteristics. This method is one which incorporates some features amenable to 'scientific' treatments such as tabular breakdowns in statistical form,[5] but its basic features depart markedly from natural-scientific criteria of excellence such as precision and a use of clear-cut variables.

This method consists in a relatively informal amalgam of procedures to which I shall refer as an 'epitome'. This amalgam seems to me to play a large though not exclusive role in communicating sociological understanding when the central question to be asked is, what sort of people are these? (Some other types of understanding are discussed below.) An epitome may include results obtained by conventional 'qualitative' methods such as interviewing; it necessarily involves rhetorical methods such as the use of components which prompt the reader to make his or her own extrapolations from them, and the selection of details on the grounds of their communicative power rather than their strict typicality.

These variegated methods contribute to the image of a single figure whose textual function is to demonstrate what can be expected from members of the group in question. An epitome of this sort can more usefully be judged in terms of the coherence of the characteristics it assembles, and its effectiveness in presenting them to the reader, than according to more easily quantifiable criteria. This of course adds considerably to the difficulties of assessing a text, but if we look at the methods actually followed by sociologists there seems to be no alternative to accepting that these difficulties are corollaries of methods compatible with everyday forms of understanding, and which tell readers the kinds of thing they want to know.

Goldthorpe *et al.* present the empirical details making up their epitome of the affluent worker in a necessarily selective manner: in one text they cannot record every detail, or even every salient detail, of all the observations they have made. Their method of selection functions so as to overcome these limitations of textuality; it is a recurrent feature of the details they choose that they have the capacity to communicate further, unstated information. Both the stated and the unstated details they convey have some relevance to the general predicament shared by the authors' subjects, though this relevance is not really straightforwardly representative.

The authors introduce their subjects' remarks not only as 'typical' but also as 'characteristic' or 'illustrative'; they use locutions such as 'As one assembler put it . . . ' (I, p. 49) or 'The following remarks captured the spirit of many others . . . ' (I, p. 88). But the 'particular illustrations' given in the text provide 'qualitative insights' which are '*backed up* by quantitative analysis of data' from the whole sample (III, p. 102, my emphasis).

Rather than claiming to have deduced conclusions from quantitative analysis, the authors say that their analysis 'confirms' that their conclusions apply to the whole group (ibid.). Though it is prudent and valid to check as much as possible using methods which are as various as possible, quantitative methods can at best confirm only that given proportions of those interviewed seemed prepared to agree with the rough tendency of the observations which have been given textual status. These remarks are presumably selected for the fact that they are more telling than those which are not chosen, and they therefore function on more levels than it is practicable to check by means of separate surveys.

An epitome can thus be said to communicate in a more natural fashion than could a strictly assembled ideal type or homunculus – as can be seen from the fact that Goldthorpe *et al.* do not feel the need to categorise and define every single attitude expressed by their respondents. The informality, and to a great extent the effectiveness, of their epitome of the affluent worker can be described in terms of their use of textual items whose interpretation depends on the reader's assessment of what they imply and on his or her reactions to their rhetorical components.

Among these components, order again plays a role which has both moral and argumentative significance. In volume I as a whole, qualities such as concern for one's family and interest in other people are suggested *before* the workers' desire for material goods is examined in any detail. This buttresses the plausibility of the authors' interpretation of their subjects' material wishes in terms of creativity rather than cupidity in vol. I, chapter 7 and at the end of ol. III – their account, that is, of how *we* are to *take* these wishes.

In vol. II, the authors' entire argument about their sample's nstrumental' attitude to politics is foreshadowed by a single uotation:

'I consider myself a working man, so a working man should always vote Labour. They say Labour is·for the working man, to try and better the working man, and that's more or less the reason. We've had it rough under a Tory government in years gone by, and it's been drummed into us as kids, the hard times. I'd be the first to vote Tory, though, if a Labour government started mucking us about' (II, p. 18).

˜his early presentation of a concise and forceful version of the uthors' case has the argumentative function of stimulating the eader's responsiveness to subsequent elements in its support.

One further characteristic of this relatively everyday, noncientistic mode of communication is that the quotations used by the uthors do not function as isolated entities but interact with each ·ther as do segments of everyday conversation. This phenomenon ontributes to the fruitfulness of the impressions which form the pitome. A respondent I have quoted above says, 'As a setter you ave to use your mind more and it [the job] is more responsible. You el as if you *are* somebody' (I, p. 13). This has standard associations ɔ the effect that the speaker's pleasure in his work affords him an nhanced self-respect; this influences the meaning of the following: You're left alone – there's only myself on the job. You go along icely on your own' (ibid.). Taken singly, this would merely convey dislike of supervision: its textual setting controls its meaning by larifying the motivation behind it.

In constructing their epitome of the affluent worker, Goldthorpe *t al.* give presence preponderantly to quotations in their subjects' ·wn language. This language is the only part of their social behaviour vhich can be exhibited to the reader – albeit under the transformng conditions of textuality; its display can act as a rhetorical spur to he reader's perception of the worker as acting in a context of social neaning which he or she can interpret using procedures appropri- te to everyday interaction.

Just as it is hardly feasible to write intelligibly about social ituations without using actual types, it seems implausible that an uthor could show what a group of people is like without exhibiting

anything they say – that is, without using quotations which functio
in an actual-typical manner. It is not possible to gain more than
general impression of authors' reliance on quotations by countin
their numbers, since one telling example may convey more tha
several less effective ones and since effectiveness itself varies with th
reader's responsiveness; but the impression given by vol. I alon
underlines the significance of this method to Goldthorpe *et al.* (I
Chapter 2, which introduces the affluent worker, the number c
quotations is correspondingly highest, at 38; Chapter 3 contains 1(
Chapter 4, 16; Chapter 5, 17; Chapter 6, 20; and Chapter 7 ha
three extended ' "case studies" ' with actual-typical elements.)

Goldthorpe *et al.* resemble Willis in so frequently taking the vie\
that the best language for their predicament is their subjects' owr
and both are able to circumvent professional conventions c
authorial neutrality by using this language. But Willis can hardly b
said to construct an epitome. The group he is writing about is sma
enough to be dealt with in individual terms, and when one think
of 'the lads' one thinks not of a composite figure but of Joey c
Spanksy.

Moreover, not all spoken language can conveniently be used fc
textual purposes, so that some differences in the ways in whic
sociologists present their subjects are explicable in terms of th
associations readers can be expected to attach to subjects' remark
Many of Rex's and Moore's subjects use non-standard English, an
these authors rely much less than do Goldthorpe *et al.* on quotatior
and more on other actual types. In Worsley's *The Trumpet Sha
Sound*, the author quotes occasionally from his Melanesian subject
but he does not make them talk *like* Melanesians; their pidgi
English would seem comical to an English audience.

This implies that there are special problems in conveying certai
kinds of sociological understanding to an audience which does nc
share the language of the subjects of a work; and both Rex an
Moore and Worsley concentrate more on their subjects' situation
than on showing what kind of people they are, producing epitome
which are much less detailed than that produced by Goldthorp
et al. It would not be easy for them to give detailed investigation t
the question what their subjects are *like*, and they more ofte
content themselves with showing that they are in principle n
different from anyone else (see the deductive forms discussed i
Chapter 5 below). We can assume that methodological preference
interact with this question of the accessibility to readers of subjects

language; but all these texts show also that authors adapt their approaches not only to their subjects' but also to their *readers'* habits of speech and interpretation.

Given the communicative functions of epitomes, it is apposite to evaluate them in a mixed mode, consisting only partly of the standards usual in assessing qualitative work in sociology. Besides these standards, it seems reasonable to refer to the literary effectiveness with which the epitome is conveyed. Platt points out that literature does not consist of a 'systematically distinguishable' 'body of utterances' with its own 'grammatical and textual properties'.[6] It can be characterised in terms of a *concentration* of communicative functions which can, individually, be found elsewhere; sometimes in the field of sociology.[7] Thus the admission that literary talents are useful in writing sociological books does not imply that sociologists somehow 'only' do what novelists do.

In any case, sociologists show what people are 'like' in relation to predicaments which are not chosen only according to the author's personal inclinations, but whose interest derives from their location at the intersection of identifiable social forces. Sociological epitomes examine people's behaviour in a fashion which gives priority to their responses to these specifically social predicaments.

If a text is dealing with the question what particular subjects are like, it is also relevant to criticise it in terms of the coherency and consistency with which these subjects' characteristics are described. It seems to me a reasonable expectation that social and personal characteristics should be shown to cluster together in some intelligible fashion, not described as if they had no bearing on one another. Sartre rightly objects to the excessively analytic spirit which leads to looking at

> persons or characters as mosaics in which each stone coexists with the others without that coexistence affecting the nature of the whole. Thus anti-Semitic opinion appears . . . to be a molecule that can enter into combination with other molecules of any origin whatsoever without undergoing any alteration. A man may be a good father and a good husband, a conscientious citizen, highly cultivated, philanthropic, *and* in addition an anti-Semite. He may like fishing and the pleasures of love, may be tolerant in matters of religion, full of generous notions on the condition of the natives in Central Africa, *and* in addition detest the Jews.[8]

Anyone who finds this sketch of perceived anti-Semitism implausible would be bound to expect sociological epitomes to conform to some standard of internal coherence; and to be compatible with such evidence about patterns of consistent behaviour as psychology or sociology itself can furnish – or else to give good reasons why not.

But it is none the less true that criteria for coherent social action are partly culture-specific. What might have seemed ordinarily consistent in seventeenth-century Spain, say, such as a series of actions based on social pride, could seem impenetrably incoherent in twentieth-century England. This shows another respect in which epitomes are directed towards · the *reader's* expectations of behaviour – demonstrating how subjects' conduct can be made to fit in with what he or she anticipates that people will do in certain situations.

In the presentation of an epitome, attributes set down in a particular order provoke sub-textual expectations according to the patterns in which characteristics are taken to cluster together in the reader's culture. These expectations enable him or her to 'see how' it is that the author's subjects feel and behave as they do. This seems to be the rationale underlying the observation made by Goldthorpe *et al.* to the effect that their respondents' attitudes to trade unions ' "makes sense" ' in terms of their 'orientation . . . towards their employment generally' (ɪ, p. 106). They add,

> given the ways in which the work situation was most typically defined among the workers we studied, it is difficult to conceive of their style of unionism being markedly different from that we have described (ɪ, p. 114).

But if in many cases readers' expectations of consistency are accepted and exploited in explanatory structures (see next chapter), sociologists are not *obliged* to accept them. If an author considers that motives he or she has discovered in subjects are not coherent in terms of the audience's views, in order to form an intelligible explanation he or she may well try to *alter* these views. Thus Rex and Moore use actual types to change readers' expectations with regard both to Englishmen in authority and to black lodging-house inhabitants. Here it is not intellectual calculations, rather the reader's feelings of familiarity and unfamiliarity about his or her fellow human beings which are being either relied upon or disturbed.

This seems characteristic of a tension in sociology between relying on what the reader expects and attacking it. An epitome in particular incorporates so many implicit details and taken-for-granted assumptions that in practice authors use the 'etcetera principle' in their own communicative habits, not attempting to name and justify every component and depending on the reader to extrapolate on the basis of what they write. This dependence is nevertheless compatible with combining the reader's expectations in such a way that the result is to change them. Hence there is no need to associate giving accounts of what sort of people subjects are with any type of conservatism, literary or political; the contrary may be the case.

In contrast to formally constructed models, which may be suitable for specific and narrowly defined purposes such as testing predictions, epitomes attempt the broader task of making social behaviour comprehensible to personal readers, demonstrating how social processes become palpable in people's lives. Doing this involves both relying on and changing readers' anticipations, in order to bring explanatory material home to them in a rhetorically effective way – so that what the reader acquires from the text is an explanation in the mode appropriate to knowledge about people.

3 RHETORICAL INDUCTION: A GUIDE TO EXPECTATIONS

The method of epitomes is not the only means sociologists have of describing what happens at the intersection of different social influences at particular places and times. It may be that an author wishes to stress that it is not a person belonging to a particular social group but *anyone* who can find himself or herself in a given position, as Goffman often does (see below); or it may be that individuals as such are not the immediate focus of attention, as is the case with Ronald Dore in *British Factory – Japanese Factory*.

Dore is concerned with what British and Japanese factories are *like*. He examines two different social situations and tells us what we could expect if we found ourselves there – what happens to 'one' both at work and afterwards (p. 201) or how 'one' sustains the

goodwill of colleagues on whom one depends (p. 235). As professional conventions demand that he should, Dore makes clear in
introducing his work that he is writing about a small number of
researched situations only; but in fact the point of doing this is that
these situations are not unique, and that the author is able to tell us –
and tell us in a particular way, with particular effects – what can
reasonably be expected in comparable social contexts. It is this that
I should like to describe in terms of 'rhetorical induction'.

Dore himself gives evidence for believing that however these
expectations are conveyed, they are not simply statements of
probability. They have the usual rhetorical characteristics of being
addressed, in the context of a continuing discourse, to a personal
reader and of being influenced by him or her. Dore points out on
p. 10 that he expects readers to examine his text with the intention of
seeing what they can borrow from the Japanese, and because of
what the *reader* is likely to do with the book he makes his evaluations
clearly available (p. 9). (Thus on pp. 28ff. Dore gives opinions on
what are and are not the advantages of piecework, or dealing with
industrial relations in Chapters 5 to 7 he is scathing about an
obtuseness, on the parts of both management and unions in Britain,
which cannot be attributed to any rational political strategy and
which involves both sides in contradictory behaviour. Occasional
more personal interpolations of sarcasm, irritation or humour recur
in the text.) Sensitisation and self-presentation play roles of
particular interest in rhetorical induction.

What Dore says about his own feelings as the producer of a text
is in many ways exemplary as a demonstration of the proper involvement of extra-'cognitive' elements in intellectual work, and
hence as implying an account of what 'sensitisation' can involve –
whether or not as a concomitant of rhetorical induction. Dore refers
to the 'challenge to one's intellectual curiosity' (p. 10) presented by
the fact that two almost identical manufacturing processes involve
two such different sets of social and economic relations. He mentions
the humour and the occasional 'slight sense of nausea' involved in
doing his research (p. 10), and the 'great pleasure' he derived from
producing evidence against the 'popular assumption' that the
Japanese form of industrial organisation is immature and will
eventually catch up with the Western one (p. 11). Emotional
positions need to be bound up with arguments, and when they are
lacking or out of key even statements of admitted fact cannot be
properly perceived; Dore says of Japanese managers themselves that

Although they may appreciate intellectually that Japan's 'pre-modern' wage system has not prevented Japan from becoming the world's third largest economy with the highest growth rate among the developed economies, they find it hard to accept the fact emotionally (p. 317).

Even Marxist or neo-classical economists with whom the author has discussed his thesis are so reluctant to abandon the comfortable notion that the British market system is *normal* that they prefer to contradict their own theoretical positions (p. 418).

Dore takes it for granted, then, that there are emotional components *in* arguments, as well as emotional attitudes which people take *towards* arguments. What he says implies that when these emotions have deleterious effects on arguments, it is not because they are emotions – after all, acceptance of Japanese differences is as emotional as is refusal to accept them – but because they are the *wrong* emotions: inappropriate or perhaps, like indignation (p. 10), even 'dangerous'.

The sensitising components of Dore's rhetorical communication thus share a recurrent feature. He wants his readers to reach a state of mind in which they can abandon preconceived notions about the normality of their own social system – where they can develop expectations at variance with their old ones. This explains why he does not expect readers to agree with him after reading only a statement of his thesis (p. 13). This is his own version of the 'convergence' view, which anticipates that in some ways the West will grow more like Japan, not vice versa. Accepting this view is not merely a matter of gaining familiarity with new evidence, but also one of abandoning familiarity with an old point of view.

The fact that Dore has to give his readers information which is not only new but also quite possibly unwelcome is indicated by the following excerpt, which might best be described as a story.[9] Its function appears to be to make it more difficult for the reader to resist the inductive generalisation which the author wants to convey.

One meets such 'inspector generals' in English Electric dining rooms since the merger. One teases them by explaining that if this were a Japanese firm they would be playing a very minor second fiddle to a product engineer, that when you start from the premise that the only way your workforce will ever diminish is by death or

retirement, then the question with which you begin a clean-up
operation is not: 'How can we cut labour costs; whom can we do
without?' but 'What new markets or product lines can we open
up so that we can fully employ our workers?' The response is at
best an incredulous denial that that could possibly be the way it
is; at worst a faint condescending smile at the thought of the
terrible cropper these poor Japs are eventually going to come
once this American-sponsored flash in the pan has burnt itself out
(pp. 37–8).

This incorporates the generalisation where most sensitisation of the
reader is required: that Japan does not function according to the
expectations appropriate to a market economy, and people there do
not sell their skills to make a living, but instead sell a lifetime of
service to one firm. Hence if the skills they do have happen no longer
to be required by their employers, the latter see it as incumbent on
them not to dismiss the workers concerned but to train them in new
skills.

This is what not only members of British management structure
refuse to believe, but Dore's academic colleagues also; so he has
good reason for expecting his hypothetical reader to be reluctant to
believe it too, and is forced to attend to dismantling barriers against
what he has to say.

In keeping with the (rhetorical) requirement of getting the
reader to develop new expectations, Dore furnishes his text with
large numbers of actual types. On the one hand, actual types
provide a method of involving the reader actively in changing his or
her own mind without feeling bludgeoned; on the other, this author
is writing about social situations, and in any social situation there
will be far more factors than can intelligibly be written down in a
text which has to make room for a large number of such accounts.
The actual type allows the reader to make his or her own
extrapolations about the situations described, and indeed relies
upon the fact that this will happen. If the activity of extrapolating
increases the reader's feeling of confidence with regard to situations
foreign to him or her, so much the better.

Thus on pp. 167–8 Dore quotes a report from a Japanese union
newssheet on a meeting with management. In a negotiating
situation which its participants perceive as lacking a crucial *raison
d'être* for British unions – defending workers in a position where
their whole livelihoods are at stake – it is more efficient to *show* the

reader what sort of interaction takes place than to spell out analyses which put names to the styles involved. In any case, descriptions – such as 'non-adversarial' or 'cooperative' – would be bound to raise hackles in some readers.

On p. 137 Dore contrasts

> The cramped, dingy, lonely silence of an English union's mid-town district office, some miles from the factories at which most of its members work . . .

with

> the Furusato Union auditorium, its smart offices and modern equipment, the constant lunch-hour traffic in and out of the union building directly across from the factory gates – the flocks of young girls and men going into the building after work for a five-thirty stereo concert (with two music critics to introduce each item) . . .

and the

> lengthy table showing where to go for what – for everything from getting a house loan or a burial allowance for a wife to lodging a complaint against your union section chairman or acquiring the services of a lawyer.

(Note the reference to complaints mechanisms; this may go towards counteracting automatic attributions of servility to the Japanese system.)

These details tell us what to expect from a Japanese union building and what goes on in it, in the sense of supplying the reader with a navigable account of the situation – one by which he or she could orient himself if he or she were there. This communicative function would not be served by the formulation of cumbersome generalisations, however scientifically competent they might be.

This is not precisely to say that the type of generalisation which rhetorical induction represents is informed by 'practical' interests – it is improbable that the majority of readers will ever need to know their way round a Japanese factory in an immediate sense – but the understanding appropriate here is derived from everyday patterns of understanding and in many ways analogous to them. Both in sociology and in everyday life it is usually (not always) both impossible and unnecessary to know with what mathematical probability we should expect, say, union–management discussions to take a particular tone. What is necessary, and possible, is to know what can reasonably be expected.

Here it would indeed be *possible* to discover exactly what proportion of Japanese union buildings house five-thirty concerts during a given time-period; but the point of the author's actual-typical mention of these concerts is that they are symptomatic (perhaps also symbolic) of the place of Japanese unions in the personal lives of their members. And this is not a matter with regard to which exact calculations can sensibly be made. To count as understanding a given type of situation readers surely need, first, to know approximately what to anticipate will happen in it; second, their knowledge must be flexible enough to allow them to interpret situations slightly different from the one the author describes, as well as – third – endowed with some of the insights it is appropriate for actors in social situations to have. These three functions are, I should claim, fulfilled by 'rhetorical inductions'.

Rhetorical induction, then, is a guide to expectations in which an author goes from a limited number of observations to a statement about what can reasonably be anticipated in general. It is characteristically sociological not only in being subject to the limitations intrinsic to information about social situations, but also in its strengths. It has the strength of enabling the reader to interpret situations which are not exactly like those described; it does not involve the artificial modesty of pretending that the author can *only* talk about what he or she has directly observed; nor does it imply the excessive claim that the author can infer from the observations actually made to *all* possible cases of a comparable type. (Thus it seems to me that what I offer as rhetorical induction avoids Popper's objections to the notion of induction in its usual sense.[10]) A rhetorical induction is not a matter of *mere* expectations but is modulated to the way in which anticipation functions in social situations; and it is *interactive*, relying on the reader to decide what new situations to classify as comparable with those with which the author deals.

A rhetorical induction presupposes that the type of social situation under examination will continue to occur as before, in all important respects; it must therefore be made in the knowledge that this qualifying presupposition will sometimes fail, in which case a

1ew induction will be needed. But this insecurity is by no means
ufficient to prohibit the formation of reasonable expectations
altogether.

Rhetorical inductions may be stated in so many words – as when
Dore says that in Japan 'status differences are *more likely* to be seen as
egitimate than in England' (p. 253; my emphasis), or when he says
hat in Japan, 'Foremen will talk with rather solemn pride of the
1eed in their job for skill in what they are apt to describe nowadays
1s "human rirēshonzu"' (p. 235). Or they may, as in the examples
quoted above from Dore's descriptions of union buildings, be left to
be inferred by the reader from actual types, epitomes, historical
1arratives or stories (which themselves may often epitomise social
processes).

The practice by authors of using actual types to convey rhetorical
inductions is the one which most clearly reveals the textual functions
of each. An actual type displays an example of the sort from which
the rhetorical induction infers, does so in a manner which provokes
the reader's involvement in the text, and casts some light on the type
of insight 'apposite for actors in social situations' (see above) which
rhetorical inductions can communicate. It seems reasonable to
assume that these insights consist not just of causal and historical
knowledge, but also of the ability, mediated by the reader's own
social experience, to interpret features of social situations as
symptoms or symbols. Textual provision of an actual type depends
on this ability but also extends it.

The provision of examples which function as actual types, and
generalisations in terms of rhetorical induction, accounts for a very
large proportion of Dore's text. Features common to both may also
account indirectly for aspects of his historical narratives – for
example, that on the rise of the Japanese trade union. Historical
knowledge of a situation itself generates the ability to interpret
contemporary features as symptomatic or symbolic of states of
affairs which have arisen in the past. (They may of course also
suggest causal explanations.)

But there is one more question which must be asked about
rhetorical induction. If it does not claim logical stringency for the
inferences it offers from a limited number of cases to reasonable
expectations about the future, why should we believe what the
author says, rather than dismissing it as simply impressionistic?

The answer to this lies chiefly in the author's self-presentation. It
would be impossible for Dore to support all his generalisations in

terms of evidence conforming to statistical criteria which forced the
reader to accept his rhetorical inductions. This is compatible with
what Goldthorpe *et al.* write (see above); when checks are made on
individual features of a rhetorical induction, this serves as backing
for the main operation – not vice versa. Such checks cannot account
for all the features which the rhetorical induction conveys, and a
statistical communicative style is not intrinsically multifaceted
specifically appropriate to social action itself. None the less, Dore
does present the reader with an enormous wealth of detail, statistical
and otherwise. If this leads the reader to accept that Dore has
competence in and mastery of the situations he describes, he or she
will be prepared to accord at least tentative acceptance to what
Dore says.

In effect, then, the reader accepts Dore's rhetorical inductions
because they have Dore's authority. In the absence of writers on the
Japanese factory who can show themselves to be even more socially
competent and better informed, it is reasonable that he or she
should do so. In the last analysis, it is the *author* whom the reader
believes on the grounds of his self-presentation, not primarily the
evidence.

4 SUMMARY

This chapter began by pointing to the functions of rhetorical
meaning in *The Affluent Worker*; rhetorical uses of standard implications and associations, and rhetorical figures such as presence and
order, extend the meaning of the text with considerable effect on its
evaluative and explanatory content.

Next I examined the way in which Goldthorpe *et al.* write about
the sort of person they take the affluent worker to be, suggesting that
instead of using a formal model for this purpose they construct what
I term an 'epitome'. An epitome conveys understanding by telling
readers the answers to questions they are likely to have about the
sort of person the subject is; it is composed of an amalgam of
procedures, some with natural-scientific affinities and standards,
and many without – such as details chosen for rhetorical rather than
statistical characteristics and specially adapted to the *reader's* habits
of assessing social phenomena. Correspondingly, epitomes should
be evaluated in a mixed mode, in which criteria such as precise
definition cannot always take first place.

This applies too to the 'rhetorical inductions' which play a central part in Dore's *British Factory – Japanese Factory*. Resting heavily on the rhetorical components of sensitisation and self-presentation, rhetorical inductions infer from the author's observations to what he can advise the reader to expect in the future, even in cases which are not identical with those seen in the past. Rhetorical inductions, I claim, allow readers to understand types of social situation by answering characteristic questions about them. They communicate in a manner which provides the reader with specifiable insights about the situations concerned. This is not itself practical knowledge of a social situation, but it is knowledge which readers want to take the form it does *because* of the experience they have of the social world.

5 Rhetorical Deductions in Sociological Texts

We have seen that there is a contrast between the methodological conception of induction and what can be found in sociological texts: not mere statements generalising about social phenomena, but three-dimensional argumentative structures, inevitably intervening into the social worlds of the readers to whom they are addressed. The same contrast occurs in the case of deduction.

The Aristotelian notion of the rhetorical deduction – the enthymeme – has not been much current in recent philosophy, and I should like to define it here as a deduction set out in such a way as to heighten its argumentative impact on its recipient (this often means that it is set out incompletely, demanding audience participation in its reconstruction); a deduction which commonly argues from premises with no ambitions to form universal empirical generalisations; and which incorporates self-presentation and sensitisation into its functioning.[1] Its uses in sociology cast light on some of the ways in which an understanding of social behaviour is achieved.

I shall argue that as a matter of empirical fact, two types of enthymeme hold places of special importance in sociological texts. I call them the 'ordinary person' enthymeme and the 'reasonable person' enthymeme, distinguishing them according to the sorts of premise from which they argue. These premises may be derived from rhetorical inductions; or they may constitute 'topoi' or taken-for-granted 'reputable opinions' about what is likely to happen in the social world. In my view 'ordinary person' and 'reasonable person' enthymemes share the recurrent sociological characteristic of relying on some of their readers' beliefs at the same time as changing others. In these two major types of enthymeme, the beliefs involved concern what it *is* to be an ordinary person or a reasonable one, what behaviour the reader ought or ought not to take as symptomatic of ordinariness or reasonableness. Both using and

110

changing such beliefs have marked personal, ethical and political consequences.

Continuing to examine the texts used in the last chapter – *The Affluent Worker* series by Goldthorpe *et al.* and *British Factory – Japanese Factory* by Dore – I shall look here at the role of the ordinary person enthymeme in first using, then changing its audience's accepted bases for arguing about and understanding happenings in the social world. Next I shall turn to the same authors' uses of the reasonable person enthymeme, which account for many of the justificatory features of their explanations. I shall also comment on a standard function of ambiguity in sociological enthymemes: they may be so constructed as to yield different deductions according to the requirements of different audiences.

In all these cases of enthymematic explanation, we can discover how understanding is conveyed by asking to what questions from their hypothetical readers the authors concerned are providing answers. In general these questions emphasise interaction rather than, say, empathy; they are questions about how to react to the subjects involved rather than about the inmost workings of their minds.

In discussing the interaction between author and reader in making sense of sociological texts, I have so far paid more attention to the reader's activity, only remarking by the way on authors' expressions of social, moral or political attitudes towards both subjects and readers. Here I shall focus on these expressions, treating them as defining the 'communicative attitudes' which I shall claim that authors display in texts.

These attitudes are by no means disconnected from writers' explanatory tasks nor from their communicational strategies. The attitudes which Goldthorpe *et al.* show to 'the' affluent worker are highly consistent with their use of the natural, non-theoreticised form of the epitome to portray him, and with their uses of the ordinary person and the reasonable person enthymeme. Dore's attitudes to the reader, rather than to his subjects, can be shown to have a bearing on his uses of the same enthymematic forms. Here I do not wish to suggest that communicational attitudes in some way blemish what should be the neutrality of sociological texts. On the contrary, we should welcome the fact that conveying personal positions is characteristic of the enterprise of sociological explanation.

1 'ORDINARY PERSON' ENTHYMEMES

The point of an 'ordinary person' enthymeme is that it makes
attitudes and behaviour intelligible by showing that they are what
could be expected of anyone in a comparable situation. Thus it
seems to me that sociologists' practice shows that a question of prime
importance in understanding other people is, 'Is their behaviour
usual or not?' I do not think this question arises from an unthinking
impulse to conformity, but for the practical reason that people wish
to know how to react to others. Should they expect interaction with
them to run along accustomed lines or not? Can the behaviour in
question be allocated to the categories normally used in making
sense of the social world, or must they be added to or changed? And
of course what can make this type of question *sociological* is the
situation in relation to which it is asked: the usefulness of this
situation in displaying what happens at the meeting of phenomena
of explicitly social interest.

In this section I shall examine some features of the rhetorical
deductive structure which sociologists use in this connection: first,
the kinds of major premise it incorporates and the sense in which it
can be said to infer; second, the aspects of this type of enthymeme
which presuppose a consensus with the reader. In the next section I
shall go on to those of its aspects which tend to change the reader's
conception of what ordinariness is.

Any kind of enthymeme, whether 'ordinary person' or not,
provides a means of inferring from premises which are not scientific
laws or hypothetical generalisations claiming universal validity.
The premises which an enthymeme does use can be divided into two
very broad types: 'general' topoi[2] or assumptions on the one hand,
and on the other often standardised claims about parts of reality
which count as, or can be established as, acceptable within a given
culture as supplying workable expectations about what is likely to
occur within it.[3]

Enthymematic premises very markedly display the rhetorical
characteristic of serving several communicative purposes at once.
They are not premises only in the sense of being starting statements
for arguments; they *legitimise* processes of arguing (this is most
obvious in the case of general topoi), and they generate forms
which *show* people how to argue. It seems to me, then, that they are
distinguished by this mixed argumentative *role* rather than by some
clearly identifiable shared form.

Here I shall treat general topoi as premises which, if they make assertions about reality at all, make extremely general ones. The strategy of the critical case', common in sociology and used in *The Affluent Worker* by Goldthorpe *et al.*, is in fact an argument from the general topos *a fortiori*: if something does not happen where it is more likely (the instantiation of the *embourgeoisement* thesis in Luton) it can be assumed that it will not happen where it is less likely elsewhere in England).[4] Another general topos argues that what applies to a part will apply to the whole;[5] for example, that what is true of this sample of factory workers is true of comparable factory workers in general.

General topoi are not limited to any particular field and apply even outside the social sphere. Taken together, they would outline what counts – at least in Western culture – as the basis of all valid arguing, but their exact number remains to be discovered. Since they are all by definition assumed to be valid, an argument based on a general topos cannot normally be countered on the grounds that its premise is false; only on the grounds that for specified reasons it is inapplicable to the case on hand.

General topoi share with special topoi the joint characteristics of showing a disputant how to argue, in the sense of showing him or her in what direction to look for an argument (hence their old name of *loci* or 'commonplaces') and sanctioning the argument when made. That is to say, a sociologist wondering how to deal with an unmanageably large group of subjects is directed, if he or she refers to the topos *a fortiori*, to look for the group to which any thesis he or she wishes to attack is *most* likely to apply. When he or she comes to argue on the basis of these results, it is the same topos which supplies what he or she says with its warrant as a valid argument.

Special topoi have more empirical content than general ones but claim to apply to given fields only. They claim plausibility for most cases within those fields, not universal truth; so arguments based on special topoi can be countered either on the grounds of inapplicability to the case in hand or on the grounds that what they take to be plausible is not. Thus the topos 'mothers love their children' might be used as a premise for the claim that women would be glad to refrain from going out to work if they could afford it; anyone disagreeing with this could argue that the premise, though unexceptionable in itself, is irrelevant to the present claim (perhaps by arguing that loving behaviour does not entail continuous companionship, or else by arguing that continuous parental

companionship could be achieved by work-sharing with fathers)
Otherwise it would have to be contended that the premise itself i
not as plausible as it sounds, and that motherly love is not a
common as it is claimed.

Here I shall treat special topoi as a single class with all othe
standardised or would-be standardised claims about what to expec
in a given sphere (though analytically this is an over-simplification)
Truisms, or 'gross observable behavior descriptions', [6] differ fron
special topoi in that they lack the rhetorical characteristic o
intrinsic direction towards use in deliberation and action, but no
doubt they can be endowed with such characteristics in argumentative practice. The products of rhetorical inductions as I have
described them in the last chapter may be introduced into
sociological argumentation by a single author and hence are not in a
clear sense standard, but in so far as they are offered as accounts o
standard behaviour I take it that they are candidates for becoming
generally held expectations.

It is just because the premises for enthymemes about social actior
are likely to be parts of common knowledge that they can seen
disappointingly banal when set down in plain English. But their
function is precisely *not* to give new information about how people
behave; it is to license inferences which will be accepted as making
behaviour intelligible *because* they situate it in terms of premise:
which are uncontroversial.

The enthymemes I want to examine first are those whose premises
concern what can reliably be expected of ordinary behaviour. Their
placing in a text is frequently unobtrusive; often they can be found
in the details of the scaffolding underpinning some more genera
form of argument. In the *Affluent Worker* series, Goldthorpe *et al*
sketch in their epitome of their subjects in I, Chapter 2; in the next
chapter they attack aspects of the 'technological' and 'human
relations' approaches to industrial sociology. In doing so they use
generally enthymematic arguments which rely on 'ordinary person'
enthymemes of a type which presuppose consensus with the reader
about what ordinary behaviour actually is.

In outline, their attack on the 'technological' approach runs as
follows. The technological theory implies that, since technological
conditions are a primary influence on workers' behaviour on the
shop floor, under defined technological conditions we should expect
certain defined relationships. [7] We do not find these relationships;

herefore at least that part of the theory which connects behaviour
vith immediate technological surroundings is false.

This reasoning is itself enthymematical in that the authors do not
tate it overtly; my account summarises an inferential form which is
only implicit on I, pp. 44–63. It is also enthymematical in that it
eaves a crucial inference to the reader – namely that if this part of
he technological theory is false, there is some reason to doubt the
est of it. (This inference can be justified in terms of what Peirce
erms 'abduction': [8] if the whole technological theory were false, the
nistakenness of this part would follow as a matter of course; this part
s mistaken; therefore there is some reason to believe the whole
heory false.) Moreover, the self-presentation of the technological
heorists is impugned: writers able to advance such demonstrably
alse opinions need not be trusted too readily in general.

The argumentative forms which I am terming 'ordinary person'
nthymemes occur in the details of the attack by Goldthorpe *et al.* on
the technological theory. Its assumptions include one to the effect
that workers can be expected to form comparatively strong
attachments to each other under certain conditions: for example,
when technological arrangements allow them to work within
speaking distance of each other, possibly also to cooperate on work-
tasks (cf. Table 19, I, p. 47). In order to scrutinise this claim,
Goldthorpe *et al.* use premises showing their conception of the
behaviour which can ordinarily be expected of people showing
friendship.

These premises are not stated in their text, but can be inferred
from their investigative strategy. They ask their respondents,

> 'How would you feel if you were moved to another job in the
> factory, more or less like the one you do now, but away from the
> men who work near to you? Would you feel very upset, fairly
> upset, not much bothered, or not bothered at all' (I, p. 50).

The assumption behind this question is that to *count* as feeling
attached to someone, all other things being equal any ordinary
person would have at least to mind if his or her frequent interaction
with that person were inhibited. The authors take this so much for
granted that for them it may even form a definitive constituent of
the notion of friendship. [9]

It seems to me that we have no textual evidence at all for taking it that this assumption forms part of a *theory* they have about friendship. Suggestions such as Schutz's,[10] to the effect that everyday reasoning is characterised by theories and hypotheses similar to scientific deductions, can obscure the argumentative functions of simple habits of expectation – which are able to give rise to coherent arguments although they *lack* such 'scientific' features as cogent rationales or fully elaborated criteria for falsification. These suggestions also make everyday thought sound scientific at the expense of perceiving how much of science is everyday.

There is, then, no reason to suppose that Goldthorpe *et al.* should or do see their connection between friendship and a desire for social interaction as other than part of a stock of taken-for-granted assumptions with no pretensions to being scientific, or even absolutely general.[11] This is all they need, or possess, for the continuation of their argument; and they find that 'Although more than half the group reported talking to their workmates "a good deal", only a quarter would be "very upset" or "fairly upset" if moved away from the men near to whom they presently work' (1, p. 50; cf. 1, pp. 51–2). Can it therefore be concluded that the type of relationship predicted by the technological theory does not occur?

Though in the circumstances this conclusion is reasonable and reliable, it does not obtain with deductive certainty. From the assumption that when ordinary people are friends with each other, they will desire to go on meeting, or anyway object to being prevented from meeting, it cannot be deduced that *this* person will certainly have such feelings. It can only be deduced that this is the most reasonable expectation. The plausibility of making this deduction in these circumstances can be enhanced in the text by rhetorical means.

The authors' self-presentation – the impression of reliability which ensues from their textual demonstrations of competence – can augment the reader's trust in the appositeness of applying 'ordinary' expectations to the people in question: his or her willingness to accept the authors' judgement that they *are* ordinary. The authors' attempts to display this ordinariness also have sensitising effects, making the reader more open to allowing that ordinary, everyday assumptions can safely be applied in this case as well as in others (see below).

Unless it can be shown that the authors' expectations of behaviour between friends are unreasonable, or that these workers are not candidates for the application of ordinary expectations, hen, their starting assumption forms an adequate basis for arguing. Since both self-presentation and sensitisation strengthen the reasons here are for applying the assumption in this case, it generates an argument which unites 'cognitive' and non-'cognitive' processes. Moreover, the communicative efficacy of the argument is augmen-ed by its incomplete statement; the reader participates in con-tructing the full inference.[12] All these are central characteristics of enthymematic argumentation.

Before going on to discuss the use of ordinary person enthymemes o alter readers' views of ordinariness. I should like to remark on three differing respects in which the enthymeme I have just examined is supported by 'sensitising' features which form part of its textual context. All can be seen as traditionally rhetorical strategies, yet none can be described as pernicious or in a pejorative sense manipulative.

First, in objecting to accounting for workers' interaction on the shop floor in terms of friendship, the authors have revealed an apparent anomaly in their subjects' behaviour. If the high degree of verbal interaction they show cannot be taken to be a sign of friendship, it is incumbent on Goldthorpe *et al.* to show what it does indicate. Displaying a highly effective sense of order, they have provided for this contingency *before* the problem arises. On I, p. 49 they describe a case in which

> talking seems often to have been regarded as an essential means of counteracting the stresses and tedium of the job itself. As one assembler put it: 'You've got to lark around with the mates a bit just to break the monotony'; or in the words of another, 'If you didn't talk, you'd go stark raving mad!'

On the one hand, this passage has standard implications which buttress the authors' epitome by emphasising the workers' anti-pathy to boredom; on the other, it furnishes an explanation to fill the gap left by demolishing the technological thesis. The neatness with which this explanation fits where it is needed may be taken to sensitise the reader to the plausibility of the authors' account.

Second, when Goldthorpe *et al.* go on to treat 'the *quality* of work relationships, in the sense of the value and meanings which workers give to them' (I, p. 53) in a way which augments the intelligibility of their notion of 'instrumentalism', they also implicitly *defend* the normality of the workers' conduct. They write, to the extent that work is defined as a mandatory form of activity and as one engaged in simply as a means to an end, the workplace will not be regarded as a *milieu* appropriate or favourable to the development of highly rewarding primary relationships, that is as a *milieu* where the worker's expressive or affective needs are likely to be met (1, p. 53).

This view is based on the assumption that if an ordinary person cannot enjoy intrinsic features of his or her work, he or she 'will' (we can reasonably expect it, it is coherent and consistent in the circumstances) try to make extrinsic ones tolerable. Hence, the authors imply rather than state, the workers converse for non-intrinsic, 'instrumental' reasons. This shows us what sort of behaviour can be expected under the heading of 'instrumentalism', it also claims that such behaviour is perfectly normal in the circumstances – with the sensitising effect of reasserting the legitimacy of applying ordinary person enthymemes to the 'affluent workers'' conduct.

In order for plausibility to attach to the authors' enthymematical accounts of what their subjects do, there must be a certain degree of consensus between authors and reader as to what constitutes ordinary behaviour, and the above examples show that Goldthorpe *et al.* attach value to heightening this consensus. But the 'instrumentalism' theory itself forms a material obstacle to arguing on the basis of such agreement. There is a considerable tension between explanations predicated on the assumption that workers basically behave as other people do, and accounts showing them to display attitudes which do not appear to be adopted by everyone else.

The authors deal with this problem by associating whatever is distinctive about their subjects' outlook not with the workers as people but with their *plight*. This severs the descriptive unity between a person and his actions which conventionally licenses the transference of judgements from one to the other;[13] it is a traditional rhetorical strategy, the third example I want to give here of the sensitising effects of contextual arguing – arguing which does not just collect isolated inferences but mobilises a whole context of discourse.

Goldthorpe *et al.* point out that their subjects are in a special predicament, experiencing the 'dilemma of having to forfeit direct satisfaction from work in order to obtain a level of earnings appropriate to their out-plant objectives' (1, p. 126). That is,

Comments made by the machinists and assemblers frequently revealed that a dilemma had been recognised between taking a more directly rewarding job and one which would afford a relatively high level of earnings, and that while the decision had been made for the latter, it had often not been an easy one (1, p. 34).

The authors do not claim that this choice need be seen as *rational*; on the contrary, they suggest that it may sometimes derive from the examples set by workers' white-collar friends and relations. But they do stress that the dilemma is imposed from without, by a situation. It is the *situation* which is bizarre, the situation which means that anyone within it must make an 'odd'-seeming choice – money and low job satisfaction or job satisfaction and inadequate pay. The workers themselves are entirely normal.

These uses of sensitisation in support of the authors' enthymematic reasoning augment the reader's willingness to apply ordinary chains of reasoning to what the 'affluent workers' do. They also contribute to showing the *meaning* of the workers' behaviour, by drawing attention to the nexus of ordinary expectations within which this behaviour has to be considered. Thus they constitute rhetorical phenomena which are both indirectly and directly explanatory in import. Moreover, they buttress a significant feature of the style of *The Affluent Worker* – its tendency to explain in terms of reasons, where possible reasons given by its subjects themselves.

As a rule this text does not refer to relationships in unambiguously causal terms, concentrating – as is consistent with the tenor of the authors' epitome – on its subjects' independent agency. It seems to me that it is possible for Goldthorpe *et al.* to describe regular connections between situation and attitude without insisting on the presence of a causal mechanism making the link inevitable *because* they use assumptions to the effect that ordinary people in given sorts of situation do as a matter of fact tend to take up given sorts of attitude.

Ordinary person enthymemes can be both written and read in complete agnosticism about metaphysical interpretations of causality, since they make attitudes and behaviour intelligible by relating them to what counts as normal in a social context which author, subjects and reader all endorse as familiarly plausible. In order to preserve this agnosticism, Goldthorpe *et al.* do not only not try to begin from scientific laws of cause and effect; they avoid them.

Ordinary person enthymemes do not purport to account fo₁ social action in mechanistic terms. They make it intelligible by showing how it *fits in* with what we normally anticipate in navigating the social world. This, I should claim, is more realistic than would be attempts at any type of causal explanation in thi₁ context; more realistic both in terms of what we can really claim to know about human behaviour, and in terms of compatibility with the accounts we give of each other's conduct in non-sociologica₁ discourse.

2 ORDINARY PERSON ENTHYMEMES AND RESTRUCTURING OPINIONS

It is not necessary that an ordinary person enthymeme should simply and squarely exploit a consensus which the reader is taken to share with the author about what constitutes normal conduct Characteristically for sociology, it may rely on part of such a consensus at the same time as vigorously attacking another part This does not (or not necessarily) involve what is usually thought of when authors disagree with their readers or present information new to them – namely, controversial causal analyses. The effect of an ordinary person enthymeme may be more radical than this. I₁ may restructure the reader's preconceptions about the behaviour which he or she can consistently expect from other people, forcing him or her to abandon particular views about normality and to adopt others which are urged by the author.[14]

This explanatory strategy as it is used both by Goldthorpe *et al* and by Dore highlights the interactive nature of the enthymeme Authors who wish not only to disagree with their readers in some respect but also to change their habits of mind still require *some* basis in agreement if their arguments are to communicate successfully Besides the preservation of some element of common ground, rearranging the reader's network of assumptions about the socia₁ world is also likely to require attention to sensitisation – or else the reader may refuse to consider even the possibility of abandoning familiar points of view. The position of the reader, therefore, must be weighed seriously and cannot just be cavalierly undermined.

Goldthorpe *et al.* go about this with an urbanity whose effect is to disguise the extent of the views which the reader is required to surrender. By 1, Chapter 4 we have learned that most of the workers in the authors' survey take an understandably negative view of their work-tasks and show little emotional attachment to their fellow employees. Yet, when the authors ask for views of their firms as a whole, they receive replies such as these:

> 'At the firm where I started work, they had a motto: "Harmony is necessary to achieve anything." I believe in this.'
> 'We've got teamwork in this firm, anyway. It pays in the end. Management and men are both in the same firm, aren't they? (ı, p. 74).

Though Goldthorpe *et al.* are at pains to make clear that no other sociological approach is in a better position to account for these responses than they are (ı, pp. 75–6), they are bound to admit that these results are a surprise:

> in *no* group within our sample can we find evidence of 'immediate' job satisfaction being at all closely linked with workers' attitudes towards their firms as an employer . . . The problem which now arises, therefore, is that of interpreting this state of affairs . . . (ı, p. 78).

It is natural to anticipate that a man who dislikes his work and is not especially fond of his colleagues will not think favourably of his firm either; and since the authors' explanatory techniques depend on showing that their subjects' attitudes and behaviour cluster in a fashion which the reader can perceive as coherent, these results present them with a problem in terms of communication as well as interpretation.

What they do in the face of this problem is to connect their new account with other assumptions which their readers are considered likely to accept. This ensures that the reader can go on perceiving the coherence they are emphasising at the same time as shifting the point of view from which he or she sees it.

The problems deriving from the workers' views about their companies can be traced to their offence against two general topoi: the topos *a fortiori*, [15] by which it could be assumed that if people do not enjoy what seems most likely as a source of satisfaction (work or work-mates), it is even less plausible that they will be pleased by a much more distant source (their firms); and the topos by which it could be argued that what applies to a part (work-tasks and work-mates) will apply to the whole (the firms where the workers are employed). The text negotiates these difficulties by recourse to a procedure advised by another general topos, 'pointing out that there is a reason for the false impression given'.[16] The authors suggest that

> To the extent that workers define their employment as essentially a means of acquiring a certain standard and style of living outside of work, it is clearly possible for them to take a negative view of the work-tasks they actually perform while at the same time appreciating a firm which offers pay and conditions that can bring a valued way of life within their grasp (I, pp. 79–80).

This statement can be re-expressed as an ordinary person en-thymeme starting from an opinion which the reader may well consider reputable: all other things being equal, any ordinary person who desires something strongly can be expected to take a cooperative attitude to what helps him or her to get it. These ordinary people – the workers – are helped by their firms to reach the living standards they wish for; therefore it should be anticipated that they will take cooperative attitudes to their firms.

In a classical example of topical arguing, Goldthorpe *et al.* have removed one assumption about what it is natural to expect by emphasising another view of social reality, with which the reader can make sense of the worker's attitudes. They have shown the inapplicability to their case of the two topoi which at first seemed to make it confusing. That is, they have given a reason for which firms are not really unexpected sources of workers' satisfaction – so the topos *a fortiori*, though valid in itself, does not apply here; and they have shown why the topos from parts and wholes does not apply either – firms should not just be seen as wholes of which work and workers simply form part.

The authors' new explanation gains indirect support from their epitome of the 'affluent worker' as a normally reasonable individual, taking the best choice open to him from the options his predicament supplies. It is an explanation, then, which harmonises with what the reader has already read, and it has apparently been produced without requiring him or her to believe anything which he or she does not accept already. This is the aspect of their arguing in which the authors' attention to the sensitisation of their readers to what they say, and their respect for their readers' own interpretive frameworks, shows most clearly.

But what this seemingly harmless reorganisation of the reader's own received attitudes in fact entails is the abandonment of an image of the industrial worker as a person who interprets the world of work from the point of view of class allegiance; and this (if the reader accepts it) is anything but a slight concession.

The above example shows that arguing from topoi involves searching for the location of an appropriate starting-point for interpreting a state of affairs; this starting-point also contains a validation for the subsequent argumentative procedure. (Why do Goldthorpe *et al.* look about for reasons for the workers' attitudes to their firms? They are hoping to be able to point out that there is a reason for the false impression of incoherence given by their subjects' replies.) Since all general topoi are correct as far as they go – they do not claim absolutely general validity, and the topos just alluded to is a piece of advice rather than a proposition – *appropriateness*, not truth or falsity, is the key concept here. Similarly, when less general topoi, or simply reputable opinions, are being used, major premises can be assessed in the light of their plausibility in relation to the situation concerned. The following case from *The Affluent Worker* shows how these notions can be combined with conventional survey methods of testing sociological claims.

In ii, Chapter 4, Goldthorpe *et al.* find that a further apparently plausible 'ordinary person' assumption is disappointed; again they repair the situation by recourse to views which can be attributed to the *reader*. The view which they reject is embodied in the suggestion that manual workers 'living in a middle-class *milieu*' are 'not only more likely to be cut off from the community influences of the working-class district, but they are also more likely to be exposed to new patterns of personal influence' (ii, p. 59). For instance, people 'owning houses in middle-class residential areas are more likely to be surrounded by persons for whom voting Conservative is the normal thing to do' (ibid.). Therefore it would seem 'plausible' to expect such workers to 'react by giving fewer of their votes to Labour' (ii, p. 60). The authors commend this as 'certainly . . . more meaningful than the affluence thesis couched in terms merely of income and possessions' (ibid.), but none the less contend that it is not correct.

This is obviously a case in which it is necessary to quantify the voting habits of people falling into the 'affluent worker' category and living in Conservative areas, and to compare them with the

voting of similar people in Labour districts. But the conclusions of
such exercises will, alone, hardly be positively conclusive. (Harré
points out that these methods do not yield clear-cut causal analyses,
as Mill thought they did, but may contain ambiguities as to the
actual 'mechanisms' at work.[17]) Having found that voting is not
neatly affected by district, Goldthorpe *et al.* revert to the field of
reputable opinions to reassemble the interpretive network at
stake.

Though the argument they are opposing is constructed from
those of other sociologists, the plausibility attributable to it rests on a
common conception of normality: if one lives surrounded by people
for whom it is usual to do X, one is likelier to do X oneself than if one
were not surrounded by them. In so far as this *is* a plausible thing to
assume, it will not do just to counter it head-on, and Goldthorpe *et
al.* proceed by reconstructing those of its elements which they can
accept. With the backing of their quantitative analyses, they claim
that 'family and occupational white-collar affiliations' seem 'far
more important in reducing their support for Labour than
. . . residence in middle-class housing areas *per se*' (II, p. 62).

In effect this urges that the fact that someone lives surrounded by
X-ers is not a *sufficient* reason for expecting him or her to do X; but
what remains plausible and appropriate in this expectation can be
stated in 'ordinary person' terms. If people about whom one cares or
in whose terms one measures oneself find it usual to do X, one is
more likely to do X oneself than if this were not the case. This
suggests an explanation for the mistake about housing areas,
because people often do live near others of whom they are fond, and
it also yields an enthymeme to explain the workers' reduction in
Labour voting – the suggestion that they are influenced by white-
collar friends and relations. This in its turn is in principle open to
empirical investigation.

This example demonstrates the combination of topical and
survey material in an hypothesis which reorganises the reader's
assumptions in a manner which it is comparatively easy to accept. It
explains workers' voting behaviour in terms of what we already
have reason to suppose that they want – harmonious relations with
those who are emotionally closest to them. This both supports and is
supported by the authors' epitome. The 'integrated fashion' (I,
p. 94) in which they present the attitudes and behaviour of the
'affluent worker' provides not only for explanatory consistency but
also for sensitisation: the more firmly a coherent character has been

established for the affluent worker, the more reasonable it seems to hope that the reader will accept a fairly minor rearrangement in his or her accepted views in order to maintain this coherent perception.

The demands which Dore makes of his readers' views of ordinariness are anything but minor. *British Factory – Japanese Factory* incorporates a repeated strategy whose intention is to undermine and demolish the view of Japanese industrial organis-ation which Dore attributes to the British: the view that British social assumptions are the norm and Japanese ones are old-fashioned, irrational, somewhat absurd, in need of 'catching up' with our own. (This intention is also attributable to Dore's more frequent 'reasonable person' enthymemes, as the next section shows, and forms part of an assault he clearly thinks necessary on British incomprehension of foreigners generally.)

The method by which this demolition takes place is in essence simple. The reader is made to apply his or her own conceptions of ordinariness to people (the Japanese) to whom he or she is not used to apply them. This is enough to change what 'ordinary' means: it used to mean 'British', but for the reader who arrives at the end of Dore's book this equivalence can no longer be made.

The quotation below illustrates the core of this process. Dore himself points out that it is an over-schematised account (p. 410), and I cite it here chiefly because of its conciseness. Clearly, the reader will need considerable inducement if he or she is to make the intellectual and emotional transition which Dore demands, so that in its entirety the author's explanatory process is bound to be long-drawn-out. It is a remarkable feature of Dore's book that the 'hard' information it contains – the welter of facts and figures it provides about British and Japanese industry – has a vital sensitising func-tion: namely, to persuade the reader that he or she can trust the author's instincts about the situation he is describing.

In the course of his book Dore attempts to convince the reader that free market principles are not taken to be natural and inevitable in Japan, and to explain the development of non-combative unions there. He says,

Free market principles of employment have a natural appeal to employers in a world where unions do not exist or are prohibited by law. They become less attractive to employers when trade unions win their right to exist and so severely limit the employer's bargaining superiority. But by the time this happened in Britain,

by the time employers began to have material incentives for
seeking alternatives, the existing market principles were so firmly
entrenched – and so reinforced by the pattern of trade unionism
itself – that change was difficult. Employers had, in any case, lost
their power unilaterally to change institutions without the cooperation of the unions.

Japanese employers, on the other hand, could see the writing
more clearly on the wall . . . By 1922, when employment
relations were still in a fluid state, international respectability
required Japan to give trade unions an accepted place in the
political firmament by allowing them to choose a representative
to attend the Conference of the ILO. Japanese employers,
therefore, knew that they had to live with unions at an early stage;
they were able to adjust to that future prospect by institutional
innovations *before* the unions became so strong that their options
were foreclosed . . . (p. 410).

This account has an extremely simple form: it just explains the
conduct of British employers in terms of choices anyone could be
expected to take, pursuing their interests within the confines of a
given situation, and then does the same for the Japanese. Any
ordinary person employing workers in such circumstances would
try to establish cooperative relations with unions; the Japanese
employers were ordinary people, and did just that. This enthymeme
beguiles by its simplicity, and lays no emphasis at all on what the
reader is required to sacrifice. If the reader accepts Dore's unfolding
of Japanese history into a series of perfectly ordinary reactions and
decisions, where now is the fundamental bizarreness, the un-
Britishness, of Japanese industrial organisation? The implication
is that ordinariness is not as intimately bound up with the
British culture as Dore believes that his reader would like to
have it.

3 THE 'REASONABLE PERSON' ENTHYMEME

We have just looked at enthymematic reasoning based on opinions
which embody notions of normality; next I shall examine some
enthymemes based on *norms*. Here the link proposed between a
phenomenon and its social situation is one of *reasonableness*; reasonable person enthymemes explain by elucidating attitudes (say) as

those which sensible people in the situations concerned could reasonably take.

I should like to stress the distinction between arguments in terms of reasonableness and those in terms of rationality, which are concerned with aims and choices in their relationships to defined ends.[18] Rational decisions in this sense 'need not be attributed to anyone in particular' but can be considered 'hypothetically, simply as arguments';[19] they connote system, principle, logic and purposefulness,[20] and can be contrasted with irrationality – although this contrast can be dangerous, as Parkin implies.[21] Thus Weber contrasts rationality with what is 'affectually determined', giving as an example of the latter a panic on the Stock Exchange.[22] But to construct a paradigm of human action as veering between calculation and panic is to subject oneself to a neurotic dichotomy, and this the notion of reasonableness helps us to avoid.

It seems to me that many less obtrusive normative factors in texts which at first sight appear neutral in tone can be traced to the use of reasonable person enthymemes. Like ordinary person enthymemes, reasonable person enthymemes account for attitudes and behaviour to which the notion of rationality is not conveniently applicable: that is, attitudes and behaviour intermixed with feelings, relationships and general views about life (*Lebenseinstellungen*). Presumably, this mixed behaviour is by far the commonest there is.

It is mixed in the sense of possessing aspects which are conceptually distinguishable, not in the sense of being formed of an amalgam of phenomena which should be seen as empirically separable in normal cases. Under 'reasonableness', the O.E.D. mentions 'Having sound judgement, sensible, moderate, not expecting too much, ready to listen to reason'. While it is true that a person may display one of these characteristics without displaying another (but also without being reasonable), I should claim that reasonable behaviour is generally *compounded* of such traits. Normal cases of reasonable behaviour cannot without artificiality be separated out into items which are rational and other items which are subject to norms; they are naturally explicated whole. This means that reasonable person enthymemes begin from premises with normative elements, and retain these elements in their conclusions.

The fact that Goldthorpe *et al.* take their subjects to be reasonable people is of crucial importance for their explanations and it provides suppressed premises for a good deal of what they say. The exposure of these premises reveals an argumentative structure which is

particularly likely to underlie claims that given attitudes or
behaviour are 'to be expected' or 'not surprising' in the circumstances. These are conventional expressions in the (social) sciences
and appear to have neutral connotations; but this appearance is
misleading.

I should now like to examine a case from *The Affluent Worker* to
show that authors will on occasion *search* for reasonable facets of their
subjects' conduct, and take pains to convince the reader that it is
reasonable. These operations mean that the components of a
reasonable person enthymeme may be dispersed over a comparatively long piece of text – another factor which can make them
difficult to notice, and which disguises their evaluative intimations.
When this background is made clear, it will be easy to show how
further cases of the same type of argument contribute to the authors'
defence of their subjects – as well as to their understanding. Lastly, I
shall look at iconoclastic properties of reasonable person enthymemes which are important to Dore and to Willis, and which are
bound up with functional ambiguities which ensure that they are
accessible to a maximum number of readers.

The enthymeme I should like to look at first is intended to
account for the affluent workers' reluctance to abandon their jobs,
although they do not like them. This is not because they have no
feeling for alternatives; in I, Chapter 6 Goldthorpe *et al.* give
quotations including these (I, p. 133):

> 'If you have your own business, you work for yourself; you get the
> profits and you're your own boss. It's all a matter of money.
> Anyone with money and sense would work for themselves.'
>
> 'I should like to engage in some business where I wouldn't be
> limited. I don't know what that would be – catering or a
> boarding-house perhaps, or I fancy myself as a publican. But I'd
> like something where I could make my own way.'

The reader already knows that most of the workers do not enjoy
their jobs and would prefer to be able to exercise their abilities more
autonomously. None the less, few of them have serious intentions to
try to do so (I, p. 133). Why not?

The authors remove the apparent anomaly here in two stages.
Partly they rely on an explanation they have themselves given for
their subjects' lack of enthusiasm about promotion, claiming on I,
p. 134, 'just as our affluent workers were fairly clear-sighted about

he barriers to gaining promotion, so too were they well aware of the
difficulties which confronted an aspiring entrepreneur'. Like
reasonableness' according to the O.E.D., clear-sightedness is a
osition, an attitude to life which involves not only intellectual
considerations but also feelings and an apposite command of them.
The terms 'clear-sighted' and 'well aware of' *commend* the workers
or *attitudes* they take up within the limitations of their situation, not
ust for rationalistic calculations.

In the second stage of their explanation the authors assert,

> . . . given the fact that many of these men had already made
> considerable sacrifices in attaining their existing standard of
> living – particularly through enduring inherently unrewarding
> and stressful jobs – a reluctance to jeopardise their achievements
> is all the more readily understood (I, p. 135).

Goldthorpe *et al.* say that given these achievements, the workers had
often less motivation than others to struggle . . . against the odds
vhich would have faced them' in new careers (I, p. 136). Again this
account refers to attitudes of the whole person, as is shown by
sacrifices', 'enduring', 'unrewarding', 'stressful', 'reluctance',
jeopardise' and 'struggle'; the term 'motivation' refers not to the
workers' rationality but to their feelings.

The enthymeme underlying what the authors say can be
expressed as follows: No one who has made great sacrifices to attain
a goal which is important to him or her can or ought to be expected
o risk these gains by aiming at further goals which it is highly
uncertain that it is possible to reach; these workers are in such a
osition; therefore they ought not to be expected to change. That is,
their reluctance is justifiable as perfectly reasonable; and to see its
reasonableness is to understand it.

The point of a reasonable person enthymeme is lost if the reader
will not agree that the behaviour in question *is* reasonable, and
Goldthorpe *et al.* take pains to search for considerations which will
convince him or her of this. They precede the explanation we have
ust examined with an uncharacteristically ironic passage derogat-
ng political positions which prescribe attitudes different from those
the workers in fact hold. They remark that setting up one's own
ousiness was 'of course'

> the mode of economic and social ascent classically prescribed for
> ambitious members of the industrial labour force by the ideo-

logues of capitalist society in its 'heroic', nineteenth-century
phase. However, in the context of modern, 'post-capitalist'
society it has appeared generally more appropriate to emphasise
the opportunities offered by other channels of upward mobility
(I, p. 131).

Besides thus casting doubt on the reasonableness of expecting the
workers to take different positions from the ones they actually
display, Goldthorpe *et al.* again associate the workers' less standardly commendable characteristics with their plight rather than
their personalities:

> . . . the specific nature of their aspirations reflects the fact that
> these men are still wage-earners who have achieved their present
> affluent condition primarily through selling their labour power to
> the highest bidder, and whose future life chances are fairly clearly
> delimited by the nature of the position and role which they
> occupy within the total economic system (I, p. 119).

The authors both stress that the workers have little reasonable
alternative to their position and discuss the contents of their
aspirations in terms likely to commend themselves to some readers
at least. The workers' hopes are said to focus first upon 'increased
consumer capacity' and 'higher standards of domestic living': 'more
money to spend and more goods and possessions' (I, p. 136). The
interpolation of 'domestic' softens the impression given here and has
standard implications connected with the authors' reference to the
workers as 'home-makers' (I, p. 143) and with their *derivation* of
' "money-mindedness" ' from 'the increased importance of a family-
centred life' to men for whom work offers few other rewards than
cash.

The workers' next-mentioned hopes (in the service of which they
can be taken to use their money) are described in a fashion which
may commend them to a different section of the authors' readership.
These hopes comprise 'aspirations for children and aspirations
which . . . reflected a desire for a less taxing, more pleasurable
existence' and they are not bound up with aims for ' "success" in
any individualistic sense' (I, p. 136). This has implications which
may invoke some approval from the workers' left-wing critics,
against whom the authors argue overtly in volume III.

It is, indeed, because of the fact that their subjects' way of life has been so often attacked that Goldthorpe *et al.* need to make special efforts to get the reader to perceive the reasonableness of their stance, which is repeatedly reiterated towards the end of volume I, Chapter 6. Redoubling their efforts to combat moral estrangement from the worker, no less than five times the authors stress their subjects' powerlessness to exert individual control over their own fates – so that their hopes for the future will be realised 'along with their fellow workers or not at all' (I, p. 138).

The implications of this are emphasised in the last two paragraphs of the chapter, which return to the workers' *plight* and both justify the attitudes they take within its limitations and invite the reader to sympathise with them.

> It is essentially through work that these men seek to realise their projects; yet their working lives do not figure significantly in these projects. Their existence outside of work represents for our affluent workers the realm of at least relative freedom; as consumers, as home-makers, they can exercise some autonomy and creativity in shaping the patterns of their lives. But the price of this is that work itself must be accepted as the realm of necessity (I, p. 143).

Other writers dismiss these workers as ' "stunted mass-produced humanity" ', ' "made-to-measure consumers" ' or ' "sublimated slaves" ' (III, p. 184). The rhetorical features of this chapter by Goldthorpe *et al.* are concentrated upon the opposite end: to justify their values not as right, but as reasonable in the circumstances.

This justification itself has considerable explanatory power, and supplies the enthymematical form of a good many explications. In III, Chapter 5 Goldthorpe *et al.* wish to explain why their subjects would prefer non-manual jobs for their children. Instead of ascribing this to displaced ambitions to middle-class prestige, the authors account for it in terms of a desire that the children should be spared their parents' dilemma of having to choose between good incomes or rewarding work. The reason for the parents' aspirations is this wish; the explanation for their having the wish is that it is a reasonable one for anyone in their situation to have.

> [I]t is readily understandable that, for their children, they should hope for occupations that offered a high level of material reward *and* of inherent attractiveness, and for the type of education that is

generally necessary in order to open the way into such occupations (III, pp. 133–4).

In order to perceive this as 'understandable' it is not necessary to undergo some form of intuitive identification with the affluent workers; only to perceive the reasonableness of their point of view.

Elsewhere, Goldthorpe *et al.* admit that a 'discrepancy' exists between their respondents' view of the class structure and 'the "reality" of this society' (III, p. 151); but they explain this view by insisting that it is reasonable in the light of their subjects' experience.

> [I]n the more visible aspects of their social lives, they could quite reasonably regard themselves as being in a broadly comparable position to that of many, if not most, of the white-collar persons they saw around them; they owned similar goods and possessions, housing standards differed little, they could afford much the same sort of outings and holidays, and so on (III, p. 152).

The authors do not attempt to give explicit *proofs* of the sense in which this is reasonable; rather, they *expose* the ways in which the workers' attitudes conform to standards of reasonableness which the reader is taken already to have.

Thus it is 'scarcely surprising' that the affluent workers 'should tend to think far more of advancing their welfare within the existing order of society', which they accept as a natural phenomenon, 'than of pursuing their goals through action directed against this order' (III, p. 154). The reader is expected to bring his or her own assumptions about reasonableness into play to see that any reasonable person might easily (whether or not correctly) think the same.

Similarly, if we bear in mind the workers' consciously successful efforts to raise their standards of living, 'it is not perhaps so remarkable after all' that their subordination at work should not seem to them the most crucial feature of their social surroundings (III, p. 155):

> it is important to recall that the social experience of many of our respondents was of a kind that could reasonably lead them to be less impressed by the weakness and vulnerability of their class position than by the extent to which they had been able to

achieve economic advance within the existing social framework (ibid.).

Goldthorpe *et al.* are arguing from the premise that any reasonable person could be expected to react as do the workers in their situation. The chief function of a large portion of the evidence they proffer about what their subjects do and say is to get the reader to admit this premise. As in the case of Dore, their 'hard' information can properly, but not adequately, be assessed in terms of factual correctness. Its part in the text falls into the technical category of sensitisation; the enthymematical accounts to which this sensitisation belongs procure the reader's understanding of the affluent worker by getting him or her to perceive the applicability of accustomed standards of reasonableness where he or she might otherwise have been reluctant to do so.

This explanatory operation is both simpler and less devastating to describe than to practice, and its evaluative components are at least as important to Dore's book as to *The Affluent Worker*. An apparently straightforward version of the reasonable person enthymeme is contained in his explanation why Japanese engineers do not take the trouble to gain state qualifications:

> Given that an Hitachi engineer is unlikely to envisage that he might one day be in the market *needing* an objective certification of his competence, given that he is likely to define himself as an Hitachi man first and as engineer second; the difference is not surprising (p. 48).

As often in the case of Goldthorpe *et al.*, Dore's last comment here might well be construed to mean that it *ought* not to be surprising; to the ordinarily uninformed British reader, of course it is surprising to hear that in Japan professional men go confidently through life without paper qualifications, and that is why Dore takes the trouble to explain it.

The enthymeme he supplies to do so can be reconstructed in either of two ways, according to the reader's own perception of Japanese life and his or her need for instruction about it. Dore takes for granted that the reader shares his opinions about the internal details of what reasonableness actually is, and what he writes down can be taken as claiming *either* that it is reasonable not to bother with examinations in such a situation, and these engineers do not bother,

so their behaviour is reasonable; *or* that it is reasonable not to bother
with examinations in such a situation, and these engineers are
reasonable people, so they do not bother.

Both these apparently harmless alternatives have considerable
rhetorical implications. As far as the second is concerned, I should
like to quote the remark by Perelman and Olbrechts-Tyteca that
'An ambiguous act often achieves its full significance and meaning
through what we know of its author.'[23] We can use this to infer that
as long as the reader is convinced that the Japanese *are* reasonable
otherwise mysterious actions are susceptible to explanation. If the
reader already takes this view of the Japanese before approaching
the book, so much the better; Dore makes it clear that he does not
expect this to be the case, which is why the first interpretation I gave
for this usefully ambiguous enthymeme is so important. In order to
obtain enough explanatory leeway to account for his subject
matter, Dore must give the reader grounds for agreeing that the
Japanese and their industrial behaviour are reasonable – and this
means defending them as such.

Quite apart from Dore's personal intentions as an author, this
evaluative strand in his accounts is ineradicable. Showing that
people have good reasons for what they do *is* to explain and it *is* also
to defend those actions. The impact of such a defence is
strengthened if the reader has previously viewed the phenomenon in
question as outlandish; an instance where this is likely is the
Japanese custom of employing workers for life.

Dore points to the social circumstances involved in the late, rapid
industrialisation of Japan, when, for example,

> The Japanese employer had reasons for recruiting young school-
> leavers and training them that the British manufacturer hadn't –
> their easy availability, their cheapness, their disciplined willing-
> ness to learn, and the fact that, because of the technological leap
> and the faster rate of growth, the market could not provide for his
> needs so that he would have to do his own training anyway
> (p. 413).

Here there is a repetition of the ambiguity about whether the
reasonableness of Japanese employers serves as a suppressed minor
premise or a suppressed conclusion; just because enthymemes are in
their nature partly suppressed, Dore is able to turn this ambiguity to
account in what is for him a very common form of argument.

Continuing to explain ' "the Japanese system" ' (p. 401), Dore refers to the fact that this system (and its perceived oddness) is often attributed partly to Confucian ideology (which is also perceived as odd, though he does not labour this point). Sweetly Dore admits that this 'is not a bad answer' (p. 401) – and goes on to confound the reader by implying that in many ways Confucianism is more reasonable than equivalent Western points of view. It

> assumed original virtue rather than original sin. Confucianists in positions of authority . . . have been rather less predisposed than their Western counterparts to see their subordinates as donkeys responsive to sticks and carrots, and more disposed to see them as human beings responsive to moral appeals. Japanese industrialists' view of man (like Robert Owen's, for that matter) made them believe in the *efficiency* of benevolence . . . (pp. 401–2).

(In view of the political provenance of many critics of Japan, note the rhetorical role of the reference to early socialism included here.) Exploiting such consensus about reasonableness as he and the reader enjoy, Dore makes the reader apply his or her own views in circumstances where it is unlikely that he or she had ever dreamed of doing so.

The structure of Willis's *Learning to Labour* is enthymematic on a large scale: its first part provides the evidence and other inducements which the reader needs in order to accept conclusions made explicit in the second part. (Other, small-scale enthymemes do also occur in the course of the text.) Like both Goldthorpe *et al.* and Dore, Willis's greatest problem is to get the reader to *apply* an enthymeme in terms of reasonableness with which he or she would have no difficulty in other cases; like both Goldthorpe *et al.* and Dore, Willis can anticipate that the reader's reluctance stems from two sources. These are his or her perceptions of the writer's subjects as people, and the alterations which would be required of his or her worldview – in particular, his or her political worldview – if these personal perceptions were changed.

We saw above that the first part of *Learning to Labour* establishes the author's self-presentation, displaying his competence in collecting evidence about his subjects and his ability to gain insights into their situation. It sensitises the reader to the author's viewpoint by exhibiting 'the lads' ' humour and vulnerability as well as their uncooperativeness at school, and gradually it edges the reader into relaxing his or her prejudices against its subjects. Self-presentation and sensitisation form the first two elements in the enthymematic structure; the third and most purely argumentative element becomes apparent only later, after Willis has given his opinions on the British social structure and the place of school education within it.

Like Dore's, Willis's enthymemes have a logical structure which is ambiguous in the sense of being usable from either of two standpoints according to need. Like both Dore and Goldthorpe *et al.*, Willis instils an element of approving evaluation into his reasoning as he takes his subjects' side on certain questions and tries to get the reader to do likewise. He asserts not just that the lads' views are normal under the circumstances but that they can be justified (and understood) as reasonable.

On p. 100, Willis quotes from a 'lad' named Spike, represented as expressing a view typical of his associates. Spike claims that 'Every job is the same. No, I've gone too far in saying that . . . The jobs what are the same is where you've got to fucking graft, when you'm a grafter, see, all jobs are the same.' Later, on pp. 133–6, the author gives expression to similar views. 'It is indeed the case that what is common to all wage-labour work is more important than what divides it' (p. 133).

> [D]eskilling is a very real process. Concrete labour is regressing more and more to a mean standard de-skilled labour . . . Whether particular individuals . . . have degrees or CSEs matters not at all. The particular concrete form of their individual labour power is irrelevant so long as it does not stop the line (pp. 135–6).

The plain implication is that the lads' view of the types of employment open to them is quite correct. But the logical structure of what Willis writes can be reconstructed in either of two ways. If the reader is not yet certain whether the lads are or are not to be regarded as reasonable, he or she can take the text as supplying *evidence* that they are:

To perceive that labouring jobs are similar in essentials is a sign of reasonableness;
The lads perceive this;
So we have good reason to think them reasonable.

If the reader already accepts that the lads are reasonable people, he or she can take the enthymeme to establish the nature of the conclusions they come to:

Reasonable people are able to see that labouring jobs are similar in essentials;
The lads are reasonable people;
So (as we would expect) they see that labouring jobs are essentially identical.

Willis's text is not ambiguous in the sense of being undecided; from the author's point of view, both these enthymemes are valid and true. It has the Janus-like property of functioning coherently from each of two different positions; and in both of these, the evaluative aspect is indispensable.

Willis himself argues against romanticising the working class or holding that his subjects are equipped with exhaustive insights into their own position (p. 122), but he does wish to establish their right to be seen as competent commentators on society, in some respects at least. To do this he must refute the view that they are irrational or psychotic, and show in which of their perceptions reasonable judgements on society lie. Hence the dual importance even to a Marxist writer of showing what sort of people his subjects are: he wishes to endorse some of their views (and not others), and if the reader can be encouraged to see them as reasonable people, this endorsement will become effective. But the reader will have to alter his or her own (socio-political) views as a corollary of extending his or her notion of acceptability to a social viewpoint it previously excluded.

This is made clear in the following. Willis writes,

Insofar as knowledge is always biased and shot through with class meaning, the working class student must overcome his inbuilt disadvantage of possessing the wrong class culture and the wrong educational decoders to start with. A few can make it. The class can never follow. It is through a good number trying, however, that the class structure is legitimated . . . The refusal to compete, implicit in the counter-school culture, is therefore in this sense a radical act: it refuses to collude in its own educational suppression (p. 128).

This concludes an enthymeme whose premises are embedded in Willis's account of the lads' recalcitrance in school in the first part of the book, together with most of its self-presentation and sensitisation components. Either,

Any reasonable person would resent a system which loaded everything against the group to which he or she belongs, and would express this resentment;
These are reasonable people;
So they resent the system – and express their resentment (by refusing to cooperate with it).

Or else the reader can take Willis to say,

Perceiving the hopelessness of trying to compete in this educational system is a sign of reasonableness in working-class lads;
These working-class lads do achieve this perception;
So we have grounds for concluding that they are reasonable.

It would be neither necessary nor effective for Willis to state either of these doubly enthymematic inferences; none the less they are significant ones. For all the authors investigated here, asking what sort of people their subjects are bears the sense of asking how we (author and readers together) are to take what they say and do. This does not arise simply from interest in these subjects for their own sake – though these writers all do display such an interest – and certainly does not imply a covert commitment to a sociology of bourgeois individualism. Its importance derives from the question which of their statements and actions we can sensibly endorse.

Since rhetorical communication does not confine itself to a strictly cognitive level, and since rhetoric is endemic to sociology, it should not be surprising that sociological enquiry entails operations on such a variety of levels – including the operation of providing subjects with moral and political defences. Nor, perhaps, should one be surprised by the implication this has that such defensive operations play an everyday role in conveying understanding.

In showing that given actions, views and feelings *are* reasonable, reasonable person enthymemes show in what light we should see them; the proper sort of response to make to them; and how they fit in with daily assumptions and standards which reader and subject share (or can be brought to share). It seems to me that if one knows as much as this about someone's conduct, and if one has undergone sensitising processes dismantling barriers against comprehension of this conduct, it would be absurd to claim that one did not understand it.

4 COMMUNICATIVE ATTITUDES IN TEXTUAL ARGUMENTATION

Except among writers who would like to insist on the adoption of some particular set of values by sociologists, it is commonly held that values ought not to affect treatments of sociological phenomena at all, even if they do determine choices of subject.[24] I do not wish to support either of these positions, but to discuss what I term the 'communicative attitudes' I see as integral to sociological texts. These are less easy to identify than straightforward 'values' or statable opinions; they are rather resistant to prescriptions about what sociologists ought to write, and they wholly defy eradication.

'Communicative attitudes', I should like to claim, are formed by a text's patterns of emphasis, the partly formulated points of view and the explanatory preferences which rhetorical analysis brings to light. They are not the same as an author's personal motives as an empirical individual – the aims and desires which move him or her in the composition of the text, and which may be impossible to reconstruct afterwards. Nor are they identical with the author's evaluative *opinions*, statable views which are much more easily amenable to argument, proof and disproof. In order to further the impartiality of sociology, Rex concurs with Mannheim and Myrdal in urging that authors should state their personal value-positions openly before they write.[25] Reasonable as this suggestion is, it is not wholly applicable to communicative attitudes, for at least two reasons.

First, it is likely that views and attitudes which are relatively vaguely specified will be less obvious to a speaker or writer than to the audience which is able to observe their symptoms. A 'communicative attitude' may be *constituted* by patterns of order and emphasis – that is, by rhetorical behaviour of which its author may be partly or entirely unconscious. Second, as I have often observed already, statements may count as expressing some moral or political

attitude in view of their communicational contexts – quite irrespect
ive of their authors' intentions. Even if an author wished to give hi
or her subject an unbiased treatment, it would be unlikely to be
possible for him or her to formulate all the communicative
attitudes expressed by the text.

Moreover, it is improbable that the authors examined in thi
book would see their communicative attitudes as values ir
precisely the sense of sources of possible bias with regard to thei
subjects. The communicative attitudes to be described here
diverge from absolute neutrality, it is true, but seem more likely to
be seen by their possessors – in so far as they are conscious of them or
can be made conscious of them – as merely the proper fashion ir
which to treat other people. In their argumentative practice the
authors examined here do not behave as impartial, impersonal
judges; but to do so would entail not an *absence* of communicative
attitudes, but the display of rather unpleasant ones.

The communicative attitudes these authors do show are of
great significance. They have considerable impacts upon the nature
of their sociological treatments of their subjects, and to some extent
they predetermine the conclusions that are reached. For example,
when Goldthorpe *et al.* refuse from the start to examine isolated
aspects of their subjects' lives, they are expressing a basic communicative attitude which determines the type of sociological method
they choose. They wish to treat their subjects 'not only as industrial
employees but also as husbands and fathers, as neighbours and
friends, as individuals with certain life-histories and objectives and
so on' (1, p. 8). This is to say that these authors' attitudes to their
subjects as *people* prohibit them from using any method which relies
on the manipulation of isolated 'variables' – even their use of 'and so
on' indicates an aversion to any method based on limited numbers
of hard-and-fast categories. Instead, they choose the non-
theoreticised communicative mode of the epitome in which to
discuss the people they are writing about.

Their text also reveals Goldthorpe *et al.* as seeing their subjects as
reflective, decision-making individuals; this is highly compatible
with their strategy of seeking explanations for what the workers do
or feel in terms of the choices they have made in particular
predicaments. Again, this shuts off various types of possible
explanation and makes others more likely. Goldthorpe *et al.*
implicitly contrast a deterministic image of the person with their
own when they ask whether 'patterning' in industrial behaviour

hould be seen as 'determined primarily by features of the work-
ituation itself' or whether it is rather

> that any such pattern may equally, or perhaps more basically,
> derive from a particular orientation which workers have taken
> towards employment – from the wants and expectations they
> have of it, and thus from the way in which they *define* their work
> situation rather than simply respond to this (i, p. 8).

The authors' support for the second part of this alternative forms the
central theme of their trilogy.

They present the workers as having chosen their current jobs
rather than having been forced into them (e.g. i, p. 33; iii, p. 64),
and search for adequate reasons for this choice. Or in i, Chapter 5
they stress that their subjects 'themselves are changing the character
of unionism and are creating, in effect, a new type of unionism
consistent with the wants and expectations which they bring to their
work' (i, p. 114). This view of the worker as an active agent is highly
consistent with the authors' use of the epitome, and with their
rhetorical use of perspective – whereby the worker himself, rather
than given aspects of his surroundings, is assigned the most
prominent place in their text.

It seems clear that these communicative attitudes cannot be
accounted for in terms of conceptual accretions on the text of *The
Affluent Worker*. To erase them – for example by altering the
rhetorical perspective of the trilogy or by presenting the worker in a
less active light – would be to change the text's entire explanatory
approach, and to change it in a direction which the authors would
presumably condemn as mistaken. The text gives us evidence for
believing that they would do so, for though the communicative
attitudes I have described may be unconscious, they are fully in
accord with the values which the authors do make explicit. Stating
their objections to regarding the affluent worker *'de haut en bas'* (iii,
p. 184), the authors standardly imply an intention to treat their
subjects with respect; they avoid explaining their conduct in terms
of accounts which could involve taking derogatory attitudes
towards their respondents or presenting them as eccentrically
motivated.

As we have seen, what the authors consider normal, understandable or reasonable in given circumstances repeatedly forms the
groundwork of their explanations of what the 'affluent workers' do.

Their predictions, such as those about possible developments in the workers' attitudes to unionism and politics in general, have the same basis. This is borne out by their style: many of the authors' explanations for workers' attitudes are provided in terms of quotations from their subjects themselves. Had the authors refrained from this textual behaviour, their text would not have exhibited *fewer* communicative attitudes; it would have exhibited different ones.

The case of Dore differs from that of Goldthorpe *et al.* in that Dore's communicative attitudes are not only concerned with his subjects but also have a great deal to do with the *reader*. For Dore, indeed, the two go together. We have seen that he is concerned to defend much of what goes on in Japanese industrial organisation; he does not maintain that everything the Japanese do is reasonable, but that, other things being equal, it is reasonable to expect them to be reasonable. It is just this latter expectation which he considers to be missing among the British, and one of his most striking communicative attitudes is an impatience with national blindnesses, prejudices and self-deceptions. This attitude is characteristic of all those of Dore's accounts which explain in terms of reasonableness or normality where the British reader might have expected premises featuring eccentricity, feudalism, or mysterious and irrational Eastern ideologies.

This feeling that the British reader needs to be *épaté*, or shaken up a bit, becomes explicit in references to the 'philistinism' of British culture in comparison with Japan's (p. 295), or to the fact that the British do not notice changes ' "in a Japanese direction" ' which are taking place in their own employment system. Tartly, Dore attributes the latter failure in perception largely to the 'neurotic national preoccupation with unofficial strikes' (p. 340).

It is characteristic of Dore, as of most of the authors examined here, that his reproofs are applied to recipients scattered over the whole political system. He is scathing about the fact that

> Organizations are based on the assumption that interview boards will always choose, or at least seek to choose, the 'best man for the job'. To cast doubt on this assumption, to suggest as a general principle that men find it difficult to assess their colleagues impartially and uninfluenced by personal feelings, is to threaten the very principles on which organizations are based and to threaten the conception of 'integrity' on which British Establishment Man founds his self-respect (p. 230).

On the other hand, Dore attacks both sides involved in what he sees as the bogus adversarialism of British industrial relations, and he is scornful of the fact that left-wing commentators are so far deceived by their own political strategies that they are unable to perceive whether management-initiated workers' participation could actually advance the cause of industrial democracy or not (p. 366).

While it is clear that Dore's overtly evaluative attitudes could in principle be removed from his text, it is doubtful what this would achieve – since his whole explanatory approach has a similarly non-neutral tendency – or whether it would be advisable. Dore himself points to the emotional difficulties people have in accepting even the plainest facts if they run counter to what everyone expects (p. 317). He refers to the reluctance even of 'Marxists and neo-classical economists' to see that ordinary material interests meant that a seniority wage system was rational for Japanese employers, irrespective of cultural values; 'it is just more comfortable to take it as self-evident that the Japanese are peculiar' (p. 418). It follows that if Dore wishes to communicate a point of view which he takes to be perfectly correct, he has no option than more or less occasionally to attack the taken-for-granted prejudices which would prevent the reader from understanding what he means.

The fact that writers are influenced by the attitudes which are expressed in their communicative approaches is not one, it seems to me, which needs deprecating. It is true that it means that sociological conclusions are to a certain extent (only) foregone. It could have been stated with some confidence before they started their work that none of the sociologists investigated here was likely to reach a conclusion in terms of social pathology, say. Or, much as Willis may have wished to see their actions from 'the lads'' point of view, it might have been predicted that he would not arrive at an explanation in terms solely of reasonable choice, because his personal view of the decision to enter a lifetime of manual work in a British factory is that no reasonable person *could* take it if in possession of all the facts. It could therefore have been forecast that his final explanation would be composed of a blend of reasonable person enthymemes and an account of why it is impossible for the lads to possess all the facts which bear on what they do.

But this is to say only that the broad outlines of what an author writes will – in my opinion they should – have something to do with the sort of person he or she is. On the one hand, a writer has to be some sort of person, and being a person entails having attitudes towards other people. A sociological text with no communicative attitudes would be one with no attitudes towards people. This would be very odd indeed and much more harmful than what is actually the case.

On the other hand, an author equipped with the outlines of a point of view still has to *demonstrate* its reasonableness: to himself or herself in the course of research, during which he or she may undergo changes in personal standpoint, and then to readers. That is, the argumentative paraphernalia required by academic work is not rendered dispensable by its author's personal commitments; quite the contrary. It is from the details of a standpoint rather than the general stance itself that usable explanations arise. A general respect for the 'affluent worker' *governs* what Goldthorpe *et al.* (say) write, but alone it is not enough to generate the contents of their work. For this, they require all three: the available techniques of sociological investigation, a form of argumentative communication, and a set of relationships with other people.

5 SUMMARY

This chapter deals with the interactive nature of enthymematic accounts based on notions of normality and on norms of reasonableness, and examines the types of explanation and understanding they convey. These accounts make what people do intelligible by situating it in relation to standard anticipations and habits of response which the reader is assumed to use in negotiating social life; they answer questions relevant to the reader's interaction with other people. Moreover, the reader is relied upon to do some of the work involved in constructing the account which the author proposes.

At the same time, the text may radically alter the reader's views about what ordinariness and reasonableness consist in, and about what he or she can sensibly expect to happen in the social world. A sociological account may be equipped with surprises which force the reader to change his or her moral, social or political views – as Goldthorpe *et al.* or Willis require the reader to alter views about participation in the class structure of society, or Dore requires him or her to abandon ethnocentric preconceptions about Britain and Japan.

The argumentative reassortment and reconstruction of accepted opinions is a chief characteristic of both ordinary person and reasonable person enthymemes, and it allows us to appreciate some of the workings of 'understanding' in social life itself as well as in sociology. Understanding is conveyed by these enthymemes when they succeed in exposing aspects of subjects' behaviour which justify us in reacting to it in terms of our everyday 'topoi', the assumptions and inferential patterns which underpin argumentative interchange. This explanatory process is not always compatible with leaving readers' everyday assumptions exactly as they were; hence the authors' need on occasion to interfere with readers' topical systems. But what it does *not* do is to attribute strict rationality to the people concerned, nor to apply to them empathy or intuition, nor to produce causal histories of internal motivations. It may be that these forms of understanding are comparatively infrequent in non-sociological discourse too.

To show that it is legitimate to apply ordinary or reasonable person enthymemes to their subjects, authors must establish what sorts of people these subjects are, and this is a textual activity prominent in the work of Goldthorpe *et al.*, Willis and Dore. Here both Willis and Dore supply enthymemes with a functional ambiguity: the type of people their subjects are appears as either a minor premise or a conclusion in their arguing, according to the different rates at which readers are prepared to accept the author's classification. Accepting that someone is normal or reasonable implies, other things being equal, a readiness to apply the same description to what he or she says or does: endorsing at least some aspects of his or her views. Hence explanatory processes often justify at the same time, and can force readers to change moral, social or political ideas to make room for the subject's.

The importance of enthymematic reasoning to sociological texts underlines a further point: that we should reorganise our conceptions of the relative roles played by the different components of a sociological work. The central theses in the projects dealt with here are argumentative rather than, in the first place, factually assertive, and blended of social and personal reasoning rather than strictly 'cognitive'. Authors often place more weight on exercises in terms of self-presentation and sensitisation than on, say, causal analyses, which seem much less significant than we might have expected; and these exercises are often located in unexpected places. What is thought of as the 'hard' information provided by a text may well perform the *communicative* function of displaying an author's competence or persuading the reader to relinquish hostility to some point of view. It may *support*, rather than constitute, the work's dominant argumentative theme.

Lastly this chapter dealt with what I term 'communicative attitudes', which are expressed in terms of patterns of emphasis and order, of perspective and explanatory preference, and which rhetorical analysis allows us to identify although authors may not be conscious of them. Communicative attitudes do not generally take the form of explicit conceptual additions to texts, and it is not possible even in principle to remove them from sociological works. To alter an author's sociological perspective, say – to remove the 'affluent worker' from the centre of the trilogy by Goldthorpe *et al.*, or to subtract from the emphasis which Dore gives to reasonable person enthymemes – would be to alter the contents of the explanations concerned, and to make the book in question *mean* something its author considered false.

In any case, there is no reason to suppose that authors would wish to see the communicative attitudes removed from their work, or that they ought so to wish. Rather than being simply sources of bias, such attitudes are bound up in the way an author both conceptualises and responds to other people. The people most in question may be his subjects or his readers; Dore clearly takes his sensitisation processes to remove rather than to generate bias, and to be legitimate and necessary responses to the sort of person he believes many of his readers to be. This is not to claim that any and every intrusion of an author's personality into what he or she writes is justified. It does show that sociological works are properly to be understood as personal communication, and judged in the terms appropriate to it.

by dwelling on parallels or analogies between this area and more controversial cases.

The necessity which sociological authors perceive for communicational strategies such as this means that they by no means try to address 'universal audiences', even though they are trying to propound *statements* which in some sense have universal validity. Just as Rex's and Moore's uses of actual types indicate that there are some things which (at least in some circumstances) cannot be *said* at all, in practice sociologists accept that there are some true statements about society which are likely to be accepted only by some people. This number they try to expand as much as is feasible – so Blau and Duncan or Rex and Moore try to include in their audiences those who disapprove of racism but are reluctant to accept that it is pervasive in their own societies – but they do not assume that they can communicate with everyone at once.

Inevitable as this approach is, the admission that there are some things which can be perceived only by some people at some times is one which brings with it dangers of sectarianism which ought to be guarded against. Still, this approach does *not* imply that there is one complete interlocking set of true statements about society, perceptible only to some people. On the contrary, a rhetorical account of truth-telling allows for a range of alternative adequate accounts of reality (see below). And in fact the authors in this survey could not be convicted of administering propaganda from one defined quarter to another. They all object to a catholic spectrum of political points of view, and require their readers to be prepared to revise a variety of received views about social reality.

Goffman is no exception. He too wishes to bring the reader eventually to explain as normal what he or she might once have rejected as bizarre, or to defend as reasonable conduct which might have seemed absurd (occasionally, vice versa: Goffman attacks as absurd what once looked reasonable). The corollary of searching for reasonableness in unlikely places is that Goffman's work has a levelling effect. His mental patients are shown as more worthy of respect than has been supposed, and other people whose status is not in general doubted – doctors or businessmen – are shown as less so. There must be some potential readers whose personal dispositions are opposed to this type of shift; indeed, the rhetorical techniques of order and emphasis which Goffman (like the other authors here) uses to defend his subjects presuppose that there is a point of view to defend them against. Hence Goffman's work too exhibits a tension characteristic of sociology: he treads a delicate balance betwee agreeing with his hypothetical reader and – since there would k little point in writing at all if he were *only* to agree – assaulting an altering his or her views.

The connections between sociology and the reader's perceptior are stressed by those sociological methods which in effect prescrib rhetorical operations to influence the reader's frame of mind. Two (these are taking the position of the agent, and introducin conceptual innovations; Goffman's uses of them are examined in th next section. As far as the first is concerned, Goffman claims tha 'any group of persons . . . develop a life of their own which becom(meaningful, reasonable and normal once you get close to i (*Asylums*, p. 7). This implies that in order to perceive the reasonabl(ness the reader must be *brought* close to the subject, which in som cases requires a good deal of rhetorical effort.

Conceptual innovation entails the redistribution of presence an emphasis among ideas about society, and its chief rhetorical impa(derives from the fact that the concepts which sociological autho challenge are *taken* from the social world. They are likely to be tho: according to which the reader *lives*. He or she will have habit feelings and dispositions bound up in them, as well as emotional an intellectual investments in them. To a considerable extent, reade of sociology books are reading about themselves.

It therefore cannot be the case that sociological works should k simple applications of methodological analyses, presenting hyp(theses devised in social vacuums for independent perusal by the readers. There is a *feeling* as of objectivity sometimes connected wit writing, when an author realises that he or she is forced to wri down something quite different from what had been intended. N doubt this does sometimes have to do with logical implication, but think that it is just as likely to be connected with what the *reader* ca be presumed to be able to accept at a given stage of argument. I Woodward's case, the development of her argumentative structur could be explained in terms of the reader's views and capacitie Even in the case of Blau and Duncan, the most 'positivist' autho examined here, sociological communication takes the form of dialogue, with mutual influence and adaptation between auth(and reader.

It has been suggested that there is a distinction within the divisi(usually made between competence and performance; performan(is not simply an actualisation of competence but has systemat features of its own.[2] In the case of sociology, this distinction is connected with the transforming role of the reader. I have argued that his or her manipulations of implication and association are integral parts of a text's *meaning*, so that the effective components of an explanation extend right off the printed page. What is literally an assortment of fragmented descriptions can be expanded by the reader into an explication of personal action in an intelligible social setting.

In order to prompt this participation by the reader, authors compose their texts in a variety of levels and registers, relying on signs, symptoms, analogies, conventions and assumptions. Instead of using formal models, the authors investigated here *prefer* an allusiveness which each reader can develop according to need – despite the risks of misunderstanding which this involves. Sociological rhetorical techniques which exploit this allusiveness are exemplified by the actual type, which allows the reader to respond to textual versions of signs and symptoms of social states of affairs, and the epitome, which describes people in a non-theoreticised manner which is in keeping with the everyday perceptions which we evolve during social interaction with one another.

The use of such methods to replace more strictly defined devices accords well with the fact that sociological communication is not a series of discrete interchanges according to methodological rules, but a long-term interactional process; it is a series of negotiations in which both parties may be influenced in a permanent manner.

In the next section I shall look at Goffman's version of these negotiations, before going on to the question of the assessment of sociological books.

1 CONCEPTUAL INNOVATION AND PERSONAL CHANGE

Though at first sight conceptual innovation seems to be an operation of purely intellectual significance, it cannot be this in sociology – where the concepts to be changed are not only the reader's concepts, but the reader's concepts about him- or herself. These concepts may be altered indirectly, as 'labelling theory' in the sociology of deviance alters the reader's conception of his or her own normality as a result of changing his or her perception of deviance. But Goffman is dealing directly with the everyday social world, deliberately trying to change the reader's apprehension of this world and the way he or she fits into it.

A 'chief concern' of Goffman's *Asylums* is 'to develop a sociological version of the structure of the self' (p. 11). This involves applying a version of the self initiated by William James[3] to the social world of the mental hospital, using this as a basis for accounting for the behaviour of its inmates. Like James, Goffman holds that there is a 'sense' in which the self 'is not a property of the person to whom it is attributed, but dwells rather in the pattern of social control that is exerted in connexion with the person by himself and those around him' (p. 154).

This position on selfhood is different from that by which the reader is likely to live. If one accepts that Goffman is right, one's liability to derogate the conduct of mental patients is likely to decrease; but so is one's right to congratulate oneself on one's own achievements. This forces Goffman to attend to sensitising the reader, a process which is begun by his choice of subject itself. The reader is *offered* an extension of his or her social understanding to people whose behaviour may not have seemed clearly comprehensible before. He or she is much less openly requested to resign illusions about his or her own life.

Goffman approaches the view of self he wishes to develop by classifying institutions according to their effects on inmates' conceptions of self; the reader's viewpoint is shifted to the question what can affect (other) people's self-images. The author presents 'total institutions' as a single category, on the grounds that all are 'encompassing' of their inmates. They share the following features:

> all aspects of life are conducted in the same place and under the same single authority . . . in the immediate company of a large batch of others, all of whom are treated alike and required to do the same thing together . . . [where] activities are tightly scheduled . . . [and] imposed from above . . . [as part of] a single rational plan purportedly designed to fulfil the official aims of the institution (*Asylums*, p. 17).

A new categorisation such as this *entails* the rhetorical operations of distinguishing among items formerly taken to be indissoluble and collecting together others seen as disparate. It emphasises features formerly thought insignificant and reduces the prominence of others previously considered important. This reassorts the presence accorded to different aspects of the institutions concerned and provides a new perspective from which to view them. It problematises situations which had been taken to be clear under the old concepts, and re-solves them under the new ones – which has the persuasive effect of demonstrating their success.

The fact that this conceptual innovation demands *personal* changes from the reader is made clear by the implications of Goffman's use of it in support of the claims that as a rule mental patients are 'more like ordinary persons than like anything else' (p. 57), and that 'the craziness' attributed to them is 'by and large a product of the claimant's social distance from the situation that the patient is in' (p. 121). The grounds for these assertions are that in a 'total institution'

> the new inpatient finds himself cleanly stripped of many of his accustomed affirmations, satisfactions, and defences, and is subjected to a rather full set of mortifying experiences: restriction of free movement, communal living, diffuse authority of a whole echelon of people, and so on (p. 137).

In a mental hospital 'humiliations' deflate the patient's view of himself (*sic*) as a 'full-fledged person' (p. 141), and 'denigrating facts' are repeatedly brought up to challenge his own version of himself (p. 146). Using personal pronouns which incorporate the reader's viewpoint into what he says, Goffman writes, 'Here one begins to learn about the limited extent to which a conception of oneself can be sustained when the usual setting of supports for it are suddenly removed' (p. 137). That is: the author is writing about the *reader* too.

This is not a point which Goffman labours directly; but his claim is that conduct usually regarded as symptomatic of mental illness is susceptible of reinterpretation, and his reinterpretations commonly centre round the theme: *anyone* would behave like this in the circumstances.

This theme is one which possesses explanatory power. For example, Goffman asserts that one result of the above-mentioned experiences can be that inmates 'discover that deflations in moral status are not so bad as they had imagined' (p. 150). The 'unserious yet oddly exaggerated moral context' in which they move results in 'a kind of civic apathy' (p. 151), a 'moral fatigue' (p. 152). This explains why patients form relationships 'in a temporarily steady

way' with others of the opposite sex, although both partners may b
married. This does not, then, arise from a weakness of characte
typical of people suffering from mental disease; Goffman ascribes i
to 'the loosening effects of living in a world within a world, unde
conditions which make it difficult to give full seriousness to either o
them' (p. 152).

This is an ordinary person enthymeme to explain patients
behaviour. It implies that anyone could be expected to behave a
they do in a similar situation; given normal reactions and thes
particular unusual social circumstances, such behaviour is to b
anticipated; it is not conduct which allows us to infer to any intrinsi
peculiarities on the parts of the people concerned. Hence, this is ar
account which both ensues from and buttresses the claim tha
patterns of social control do not 'so much support the self a
constitute it' (p. 154).

This implication that the reader could expect him- or her*self* tc
behave similarly in such a position – and that the fact that he or she
now does not behave like a mental patient is also attributable tc
social circumstances – is what poses the greatest obstacle to accepting
Goffman's account. In *Relations in Public*, Goffman asserts that
sociological hypotheses ought to produce concepts which 'reorder
our view of social activity' (p. 21). As when ethologists perceive
'natural patterns' in what previously looked 'haphazard', 'Once
these behavioural sequences are pointed out to the observer, his
seeing is changed' (p. 22). But changing one's conception of self in
the way Goffman suggests involves behavioural corollaries. It
entails *reacting* to oneself and others differently, on the basis of
different practical judgements. This means that it is also a shift in
terms of morality, politics and feeling.

These shifts are most obvious to the reader when he or she
disagrees with the implications of the conceptual reorganisation
proposed. For example, someone objecting to Goffman's redescrip-
tion of sessions of group psycho-therapy as 'arranged confessional
periods' (*Asylums*, p. 139) would probably refer to the denigratory
implications of 'confessional'. But in order to combat them he or she
would have to produce moral and practical reasons for retaining the
more benificent associations of the conventional terminology.

These varied personal phenomena attendant on conceptual
innovation provide the rationale for Goffman's emphases on the
points of view from which social events are observed (*Asylums*, p. 7),
and on getting readers to adopt those points of view. With Goffman

as with other authors,[4] the form which such an operation takes is often the following: a potentially contentious description is applied to A, where there is enough common ground with the reader for the author to assume that he or she will accept the description with comparatively little resistance. A and B are shown to be in some respects similar; then the reader may agree to apply the description in question to B.

In discussing total institutions, Goffman begins with prisons, in whose destructive characteristics the (liberal) reader may find it easy to believe, *then* he goes on to mental hospitals. On the concept of self, he begins with mental patients, and leaves the reader to draw conclusions about himself or herself. The rhetorical effects of order are integral parts of these arguments, and the process of reading itself conduces to changes of attitude on the reader's part.

Goffman's techniques of humour and irony have sensitising effects to support his reorganisations of perceived 'natural sequences' in everyday reality. He remarks wryly that although people tend to think of honest behaviour as ingenuous, and see deliberately arranged conduct as dishonest, *both* contain elements of impression management. Someone acting in a perceptibly honest fashion can also be seen as a 'performer' arranging a 'show' (*The Presentation of Self*, pp. 76–7). Thus the reader can agree to see respected figures such as lawyers, economists and accountants as 'specialists in verbal fronts' (p. 156) without feeling overly attacked.[5] Or Goffman classes together institutions such as the Union League Club in New York and the Los Alamos Laboratories in virtue of the fact that both are 'felt to be somewhat snippy about who is let in' (*Asylums*, p. 15). Where a neutral tone would not be effective, still less a moralising one, Goffman's irony directs the reader's attention to aspects of social life which otherwise he or she might have preferred to ignore.

In the same way, startling comparisons can surprise the reader into perceiving and drawing inferences from phenomena he or she would not normally associate with each other. Goffman breaks social taboos by comparing people from opposite ends of the social scale – likening the territorial behaviour of mental patients who segregate themselves behind barriers of chairs to that of people availing themselves of the enclosure arrangements at Ascot (*Asylums*, p. 216). Thus he is able to stress reasons common to the conduct of each.

In common with other authors examined here, Goffman uses the pronoun 'one' in reference to subjects with whom the reader would not as a rule compare him- or herself. The implied interchange-ability between the reader and the subject normalises conduct which otherwise seems strange – such as choosing to spend one's free time in the lavatory. Goffman reflects that places like this 'seemed pervaded by a feeling of relaxation and self-determination, in marked contrast to the sense of uneasiness prevailing on some wards. Here one could be one's own man' (*Asylums*, p. 206; cf. pp. 165–6). Once more the processes involved in reading themselves equip the reader with enabling experiences which allow him or her to complete the enthymematical reasoning offered by the text.

These experiences do not leave the reader as he or she was. In sociology, conceptual innovations do not just affect what the reader is prepared to *do* in the way of looking at social phenomena; they tend to affect what he or she *is*, in terms of participating in social phenomena. Like the other authors investigated here, Goffman intervenes into the reader's moral reactions to what happens around him or her. In effect he attacks the ways in which mental patients are perceived, judged and treated, and in doing this he indicates reappraisals of accepted notions of ordinary behaviour.

Goffman's work attempts to contribute to these reappraisals by making the reader more alert to and critical of the minutiae of social life, and getting him or her to incorporate the results of these observations into interaction with other people. (Work such as this may have had effects which are traceable, though perhaps not radical; Weitz remarks that observing non-verbal communication has become a 'popular pastime' in the United States. [6]) The fact that this has moral implications is on occasion made explicit. In *The Presentation of Self in Everyday Life* Goffman rejects the tendency of 'Individualistic modes of thought' to

> treat processes such as self-deception and insincerity as charac-terological weaknesses generated within the deep recesses of the individual personality . . . Self-deception can be seen as something that results when two different roles, performer and audience, come to be compressed into the same individual (pp. 86–7, n. 6).

With contentions such as this, the reader's normal uncritical moral 'immersion' in social life is shattered and destroyed.

2   APPRAISING SOCIOLOGICAL TEXTS

Accepting the legitimate role of rhetoric in sociological reasoning has implications for the notions of meaning and understanding, and it shows that sociological *objectivity* is an abstraction which cannot be instantiated in actual communication. In the texts examined here, self-presentation and sensitisation form integral parts of rhetorical reasoning, and these phenomena and their effects have ineradicable elements which are personal, social, ethical or political. These elements are so bound into textual meaning that to alter or diminish them would not bring a work nearer to objectivity, it would merely make it mean something else.

Since this is so, in place of attempting objectivity sociologists in fact proceed as follows: they try to tell the truth in a manner which complements, and is complemented by, the knowledge and dispositions which their (selected) audience already has. Consciously or otherwise, writers try to gauge the personal and political commitments of the audience they wish to address, or are forced to address, and they adapt the personal and political tenor of their own communication so as to complete or correct their readers' views. Strictly speaking, truthfulness is a product of the joint communicative efforts of both.

This rhetorical notion of truthfulness allows for alternative truthful accounts because it implies that different audiences require different treatments to arrive at equivalent points. An audience with given feelings and beliefs will only accept, and indeed only comprehend, communication in certain directions; any author's views will be similarly limited and incomplete, and he or she is well advised to look for the audience which can yield the most productive combination, together with what he or she can contribute. Another author will need to say other things – perhaps to another audience.

The correctness of what is jointly achieved in rhetorical communication, and the appropriateness of the inducements which both author and audience are offered in the process, must be evaluated in terms which themselves are not reducible to 'objective' elements. Dore, for example, has to give an English audience social and emotional considerations in favour of accepting explanations in terms of Japanese ordinariness which would be neither necessary nor useful in Japan. But the question in terms of what expectations ordinariness should be construed, or whether Dore uses acceptable methods of communicating them, must be answered in language which is itself partly moral, social and emotional.[7] It is language whose use means that speakers cannot assess particular contentions by standing outside the whole subject – but they can develop relatively good or bad reasons for accepting or rejecting them.

The fact that different readers have different preconceptions about social events is one reason why the notion of communicated truth, or what I call rhetorical truth, cannot be explicated by linking good or bad reasons to consensus among a 'universal' audience.[8] History gives us no grounds for assuming that any all-embracing conglomerate of actual audiences would ever have personal and political preconceptions which balanced each other into a transcendent accuracy. Instead of taking it that they would (and aspiring to objectivity by setting out for this transcendent point by themselves), authors try to communicate appropriately by their own non-objective lights; those assessing the results have no option but to do the same.

This does not mean that no value at all attaches to the criteria which have been worked out for evaluating, say, statistical procedures in survey mateirals. In so far as statistical criteria can yield good reasons for particular claims, it ought to go against their professional standards for sociologists to ignore them. But these criteria are not absolute; their usefulness is relative to the parts played by the relevant materials in overall communicative processes, whose total components will be of mixed constitution.

The necessity for standards of mixed provenance and status can be seen in the case, for example, of the actual type, in whose use authors pointedly refrain from conforming to methodologically-preferred standards of procedural completeness. Here notions such as accuracy and precision are by no means the first consideration. It makes no sense to ask how many cats Rex and Moore have observed in Claremont Road and what relationship this number has to the cat population in Sparkbrook as a whole.

I explained actual types as textual uses of signs or symptoms (cats may not be intrinsically symbolic, but their textual appearance here is), not selected according to strictly evidential criteria but according to their suitability for the reader's creative use of them. If the reader's system of associations does not overlap with the author's, he or she will not know to what the author is referring. As long as it does, the reader's manipulation of signs and symptoms in the text can form a substitute for the experience necessary in order

᠊ be convinced by a general observation which only the author has ᠊een able to make first-hand. I suggested too that the types of ᠊eneralisation to which actual types point can be described as ᠊hetorical inductions'. Looking at rhetorical inductions can show ᠊ more detail how conventional methods of sociological assessment ᠊an be related to rhetorical forms.

I have argued that a rhetorical induction is a non-universal ᠊eneralisation which enables its holder to know what as a rule to ᠊xpect in a certain sort of social situation – even one somewhat ᠊ifferent from the one whose analysis he or she has read. These ᠊xpectations are of the same type as those we use in ordinary social ᠊fe; that is, they are *not* simply *predictions* about what is liable to ᠊appen in a situation. (Predictions pure and simple are more useful ᠊n the race-course than in most ordinary social interaction.) ᠊hetorical inductions show how features of given types of situation ᠊an be taken as signs or symptoms, and of what. Dore's rhetorical ᠊ductions, for example, equip the reader with the ability to decide ᠊hether the opulence of Japanese union buildings is a sign of ᠊bservience to management or not. But their purpose is not to ᠊quip the reader for directly practical survival in the situation ᠊oncerned. Sociological rhetorical inductions deal more pointedly ᠊ith the interpretation of situations than everyday ones need do, ᠊nd they connect these situations more selectively with phenomena ᠊f social, political and economic interest.

Though rhetorical inductions are not universal generalisations, ᠊hey are not genuinely limited to the small number of situations ᠊hich single authors can examine. The point of Rex's and Moore's ᠊ork is to tell us about decayed inner-city areas in general, of ᠊Villis's to tell us about disaffected working-class 'lads' in general, of ᠊ore's, to tell us about larger Japanese factories in general – ᠊egardless of whether the author actually mentions these wider ᠊onclusions or not. (The generalisations implied by this book have ᠊he same argumentative form.)

In deciding whether to accept a text's rhetorical inductions – ᠊ven those parts of them which are limited to what has actually been ᠊nvestigated – the reader has to decide whether to believe the *author* ᠊r not. Since rhetorical inductions are not just summaries of the ᠊requency of events, and would not be supremely useful in ᠊nterpreting the social world if they were, in the nature of the case an ᠊uthor cannot supply evidence which *forces* the reader to accept his ᠊r her claims. He or she can only assure us that in his or her own experience the expectations the text recommends hold good.

At this point conventional standards of evaluation can be used in two ways: to evaluate the factual assertions which support the author's self-presentation, in order to decide whether his or her social competence and judgement can be trusted; and to evaluate parts (only) of the expectations which rhetorical inductions convey. These evaluations, though important, have a chiefly negative potential.

Dore's claim, say, that a certain percentage of Japanese workers are unionised is open to check. If he were wrong, this would militate against the convincingness of his self-presentation, and it might mean that some of the rhetorical inductions he offers are misleading. (This would depend on the extent of his miscalculation and on its place in his arguing.) If he is right, this means not that his argument is correct *but that it can go ahead.*

The claim that so-and-so many Japanese belong to unions means nothing in social or in sociological terms until it is embedded in a setting of discourse which gives it an argumentative function. To *call* it a factual claim is to label it according to its chief or most obvious characteristic; it is not to imply that as a rule we can expect authors' statements to be *purely* factual. And it is the argumentative function of the claim which shows which are the *crucial* standards by which to judge it. These depend on its point and its composition: its appropriateness and usefulness as a guide to social situations, its communicative efficiency, the social, political, ethical and personal impacts which would ensue from accepting it and the argument of which it is part.

In the same way, sociological uses of the epitome depend on certain claims about facts, which take on different implications according to their argumentative roles. The propensity of 'affluent workers' to buy domestic items such as washing machines is taken to signify different things by Goldthorpe *et al.* and by Marcuse, but both assume that these purchases do take place. As long as it can be accepted that they do, the important question is what links in terms of consistency and coherence can be argued for between this tendency and others which the workers show. Which of these others – their stress on family life, say – need more emphasis, which are insignificant, which are signs or symptoms of which others?

Epitomes are a form of communication consonant with the fact that in everyday life we learn about social situations by learning what people do in them. And I should claim that as a rule we learn about other people fragmentedly, in terms of selected symptoms or propensities in their behaviour (explicitly causal theories about other people are, it seems to me, given an unusual emphasis at middle-class dinner-tables). It is compatible with this that epitomes do not usually feature cut-and-dried relationships between variables, but take a less stringent, more allusive form, in which in the end everything depends on the sense made by the argumentative structure involved. Once more, 'the sense' is judged by standards which take for granted a certain factual and logical consistency but which include, more importantly, terms which are pragmatic, political and personal.

This mixed and personal mode of communication is displayed in paradigmatic form in the rhetorical deduction or enthymeme. This is an inference whose expression depends on its hypothetical reader: the parts which are stated in particular ways, and those which are suppressed, are determined by what the author takes to be the reader's position. (Thus Willis or Dore increase the flexibility of their arguing by making the written parts of their enthymemes ambiguous in a fashion which fits them for use by readers with different explanatory needs.)

Both author and readers take part in this type of deductive interchange in their capacities as persons, not just as intellects. Enthymemes are composed partly of the author's self-presentation, which offers the reader good reasons for weighing seriously what he or she says, and sensitisation, which can be essential in order to make a piece of reasoning accessible to particular readers. Thus Goffman conforms to the practice of all the writers examined here in using rhetorical devices to shift his reader out of the habit of taking received social conduct at face value. This habit forms the greatest barrier to perceiving the point of what Goffman writes. Once it has been dislodged, the author leaves the reader to reconstruct the text's reasonable or ordinary person enthymemes alone.

Hence the fact that statedly deductive forms are not central to the written parts of a text does not exclude the possibility of their centrality to the arguing between author and reader. Nor need sociological writers be required to insist on universal empirical generalisations in order to count as inferring properly.[9] Enthymemes deduce from premises with no aspirations to be lawlike, and which are generally, not inevitably, valid. Often they consist of the topoi which form our basic stock of workable anticipations about the social world. Sociological enthymemes, therefore, should not be seen as

aspiring or failed hypothetico-deductive structures. They are
special type of arguing with a purpose of their own: to combine
explanation which is as deductively sound as inherently uncertain
circumstances will allow with maximum intelligibility from the
reader's point of view.

The rhetorical methods described here – rhetorical induction and
deduction, actual types and epitomes – together account for a good
proportion of the way understanding is conveyed in sociology. What
is common to these methods is that authors do not just concentrate
on their subjects; they try to make what their subjects do assimilable
for the reader, to answer questions he or she can be expected to feel
are important, to locate their subjects' behaviour in terms of the
reader's apprehension of the social world – even if this involves some
interference with what readers take the social world to be.

In negotiating with readers about what they can understand or be
brought to understand at given stages of arguing, authors intervene
into readers' personal habits of living. They strengthen those of their
readers' assumptions about the social world with which they agree
and try to get them to abandon others, or to use them differently.
Thus enthymemes make behaviour comprehensible by getting the
reader to situate it in relation to uncontroversial premises, but the
reader may be very surprised by the fact that they are these
particular premises. He or she may not wish to dispute the premises
in themselves, but also may not in the past have wished to connect
them with the behaviour in question.

It seems to me that this is part of what we mean when it dawns on
us that some piece of conduct is understandable after all. A
rearrangement has taken place in our structure of topical preconceptions about what we can reasonably and consistently expect from
other people. In this way we are brought to understand the
intransigence of Willis's 'lads' at school. We are shown the
considerations which make their actions follow from quite normal
premises, and we are made to abandon our prejudices against
connecting these premises with the lads' conclusions. Sometimes
sensitisation alone is enough to get readers to make such a
connection. To refrain from thinking of people with whom we do not
agree as if they were abstract entities, and instead give *presence* to the
fact that they are people, is not merely a matter of sentiment. It
licenses us to understand them by applying premises in terms of
ordinariness or reasonableness to what they do; it incorporates their
conduct into a familiar topical system.

A further contribution to what is meant by understanding a person or situation is supplied by rhetorical induction and the actual type. These do not only help the reader to grasp what is liable to happen in a situation and how to order it in terms of the social assumptions he or she already has, but convey intimations about interpreting signs and symptoms in these situations. (Probably 'empathy' is achieved by interpretations of the same variety.) It seems to me that these are some of the elements of everyday understanding; sociological understanding reorders their contents and the relations between them, it insists on significatory or symptomatic functions which in everyday life may be ignored, and it selects for this treatment states of affairs for which social or political significance can be claimed.

This form of understanding depends on personal communication and it involves personal changes to the reader. That is, it affects the habitual patterns of attention, attitude and feeling which make one into a person of one sort rather than another, liable to react to people of particular kinds in one way rather than another. When a reader of a sociological text is required to see its subjects as ordinary or reasonable in certain respects, he or she is offered not just an explanation but at the same time a justification which entails differences in behaviour on the reader's part. These are personal accounts which are politically important in that they teach readers how to take and how to react to what is claimed or done by those people whom they judge to resemble the subjects of the text.

There remains the question how much of anyone's grasp of a social situation can be portioned out into signs, symptoms, quasi-general topical anticipations, epitomised personal figures, rhetorical induction and rhetorical deduction, as well as the more familiar forms of causal attribution, historical narrative or story, and intendedly factual information which is given its point by being set into a particular discourse. This question is one for which no *a priori* response presents itself. Its answer must depend at the least on the views and purposes of the questioner, the explanatory conventions of his or her culture, and the development of the forms of understanding which immediately precede his or her own attempt and which it both attacks and extends.

None the less the conclusions reached here by observing what sociologists do in practice suggest that in the past we have been inclined to regard the wrong cases as *central* to sociological understanding. Causal questions about the formation of given motivations seem most often to be asked when something has gone wrong, so that understanding is unusually difficult and attempts to achieve it are characterised by frustration rather than by confidence. Questions in terms of empathy seem more relevant to lovers than to run-of-the-mill sociologists. The implicit questions with which the latter seem to deal in their texts focus on the sort of interaction possible between the reader and people who are like the sociologist's subjects: what the reader can expect them to do, how to take it, how it fits in with the anticipations he or she normally uses in navigating social life.

Attempts to convey sociological understanding, then, are composed not only with reference to their subjects' ideas but also with reference to their *readers'* habits of thought, feeling and behaviour. Since readers' anticipations differ, sociological questions which are identical in literal terms will have different answers for different authors, readers, times and places. The same question will be treated differently according to what common ground is shared by an author and different audiences. And since the social and political meaning of a text can be transformed by its impact on some public discourse running independently of the author's work, different meanings can be bestowed on the same text in different contexts.

If this is so, sociological objectivity cannot be defined in terms of unbiased access to the propositional contents of descriptive sentences. Propositional content itself will be identifiable only relatively, and will depend on the role of a sentence in a particular discourse. Nor will the sentences of which sociological texts are composed be descriptive in the sense of excluding evaluations. We have seen that meaning, including evaluative meaning, attaches to rhetorical devices such as order, presence, emphasis and perspective, as well as to interacting associations between parts of texts. None of these can be excluded from sociological works. Moreover, consistently patterned uses of these devices constitute authors' 'communicative attitudes': their explanatory preferences—in terms, say, of giving ordinary person explanations for some types of action and not others. There is no reason why authors should be supposed to wish to remove these attitudes from texts even if it were possible; to change them would be to change attitudes to other people which as a rule their owners can be assumed to consider justified.

As an alternative to unattainably and damagingly stringent 'positivist' standards in the human sciences, argumentative methods of reaching agreement are increasingly widely being married to a conception of science based on a consensus theory of truth. According to this view, methodology itself would be subsumed under rhetoric as a catalogue of different methods for reaching public coincidence of opinion. Ziman stresses social practices for reaching agreement and points out that they are central to the pursuit of science;[10] rhetoricians thinking along these lines take frequent recourse to the work of Toulmin, Polanyi and Kuhn. The 'process' view of truth which results for writers such as Brummet is one which maintains that no form of science is capable of observing objective reality, and denies the dichotomy between what and how people know, and reality itself.[11]

Upholders of this view need not deny that the physical world exists, but they centre their assertions on the claim that it is *we* who construct the meaningfulness of our own experiences, in interaction.[12] This view is compatible with much scientific and social-scientific practice, and it is commendable for making a firm connection between arguing and action. Seeing scientific arguing as *urging* particular viewpoints, and thus as a form of action itself, undermines the dichotomy between thought and action which I should oppose for reasons different from these writers'.

Nevertheless I do not wish to support this view of arguing in the social sciences. I do not want to endorse the notion of a bare-bones sociology which argues without being rhetorical, but neither do I want to adopt a position which introduces notions such as those of 'degrees' of truth or of truth changing over time. This seems to me tantamount to abandoning the concepts of truth and falsity altogether. I have instead argued that there are different ways of perceiving what is true, and different ways of truth-telling. This allows for more than one true account of a state of affairs but it by no means rules out that we should also claim to be able to identify some accounts which are definitely false.

A consensualist view seems to me in danger of failing to give serious consideration to (social) science as searching for opinions which are adequate to reality; and it abandons the notion of truth as a 'regulatory idea' which is postulated as in some way independent of what people happen to agree on at a particular place and time.[13] Hence this view appears to risk allowing ultimate authority in the establishment of opinions simply to the most powerful arguer.

It seems to me probable that without the support of a community of reasonable people one is unlikely to reach reasonable conclusions; but this does not settle the question how one establishes the reasonableness of a group or its views. To assume that the natural constitution of mankind is such that a 'correct' consensus will ever, even 'in principle', be reached seems to me arbitrary, or else wishful thinking.[14]

The notion of rhetorical communication makes it possible to recognise that in presenting what he or she hopes approaches an adequate view of a situation, a sociological author is completing a whole of which the reader being addressed possesses a certain part; and complementing this part is very likely to dislodge some beliefs which the reader had previously associated with it. We have seen that however convinced sociologists may be of their analyses, they do not try to communicate them to everyone at once. The notion of correctness in their communication cannot be understood independently of that of appropriateness in interaction with this particular audience.

Thus rhetorical communication is an integral part of what makes sociological texts explanatory. To give a sociological explanation is to make a social situation intelligible; if it is to be made intelligible it must be made intelligible *to somebody*, and rhetorical communication is in its essence addressed communication. Making a social situation understandable involves reorganising and resorting anticipations which do not belong only to the author, but which form part of a consensus between him or her and the reader, and which is open to change during a transaction which affects them both.

Hence it is necessary to reverse the priority usually given to following methodical procedures in sociology and to take much more notice of whether these procedures are embedded in an argumentatively acceptable process. This means that authors should claim responsibility for their possession of personal communicative attitudes, which influence the ways in which they implement their methods as well as the ways in which they perceive their subjects and persuade their readers. Taking such responsibility – making room for the fact that sociological writers are people too – entails a certain degree of rigour in inspecting the ethical and political implications of one's own stance, though it is no business of this book to say in what the standards concerned should consist. But presumably it is true to say that the personal perceptiveness needed to apply them is not immeasurably greater than that required in everyday life, where it is also usual for people to learn from interaction with other people, and not from ownerless procedural blueprints.

Appendix:
The Choice of Books

I used three criteria in choosing books to examine in this text. First, their selection should be connected with their place in modern sociology and not with any *special* suitability they might have for rhetorical treatment. Second, I wanted them to be fairly diverse in subject-matter and approach, but not so eccentric as to be unrepresentative of their discipline. Third, I did not want them to be bunched together too closely in time. I object to the idea that any work not written within the last five years is not worth reading, and I wanted to avoid the danger of paying excessive attention to some feature dictated by a passing fashion.

In order to obtain such a selection, I used the results of surveys which I had made in 1973 and 1980. On each of these occasions I wrote to a random sample of half the members of the British Sociological Association, asking respondents to name 'at least three sociological works containing explanations which [they] regard[ed] highly' (cf. Heath and Edmondson, 1981). I stressed that I was using the term 'explanation' very loosely and indeed wished respondents to give it their own interpretations.

In the answers to the 1973 survey, the most frequently mentioned works, excluding *Suicide* and *The Protestant Ethic*, were as follows. The *Affluent Worker* series by Goldthorpe *et al.*, *The Blackcoated Worker* by Lockwood, *The Management of Innovation* by Burns and Stalker, and *Family and Social Network* by Bott, were mentioned nine times. *The Social Origins of Dictatorship and Democracy* by Barrington Moore, *Relative Deprivation and Social Justice* by Runciman, and *The Social Construction of Reality* by Berger and Luckmann, were mentioned eight times. *Industrial Organization: Theory and Practice* by Woodward, *Prosperity and Parenthood* by Banks, *Race, Community and Conflict* by Rex and Moore, and *Outsiders* by Becker, were mentioned six times. *Asylums* by Goffman, *Hightown Grammar* by Lacey, and

Knowledge and Control by Young, were mentioned five times. Though Blau's name was mentioned six times, *The American Occupational Structure* was mentioned four times.

I shall not list here the other works mentioned four times or fewer. (170 respondents between them gave titles of 340 works, of which only 88 appeared more than once.) If we look at the 1973 list from the point of view of frequently-mentioned authors rather than books, the most important additions to the above list are that Goffman's name is mentioned twelve times (and Marx's only thirteen; Durkheim was mentioned twenty-five times and Weber twenty-six); Parsons appears seven times, Lipset six times, and Bernstein, Cicourel, Evans-Pritchard, Gouldner and Wilson five times.

Again excluding Marx, Weber and Durkheim, the most frequently mentioned books in 1980 were Willis's *Learning to Labour*, mentioned fifteen times, the *Affluent Worker* series and Goffman's *Asylums*, mentioned eight times; *Labour and Monopoly Capital* by Braverman, *The Social Origins of Depression* by Brown and Harris, *Social Mobility and the Class Structure* by Goldthorpe, *Race, Community and Conflict* by Rex and Moore and *British Factory – Japanese Factory* by Dore were all mentioned five times. (On this occasion a total of 162 respondents provided 431 citations.)

I did not feel myself bound to proceed rigidly according to these results, but in this book I have analysed the only three modern works to be mentioned five times or more in both surveys: the *Affluent Worker* series, *Asylums* and *Race, Community and Conflict*. *Learning to Labour* was clearly most popular in 1980, and it provided an approach which differed from the others in politics, methodology and subject-matter. *The American Occupational Structure* I chose because I wanted to deal with a strongly positivist work. Woodward's and Dore's books are respectively earlier and later examples of 'classical British empiricism', not unrepresentative of the tenor of what I think modern sociology is taken to be in England.

The surveys to which I have referred were not pieces of attitudinal research, but on occasion they generated impressions which are relevant to the present work. For example, respondents tended to select works from some area of subject-matter they found interesting, rather than because of their correctness as applications of some particular methodology. Support for a work showing one methodological direction did not seem to preclude admiration for another with a quite different methodological allegiance.

Also, though many reasons which respondents gave for citing particular works were compatible with recognised methodological approaches, many others were not; and sometimes both types of reason were advanced by the same person. Many books were commended for providing 'insights' into their fields. One respondent praised a work of ' "introspective" sociology' which, he said, ' "made sense" ' to himself as a teacher 'as an explanation of the strains and conflicts inherent in the teacher's role'. Another wrote, 'I rate highly studies which provide an account of an organisation which seems to *convey the reality* of the organisation to me . . . ' (my emphasis). A third commended books which 'spark off thought' in the reader, enabling him or her to teach with 'conviction and revived enthusiasm'. This respondent compared this effect with that of reading Bellow's novels for a teacher of English, and accounted for it in terms of providing 'illustrations and examples' which made him feel that he had 'pushed [his] horizons a bit further out'. All these remarks display an awareness and appreciation of the rhetorical effects of sociological works.

Once more I should like to take the opportunity of thanking all those who were kind enough to respond to the survey questions.

Notes and References

INTRODUCTION

1. Weber, *Economy and Society*, pp. 4–5.
2. Jarvie, *Concepts and Society*, p. 29.
3. Weber, op. cit., pp. 4ff.
4. Cf. Rex's view that religious action is not really understandable in sociology because it is not clearly directed to the attainment of a purpose; *Key Problems in Sociological Theory*, pp. 80, 92.
5. Weber, op. cit., p. 5. Cf. the first paragraph of his 'Subjectivity and Determinism', in Giddens (ed.), *Positivism and Sociology*, p. 23.
6. Rex, 'Typology and Objectivity', p. 34.
7. Weber, *Economy and Society*, p. 6.
8. Weber, op. cit., p. 11.
9. Weber, *The Protestant Ethic and the Spirit of Capitalism*, pp. 48ff.
10. Schutz, *Collected Papers*, vol. I, p. 36.
11. Schutz, op. cit., p. 65. G. H. Mead makes a point comparable with Schutz's in *Mind, Self and Society*, pp. 1–41.
12. Hempel, *Aspects of Scientific Explanation*, p. 424. In 'Communication and the Foundations of the Humanities' Apel reproaches positivist writers with failing to ask how explanations come to be understood (p. 13), but I think this reproach should be made against interpretivists too.
13. Part of the history of this view is summarised in Florescu, 'Rhetoric and its Rehabilitation in Contemporary Philosophy', pp. 193–205. (Cf. 'Can Rhetoric Provide a New Basis for Philosophizing?' by Grassi.) For its eighteenth-century flowering see *The Concept of Taste in Eighteenth-Century British Aesthetic Theory* by Tadhg Foley, whom I should like to thank for his learned and instructive conversation on this topic.
14. Locke, *An Essay Concerning Human Understanding*, part III, ch. IX, para. 4.
15. Sprat, *History of the Royal Society*, p. 113.
16. See for example Sacks, Schegloff and Jefferson: 'A Simplest Systematics for the Organization of Turn-Taking for Conversation'.
17. Habermas, 'What is Universal Pragmatics?', in *Communication and the Evolution of Society*, p. 3. For other criticisms of this notion of *Verständigung* see Keat, *The Politics of Social Theory*, pp. 180–98. For some of Habermas's views on rhetoric see his *Theorie des Kommunikativen Handelns*, which is intended to replace some of his earlier work (and, interestingly, expresses admiration for Talcott Parsons).
18. Cf. Grimaldi, 'Studies in the Philosophy of Aristotle's *Rhetoric*', *passim*.

19. Gadamer, *Wahrheit und Methode*, p. 18.
20. Dyck, 'Argumentation in der Schule: ein Streifzug', p. 137. Dyck's approach is criticised by Hess-Lüttich and Wörner: 'Konsens und Kontroverse, Plausibilität und Partei'. See also Duhamel's excellent 'The Function of Rhetoric as Effective Expression'.
21. Aristotle, *Rhetorica*, 1358b 1.
22. For example, by Cope in *An Introduction to Aristotle's Rhetoric*, pp. 30–2.
23. Plato's friendliest views on rhetoric are expressed in the *Phaedrus*, though it could be argued that even the *Gorgias* does not condemn it entirely.
24. Cf. Kopperschmidt, *Allgemeine Rhetorik*, p. 17.
25. Quintilian, *Institutio Oratoria*, vols. I, IV.
26. Cf. Murphy, 'The Metarhetorics of Plato, Augustine and McLuhan: A Pointing Essay', p. 209.
27. Cf. Murphy, *Rhetoric in the Middle Ages*, pp. 269ff.
28. This work was for a long time erroneously attributed to Cicero; its real author is unknown.
29. Cf. e.g. Brüggemann and Haas, 'Humanismus und Barock', section 2.
30. Luther, *Kritische Gesamtausgabe*, Weimar Edition, vol. 2, p. 506. Luther also describes God's communication with human beings in terms of rhetoric: vol. 40, p. 59.
31. Howell, 'Baroque Rhetoric: A Concept at Odds with its Setting', pp. 8ff.
32. According to Puttenham in *The Arte of Englishe Poesie*, 'Figurative speech is a novelty of language evidently (and yet not absurdly) estranged from the ordinary habit and manner of our daily talk and writing, and figure itself is a certain lively or good grace set upon works, speeches and sentences to some purpose and not in vain, giving them ornament or efficacy by many manner of alterations in shape, in sound and also in sense' (p. 159).
33. For modern developments of the Puttenham thesis see Plett, *Rhetorik: Kritische Positionen zum Stand der Forschung*, or Dubois *et al.*, *Rhétorique générale*.
34. Cf. Howell, *Eighteenth-century British Logic and Rhetoric*. For a view of American nineteenth-century rhetoric, see e.g. Einhorn, 'Consistency in Richard Whately: The Scope of his Rhetoric' (and bibliography).
35. Jens in his article 'Rhetorik' also associates the rise or fall of interest in rhetoric with developments affecting public participation in political affairs (pp. 433–4). Cf. Lepenies, *Melancholie und Gesellschaft*, pp. 76ff.
36. I shall refer here to (but not summarise) the 1969 translation which arose from American interest in rhetoric.
37. Sprat, op. cit., p. 113.
38. Quoted in Murphy, *Rhetoric in the Middle Ages*, p. 51.
39. Skinner, *Verbal Behavior*, p. 420.
40. Aristotle, *Rhetorica*, 1355b 26f.
41. Ar. *Rhet.*, 1357a 24ff.
42. Ar. *Rhet.*, 1357a 24f.
43. Ar. *Rhet.*, 1357a 5ff.
44. Ar. *Rhet.*, 1355b 1f.
45. Cicero, *De Inventione*, XXIX, p. 85.
46. See below, Chapter 5 section 3.
47. Hempel, *Aspects of Scientific Explanation*, pp. 463ff. On pp. 479ff. Hempel tries to apply a rational choice explanation to the conduct of a pre-eminently rational

individual – Bismarck, editing the Ems telegram – and concludes that even in this case such an explanation does not work.

48. Johnstone, 'From Philosophy to Rhetoric and Back'.
49. Cf. Toulmin, *The Uses of Argument; Human Understanding*. Fisher, 'Rationality and the Logic of Good Reasons' makes some interesting observations on this topic, though from my point of view is too much inclined to keep and combine separate notions of rationality and reasonableness.

1 RHETORIC AND SOCIOLOGY

1. Cf. 'Masculinity in Philosophy' by Keat, though the term 'masculinism' in an early version of this paper has now been replaced by 'genderism'.
2. Storr links a writer's personality traits with the type of philosophy he or she is likely to produce when he refers to the view that Descartes achieved his 'detachment and objectivity' and his creation of 'an ideal world to compensate for the disappointments of reality' as a result of 'maternal deprivation' which led him to flee 'unruly and destructive emotion' (*Human Aggression*, p. 121). To judge by the reproaches nowadays heaped on Descartes for his influence on subsequent philosophy, many people must wish that he had had a different psychological constitution.
3. Aristotle, *Rhetorica*, 1356a 2f.
4. Ar. *Rhet.*, 1378a 8f.
5. According to the pamphlet *Notes for Writers* of B Phil and D Phil theses in sociology in Oxford, examiners soon come to decide whether they 'can trust the writer's judgement' or not.
6. Perelman and Olbrechts-Tyteca, *The New Rhetoric*, p. 18; *vid.* also p. 17.
7. See Schutz, op. cit., III, p. 120; I, pp. 14–15.
8. Booth, *Modern Dogma and the Rhetoric of Assent*, p. 101.
9. Ar. *Rhet.*, 1356a 6ff.
10. Ar. *Rhet.*, 1356a 3.
11. Ar. *Rhet.*, Bk I, ch. 1.
12. Made e.g. by Willard, *The Conception of the Auditor in Aristotle's Political Theory*, p. 236.
13. Plato, *Phaedrus*, 271ff.; this edition pp. 90ff.
14. Ar. *Rhet.*, 1356a 22–25.
15. Ar. *Rhet.*, 1356a 15f.
16. Cf. Ar. *Rhet.*, 1356a 19f.
17. For a more strictly logical treatment than I am giving here, see the following articles by M. H. Wörner: 'Enthymeme–Ein Rückgriff auf Aristoteles in Systematischer Absicht', esp. pp. 96ff.; ' "Pathos" als Überzeugungsmittel in der Rhetorik von Aristoteles', pp. 65ff., and 'Charakterdarstellung und Redestil'.
18. Cf. M. H. Wörner, 'The Role and Function of Special Topoi Related to Choice in Aristotle's Rhetoric'; Wim de Pater, 'La Fonction du Lieu et de l'Instrument dans les *Topiques*'; Otto Bird, 'The Rediscovery of the "Topics": Professor Toulmin's Inference-Warrants'.
19. In general these authors make a different use of rhetorical figures from mine,

and I have selected from their work what seems especially suitable for analysing sociological texts.

20. Perelman and Olbrechts-Tyteca, op. cit., pp. 490ff.
21. Ibid., pp. 494ff.
22. Ibid., p. 494.
23. See ibid., Part III, ch. 5.
24. Ibid., p. 16.
25. Ibid., p. 116.
26. Emphasis is given a more complex treatment in the *Rhetorica ad Herennium* (pp. 401–3).
27. This is termed 'ocular demonstration' in the *Rhetorica ad Herennium* (pp. 405–9).
28. See e.g. Dubois *et al.*, op. cit.
29. Even Comte in his *Positive Philosophy* admits this (vol II, p. 96). (Though note that this work is not always as entirely 'positivist' as it is represented; see e.g. vol. I, pp. 3–4 and vol. II, pp. 97–8 on theory-laden perceptions.)
30. Perelman and Olbrechts-Tyteca, *The New Rhetoric*, p. 487.
31. I owe this suggestion to Kenneth McDonald.
32. See *The Structure of Scientific Revolutions* (where I *treat* 'paradigm' as having this meaning; see n. 34 below).
33. Cf. Wörner, *Performative und sprachliches Handeln*, p. 78, for distinctions between levels at which utterances are intended as, count as, and are taken as cases of X-ing.
34. Cf. e.g. Masterman, 'The Nature of a Paradigm', p. 61; she claims to find at least twenty-one senses of 'paradigm' used by Kuhn.
35. Achinstein, *Law and Explanation*, p. 61.
36. Ibid., p. 80.
37. Black makes this distinction in *Rhetorical Criticism*, pp. 11–14, and Pollman in *Literaturwissenschaft und Methode*, vol. I, pp. 27ff., divides literature into informative writing whose language is subservient to its subject-matter and that in which language has some special role to play. This is hardly a division which I can accept for general use.

2 QUALITATIVE SOCIOLOGY AND ARGUING FROM EXAMPLE

1. Aristotle, *Rhetorica*, 1358b 1f (see above).
2. Jarvie, *Concepts and Society*, p. 16.
3. Cf. Goldthorpe, 'A Revolution in Sociology?' and 'Trends in Class Mobility'.
4. Cf. Perelman and Olbrechts-Tyteca, *The New Rhetoric*, pp. 65ff.
5. Keat, *The Politics of Social Theory*, p. 42.
6. Schutz says that the sociologist should construct 'a set of typical notions, purposes, goals, which are assumed to be invariant in the specious consciousness of the imaginary actor-model', a 'homunculus or puppet' whose behaviour is to be 'interrelated in interaction patterns' with that of others. Then 'the circumstances within which such a model operates may be varied' while the 'elements relevant to the performing of the course-of-action patterns observed' are held constant.

Thus the sociologist can 'predict how such a puppet or system of puppet might behave under certain conditions and . . . discover certain "determinat relations between a set of variables, in terms of which . . . empiricall ascertainable regularities . . . can be explained". This, however, is Professo Nagel's definition of a theory' (*Collected Papers*, vol. I, pp. 64–5).

7. This may not always apply to sociological *articles*, for the reasons canvassec above.

8. Sitwell describes Lytton Strachey at a party as 'one of the most typical and on of the rarest persons in this assembly' (*Laughter in the Next Room*, p. 22), meanin apparently that his eccentricity itself pointed up features common to the whole gathering. This notion of typicality may refer to a feature taken to be basic to a phenomenon rather than in obvious terms quantitatively dominant in it. Wher the same author mentions someone's 'typical Irish voice, generous anc compelling' (op. cit., p. 111), he does not imply that he supposes 66 per cent o Irish people to have such voices, but that this voice expresses a quality which he himself associates with being Irish. By contrast, when Dickens mentions Miss Squeers's 'lonely cornelian heart, typical of her own disengaged affections (*Nicholas Nickelby*, p. 275), he is referring to a symbol which is significant by public convention. I suggest that all these usages and more are still to be founc in sociological books.

9. The traditional example occurs in Aristotle's *Rhetorica*, 1357b 12f. I owe this interpretation of it to Klaus Jacobi.

10. *Soziale Interaktion und literarischer Dialog*, vol. I, pp. 289ff.: 'Medialität und Multimedialität. Zum Verhältnis von Kanal, Code, Sinn und Modus in Zeichensystemen'.

11. Cf. Edmondson, *Rhetoric and Sociological Explanation*, ch. 6, for a treatment of 'gestural recording' in Becker's *Outsiders*.

12. Cf. Maier, *Die Syllogistik des Aristoteles*, vol. II, I, pp. 438ff. I am not using the term 'rhetorical induction' in an Aristotelian sense here.

3 'SCIENTIFIC SOCIAL THEORY' AS SUASIVE DIALOGUE

1. I shall deal with this topic again in Chapter 5 below.

2. I owe this point to John Goldthorpe.

3. Aristotle mentions some of the steps speakers may take in connection with 'ethos'; they include getting someone else to mention one's good qualities in an introduction or foreword (*Rhet.*, 1418b 24–33).

4. Probably Crowder is correct in attributing to Duncan an 'American egalitarian achievement ideology' ('A Critique of Duncan's Stratification Research', p. 19), though Blau and Duncan specifically deny espousing all the tenets of the 'Davis and Moore' attitude to stratification (p. 7). But cf. Goldthorpe's rebuttals both of the claim that mobility research itself is necessarily linked to one particular political position and the claim that political bias is irrelevant to it ('Mobilité Sociale et Intérêts Sociaux').

I see no reason to assume that evaluative positions need necessarily lead to mistakes in data-evaluation, though there is some evidence that this may have happened in Blau's and Duncan's case. For evidence that they are mistaken in supposing that contemporary industrial societies are evolving increasingly better relative mobility chances, see Hauser *et al.*, both 1975 papers, and Goldthorpe, 'Trends in Class Mobility'.

5. Iser in *Der Implizite Leser* analyses the reading of novels in such terms as the reader's anticipation and retrospection of different parts of a text and the possibility that such activities will prove self-revelatory to him. Iser focuses on moral and imaginative responses in reading, and is not concerned with the reader's influence on the *author*.

6. Contrast Perelman and Olbrechts-Tyteca in *The New Rhetoric*, pp. 31ff., on the universal audience.

7. These conventions remain to be made explicit, but I hope that this work goes some way towards doing so.

8. Cf. Aristotle's and Augustine's views on the relationship between speaker and hearer as an influence on the nature of the communication and comprehension between them. It seems to me that this idea should be investigated in terms of the psychology of perception and communication.

9. See also Blau and Duncan, p. 19: 'If the reader studies this table he may discern . . . '

10. E.g. ibid., p. 203, ch. 10; p. 241.

11. In Duncan's very technical ch. 4, for example, overt appeals or references to the reader occur on pp. 130, 131, 133, 141–2, 150, 151, 152, 153, 154, 155.

12. See e.g. pp. 183, 392, 398; Blau and Duncan ask for research on individuals' reactions to social mobility, and comparative studies between nations, as well as other matters. Woodward also explicitly addresses future researchers, e.g. on pp. 74, 132, 168, 233.

13. For example, the authors advocate drives against 'the vicious circle resulting from discrimination and poverty' but are reluctant to eliminate 'all *dis*advantages that flow from membership in a family of orientation' where advantages would disappear by the same token (p. 205), and they advise adjustment of educational facilities to help children from large families, as well as aid for black people 'on many different levels' (p. 442).

14. Other references to readers' preferences and attitudes occur on pp. 168–9, 377.

15. Thus I am using the term 'metaphor' in a very broad sense rather than, say, distinguishing between different types of model or image like Perman ('The Artful Face of Sociology').

16. Cf. Nisbet (*Sociology as an Art Form*) or Brown (*A Poetic for Sociology*), who insist on the centrality of metaphor to sociological thought in general.

17. M. Hesse, *Models and Analogies in Science*.

18. Parkin, *Max Weber*, p. 33.

19. Kemp, 'Controversy in Scientific Research and Topics of Communication', pp. 515, 519.

20. Cf. Popper, *Conjectures and Refutations*, etc.; but Weimer ('Science as a Rhetorical Transaction', p. 295) points out that although Popper sees science as argument, he sees argument as unrhetorical and strictly deductive.

21. The author remarks in her Preface that 'it is now difficult to understand why the booklet created so much controversy at the time it was published;' she explains this by saying that her conclusions were interpreted 'as undermining completely the principles and concepts of classical management theory' and

attacking management education (p. vi). Cf. the introduction by Dawson and Wedderburn to the 1980 second edition of the book: 'Joan Woodward and the Development of Organization Theory'.

22. I have slightly simplified this account from p. 139. It does in fact contain some explanatory terms, but none which explains the author's conclusion. She presents it as if she had deduced logically from factors a, b and c to a predictable d; but her conclusion cannot be inferred with deductive certainty, because people only *often* quarrel in such circumstances. Woodward's argument is really a case of enthymematic arguing; see Chapter 5 below.

4 MEANING, PEOPLE AND RHETORICAL INDUCTION

1. Bitzer, 'The Rhetorical Situation', *passim*.
2. Cf. Austin, *How To Do Things With Words*, ch. 4, and Wörner, *Performative und sprachliches Handeln*, pp. 42–59; Ryle, *Dilemmas*, ch. 8; Searle (*Speech Acts*, pp. 42ff.) on Grice's analysis of meaning, and Strawson, *Logico-Linguistic Papers*, ch. 8: 'Intention and Convention in Speech Acts'.
3. This contrast is made very explicit in Eagleton's *Marxism and Literary Criticism*.
4. See n. 6, Chapter 2 above.
5. But for reservations about the scientific status of interviewing results, see Hopf, 'Die Pseudo-Exploration' and 'Soziologie und qualitative Sozialforschung'.
6. Platt, *Towards a Speech Act Theory of Literary Discourse*, p. xi.
7. Cf. Worsley's praise of Burridge for writing 'graphically', 'with a novelist's touch' (*The Trumpet Shall Sound*, p. 219).
8. Sartre, *Anti-Semite and Jew*, p. 8.
9. For Aristotle on the function of stories and fables in reasoning, see *Rhetorica, II*, 20. He says that stories which are relevantly analogous to the situation with which one is dealing can present hearers with grounds for accepting a given conclusion. (For example, if someone is considering whether to take up a job abroad, the speaker might tell him/her a story about a friend who did so and suffered from homesickness. This might give the hearer a reason for not going.)

   Stories might also function in terms of sensitisation, as 'epiphanies' to remove particular blocks to comprehension, or else (like this one from Dore) to illustrate the foolishness of given attitudes. None the less it would seem unwise for sociologists to *make up* stories. The nearest Dore comes to doing so is when he quotes an account by an English Electric foreman who is imagining why it is that people fail to come to work on a wet Monday morning during a bus strike (pp. 2–3).
10. For example, *The Logic of Scientific Discovery*, pp. 315 ff. Popper says that induction interpreted stringently leads either to infinite regress or to apriorism; but I do not think that sociologists' practice suggests the need for a *stringent* interpretation of the term.

5 RHETORICAL DEDUCTION IN SOCIOLOGICAL TEXTS

1. Most accounts of the enthymeme misunderstand it as simply a shortened or informally expressed deduction; works which do not do this are the articles by Wörner mentioned in Chapter 1, n. 17, and Sprute's *Die Enthymemtheorie des Aristoteles*.

2. The articles on topoi mentioned in Chapter 1, n. 18 are suggestive and interesting; Brunschwig's Introduction to *Aristote – Topiques* is usually cited in this connection for its logical virtues (XXXVIII–XLV). But the definitive work on this subject remains to be written.

3. Grimaldi in *The Enthymeme in Aristotle* terms topoi 'the varied, particular focal points of an individual subject which throw light on the subject and the field of knowledge it represents' (pp. 119–20), and in 'The Aristotelian *Topics*' he says they are 'sources for informative, factual material upon the subject of discussion' (p. 182). I should say that they also define what *counts* as reasonable to expect within a given culture (see n. 9 below).

4. Aristotle, *Rhetorica*, 1397b 12–27.

5. Ar. *Rhet.*, 1401a 24–1401b3.

6. The explanatory value of truisms is defended by Scriven in 'Truisms as the Grounds for Historical Explanations' (see p. 463).

7. This example seems to support the contention that (social) science involves making *assertions* (Weimer's 'Science as a Rhetorical Transaction', pp. 9ff.). The 'technological' theorists do not just claim that *if* they were right, certain consequences would follow; they claim that they have found origins for states of affairs which do obtain.

8. 'Abduction and Induction', in *The Philosophical Writings of Peirce*, ed. J. Buchler.

9. Cf. Ar. *Rhet.*, 1380b 35 – 1381a 1: 'We may describe friendly feeling towards any one as wishing for him what you believe to be good things, not for your own sake but for his, and being inclined, so far as you can, to bring these things about.' Both Aristotle and Goldthorpe *et al.* define what, in general, *counts* as friendly behaviour; what we envisage in connection with it, and usually bargain for when friendship is being shown. This conception is a source of expectations, and at the same time it allows us to make inferences in connection with friendship.

10. Schutz, *Collected Papers*: 'Our knowledge in daily life is not without hypotheses, inductions, and predictions, but they all have the character of the approximate and the typical' – like ' "cook-book" ' knowledge (vol. II, p. 73).

11. Similarly, Scriven (op. cit., pp. 463ff.) denies that 'normic statements', which include the 'truisms' on which he takes many historical explanations to depend, should be expected to function as Hempelian generalisations; these are generally unavailable, or, when they can be made, too specific to provide explanations for actual occurrences.

12. Dealing with a more manipulative example, Rivera analyses Ignatius's *Exercises* to show the persuasive value of allowing active participation to those one wishes to convince (*Kommunikationsstrukturen* . . .).

13. Cf. Perelman and Olbrechts-Tyteca, *The New Rhetoric*, pp. 411ff.

14. Attacks such as this are not restricted to sociology. Feyerabend in *Against*

Method shows by taking the case of Galileo that very startling attacks on an audience's preconceptions may be made by natural scientists too.

15. For these two topoi see notes 4 and 5 above.
16. Ar. *Rhet.*, 1400a 22–29.
17. Harré, *The Philosophies of Science*, p. 40.
18. Cf. Mortimore, 'Rational Action', pp. 93ff.
19. Gibson, 'Arguing from Rationality', p. 114.
20. Cf. Perelman, 'The Rational and the Reasonable', ch. 11 of *The New Rhetoric and the Humanities*.
21. Parkin, *Max Weber*, pp. 36–7.
22. Weber, *Economy and Society*, p. 6.
23. Perelman and Olbrechts-Tyteca, *The New Rhetoric*, p. 300.
24. Cf. ch. 2 of Keat's excellent *The Politics of Social Theory*: 'Value-Freedom and Socialist Theory'.
25. Rex, *Key Problems of Sociological Theory*, pp. 165–6.

6 SOCIOLOGY, RHETORIC AND PERSONAL COMMUNICATION

1. Schutz, *Collected Papers*, vol. I, p. 55; cf. p. 44.
2. Hymes, 'On Communicative Competence', pp. 271ff.
3. See James, *The Principles of Psychology*, vol. I, ch. 10.
4. See for example Becker's *Outsiders* (commented on in Edmondson, *Rhetoric and Sociological Explanation*, ch. 6).
5. Sanders, in 'Utterances, Action and Rhetorical Inquiry', points out that the most honest of speakers must attend to what his or her actions count as, in order to communicate at all (pp. 119–20).
6. *Nonverbal Communication*, p. 3.
7. Cf. *Explanation and Human Action* by Louch, who maintains that 'observation, description and explanation of human action is only possible by means of moral categories' (p. vii).
8. Cf. Perelman and Olbrechts-Tyteca, *The New Rhetoric*, pp. 31ff.
9. Overington's claim that sociology does not deduce deductively at *all* ('The Scientific Community as Audience', p. 160) is much exaggerated. It is just that when sociologists infer deductively, their deductions need not be apparent or formally complete.
10. Ziman, *Public Knowledge: The Social Dimension of Science*. On pp. 31ff. Ziman considers the rhetorical force of these practices.
11. In 'Postmodern Rhetoric' Brummet uses Polanyi's work to try to reconcile rhetorical with experimental views of science. He is prepared to decrease adherence to the laws of logic themselves in favour of a view of the complementarity of different spheres of arguing.
12. Cf. Vatz, 'The Myth of the Rhetorical Situation', p. 157.
13. Cf. Popper, *Conjectures and Refutations*, *Objective Knowledge*.
14. And if its proponents do not expect it to be reached, its usefulness as a criterion is difficult to perceive.

Bibliography

Where there is more than one work by the same author, these are listed in alphabetical order of titles. For translations of modern works, the date in brackets is that of the original publication.

Achinstein, P. *Law and Explanation* (Oxford University Press, 1971).

Apel, K.-O. 'Communication and the Foundations of the Humanities', *Acta Sociologica*, 15, 1 (1972).

Aristotle *Rhetorica*, trans. W. Rhys Roberts (Oxford University Press, 1946).

Austin, J. L. *How To Do Things With Words* (Oxford University Press, 1955).

Becker, H., *Outsiders* (Glencoe: Free Press, 1963).

Benn, S. I. and Mortimore, G. W. (eds) *Rationality and the Social Sciences* (London: Routledge and Kegan Paul, 1970).

Bird, O. 'The Rediscovery of the "Topics": Professor Toulmin's Inference-Warrants', *Proceedings of the American Catholic Philosophical Association*, 34 (1960).

Bitzer, L. 'The Rhetorical Situation', *Philosophy and Rhetoric*, 1, 1 (1968).

Black, E. *Rhetorical Criticism: A Study in Method* (New York: Macmillan, 1965).

Black, M. *Models and Metaphors* (Cornell University Press, 1962).

Blau, P. and Duncan, O. D. *The American Occupational Structure* (New York: Wiley, 1967).

Booth, W. *Modern Dogma and the Rhetoric of Assent* (University of Chicago Press, 1974).

Brown, R. H. *A Poetic for Sociology* (Cambridge University Press, 1977).

Brüggemann, C. and Haas, E. 'Humanismus und Barock', in G. Ueding (ed.), *Einführung in die Rhetorik* (Stuttgart: J. B. Metzler, 1976).

Brummet, B. 'Postmodern Rhetoric', *Philosophy and Rhetoric*, 9, 1 (1976).

Brunschwig, J. *Aristote – Topiques*, Société d'Edition 'Les Belles Lettres' (Paris: 1967).

Cicero. *De Inventione*, trans. H. M. Hubbell, Loeb Classical Library (London and Cambridge, Mass.: Heinemann, 1949).

Cicourel, A. *Method and Measurement in Sociology* (Glencoe: Free Press, 1964).

Comte, A. (condensed trans. by H. Martineau) *Comte's Positive Philosophy* (London: Chapman, 1853).

Cope, E. M. *An Introduction to Aristotle's Rhetoric* (Cambridge University Press, 1867).

Crowder, N. D. 'A Critique of Duncan's Stratification Research', *Sociology*, vol. 8 (1974).

Dickens, C. *Nicholas Nickelby* (1839; this edn London: Collins, 1973).

Dore, R. *British Factory – Japanese Factory* (London: Allen and Unwin, 1973).

Dubois, J., *et al. Rhétorique générale* (Paris: Librairie Larousse, 1970).

Duhamel, P. A. 'The Function of Rhetoric as Effective Expression', *Journal of the History of Ideas*, 10 (1949).

Dyck, J. 'Argumentation in der Schule: ein Streifzug', *Rhetorik*, I (1980).

Eagleton, T., *Marxism and Literary Criticism* (London: Methuen, 1976).

Edmondson, R. 'Rhetoric and Sociological Explanation', unpublished D Phil thesis, Oxford, 1979.

Einhorn, L. J. 'Consistency in Richard Whately: The Scope of his Rhetoric', *Philosophy and Rhetoric*, 14, 2 (1981).

Erikson, K. (ed.) *Aristotle: The Classical Heritage of Rhetoric* (Metuchen, New Jersey: Scarecrow Press, 1974).

Feyerabend, P. *Against Method* (London: Verso Editions, 1975).

Fisher, W. R. 'Rationality and the Logic of Good Reasons', *Philosophy and Rhetoric*, 13, 2 (1980).

Florescu, V. 'Rhetoric and its Rehabilitation in Contemporary Philosophy', *Philosophy and Rhetoric*, 3, 4 (1970).

Foley, T. 'The Concept of Taste in Eighteenth-century British Aesthetic Theory', unpublished D Phil thesis, Oxford, 1981.

Gadamer, H.-G. *Wahrheit und Methode* (Tübingen: J. C. B. Mohr (Paul Siebeck), 1960).

Gibson, Q. 'Arguing from Rationality', in Benn and Mortimore (eds), *Rationality and the Social Sciences* (London: Routledge and Kegan Paul, 1970).

Giddens, A. (ed.), *Positivism and Sociology* (London: Heinemann, 1974).

Goffman, E. *Asylums* ((1961); this edn, Harmondsworth: Penguin, 1968).

Goffman, E. *The Presentation of Self in Everyday Life* ((1959); this edn, Harmondsworth: Penguin, 1969).

Goffman, E. *Relations in Public* ((1971); this edn, Harmondsworth: Penguin, 1972).

Goldthorpe, J. 'A Revolution in Sociology?', *Sociology*, 7, 3 (1973).

Goldthorpe, J. 'Mobilité Sociale et Intérêts Sociaux', *Sociologie et Société*, 8, 2 (1976).

Goldthorpe, J. 'The Experience of Social Mobility', paper to the World Congress of Sociology, Upsala, 1978(a).

Goldthorpe, J. 'Trends in Class Mobility', *Sociology*, 12, 3 (1978(b)).

Goldthorpe, J., Lockwood, D., Bechhofer, F., Platt, J. *The Affluent Worker: Attitudes and Behaviour* (vol. I), *The Affluent Worker: Political Attitudes and Behaviour* (vol. II), both 1968; *The Affluent Worker in the Class Structure* (vol. III), (Cambridge University Press, 1969).

Grassi, E. 'Can Rhetoric Provide a New Basis for Philosophizing?', *Philosophy and Rhetoric*, 11, 2 (1978).

Grimaldi, W. 'Studies in the Philosophy of Aristotle's *Rhetoric*', *Hermes, Zeitschrift für Klassische Philologie*, 25 (1972).

Grimaldi, W. 'The Aristotelian *Topics*' (1958), reprinted in Erikson, K. (ed.), *Aristotle: The Classical Heritage of Rhetoric* (Metuchen, N. J.: Scarecrow Press, 1974).

Grimaldi, W. *The Enthymeme in Aristotle* (1955), PhD diss. (Ann Arbor Microfilms, 1978).

Habermas, J. *Communication and the Evolution of Society* (1976), trans. T. McCarthy (London: Heinemann, 1979).

Habermas, J. *Theorie des kommunikativen Handelns*, vols I and II (Frankfurt am Main: Suhrkamp, 1981).

Harré, R. *The Philosophies of Science* (Oxford University Press, 1972).

Hauser, R. M. *et al.* 'Structural Changes in Occupational Mobility Among Men in the United States', *American Sociological Review*, 40 (1975(b)) (October).

Hauser, R. M. *et al.* 'Temporal Change in Occupational Mobility: Evidence for Men in the United States', *American Sociological Review*, 40 (1975(a)) (June).

Heath, A. F. and Edmondson, R. 'Oxbridge Sociology: The Development of Centres of Excellence?', in P. Abrams *et al.* (eds), *Practice and Progress: British Sociology 1950–1980* (London: Allen and Unwin, 1981).

Hempel, C. *Aspects of Scientific Explanation* (New York: Free Press, 1965).

Hess-Lüttich, E. W. B. *Soziale Interaktion und literarischer Dialog* (Berlin: Erich Schmidt Verlag, 1981).

Hess-Lüttich, E. W. B. and Wörner, M. H. 'Konsens und Kontroverse, Plausibilität und Partei. Zum Verhältnis von Argumentationstheorie und Argumentationspraxis in der Rhetorik', *Rhetorik*, 2 (1981).

Hesse, M. *Models and Analogies in Science*, revised version (University of Notre Dame Press, 1966).

Hopf, C. 'Die Pseudo-Exploration – Überlegungen zur Technik qualitativer Interviews in der Sozialforschung', *Zeitschrift für Soziologie*, Bd. 7 (1978).

Hopf, C. 'Soziologie und qualitative Sozialforschung', in C. Hopf and E. Weingarten, *Qualitative Sozialforschung* (Stuttgart: Klett-Cotta Verlag, 1979).

Howell, W. S. 'Baroque Rhetoric: A Concept at Odds with its Setting', *Philosophy and Rhetoric*, 15, 1 (1982).

Howell, W. S. *Eighteenth-century British Logic and Rhetoric* (Princeton University Press, 1971).

Hymes, D. 'On Communicative Competence', in J. Pride and J. Holmes (eds), *Sociolinguistics* (Harmondsworth: Penguin, 1972).

Iser, W. *Der Implizite Leser, Kommunikationsformen von Bunyan bis Beckett* (Munich: W. Fink-Verlag, 1972).

James, W. *The Principles of Psychology* ((1890); this edn New York: Dover, 1950).

Jarvie, I. C. *Concepts and Society* (London: Routledge and Kegan Paul, 1972).

Jarvie, I. C. *The Revolution in Anthropology* (London: Routledge and Kegan Paul, 1964).

Jens, W., 'Rhetorik', in P. Mera and W. Stammler (eds), *Reallexikon der deutschen Literaturgeschichte*, vol. 3 (Berlin and New York: de Gruyter, 1977).

Johnstone, H. W. Jr. 'From Philosophy to Rhetoric and Back', in D. M. Burks (ed.), *Rhetoric, Philosophy and Literature* (Indiana: W. Lafayette and Purdue University Press, 1978).

Keat, R. 'Masculinity in Philosophy', *Radical Philosophy*, 34 (1983).

Keat, R. *The Politics of Social Theory* (Oxford: Blackwell, 1981).

Keat, R. and Urry, J. *Social Theory as Science* (London: Routledge and Kegan Paul, 1975).

Kemp, R. 'Controversy in Scientific Research and Topics of Communication', *Sociological Review*, 25, 3 (1977).

Kopperschmidt, J. *Allgemeine Rhetorik: Einführung in die Theorie der Persuasiven Kommunikation* (Stuttgart: Kohlhammer, 1973).

Kuhn, T. *The Structure of Scientific Revolutions* (University of Chicago Press, 1962).

Lakatos, I. and Musgrave, A. *Criticism and the Growth of Knowledge* (Cambridge University Press, 1970).

Lepenies, W. *Melancholie und Gesellschaft* (Frankfurt am Main: Suhrkamp, 1969).

Locke, J. *An Essay Concerning Human Understanding* ((1690); this edn ed. A. D. Woozley, London: Fontana, 1964).

Lockwood, D. *The Black-coated Worker* (London: Allen and Unwin, 1958).

Louch, A. R. *Explanation and Human Action* (Oxford: Blackwell, 1966).

Lubbock, P. *The Craft of Fiction* (London: Cape, 1921).

Luther, M. *Kritische Gesamtausgabe* (Weimar edition, 1913).

Maier, H. *Die Syllogistik des Aristoteles* (Hildesheim/New York: Georg Olms, 1970).

Masterman, M. 'The Nature of a Paradigm', in I. Lakatos and A. Musgrave (eds), *Criticism and the Growth of Knowledge* (Cambridge University Press, 1970).

Mead, G. H. *Mind, Self and Society*, vol. I ((1934); this edn ed. C. W. Morris, Chicago University Press, 1962).

Mill, J. S. *A System of Logic* ((1843); this edn Longmans, Green and Co., 1906).

Mills, C. Wright *The Power Elite* (New York: Oxford University Press, 1956).

Mortimore, G. W. 'Rational Action', in S. I. Benn and G. W. Mortimore (eds), *Rationality and the Social Sciences* (London: Routledge and Kegan Paul, 1970).

Murphy, J. J. *Rhetoric in the Middle Ages* (Berkeley: University of California Press, 1974).

Murphy, J. J. 'The Metarhetorics of Plato, Augustine and McLuhan: A Pointing Essay', *Philosophy and Rhetoric*, 4, 4 (1971).

Nagel, E. *The Structure of Science* (New York: Harcourt, Brace and World, 1961).

Natanson, M. and Johnstone, H. W. (eds) *Philosophy, Rhetoric and Argumentation* (Pennsylvania State University Press, 1965).

Nisbet, R. *Sociology as an Art Form* (Oxford University Press, 1976).

Outhwaite, W. *Understanding Social Life: the Method Called Verstehen* (London: Allen and Unwin, 1975).

Overington, M. 'The Scientific Community as Audience: Towards a Rhetorical Analysis of Science', *Philosophy and Rhetoric*, 10, 3 (1977).

Owen, G. E. L. (ed.) *Aristotle on Dialectic – the Topics* (Oxford University Press, 1968).

Parkin, F. *Max Weber* (Chichester and London: Ellis Horwood Ltd and Tavistock Publications, 1982).

Pater, W. de 'La Fonction du Lieu et de l'Instrument dans les *Topiques*', in G. E. L. Owen (ed.), *Aristotle on Dialectic* (Oxford University Press, 1968).

Peirce, C. S., 'Abduction and Induction', in J. Buchler (ed.), *The Philosophical Writings of Peirce* (London: Routledge and Kegan Paul, 1940).

Perelman, C., *The New Rhetoric and the Humanities* (Dordrecht: Reidl, 1979).

Perelman, C. and Olbrechts-Tyteca, L. *The New Rhetoric: A Treatise on Argumentation* ((1958); University of Notre Dame Press, 1969).

Perman, D. 'The Artful Face of Sociology', *Sociology*, 12, 3 (1978).

Plato. *Gorgias*, ed. W. Hamilton (Harmondsworth: Penguin, 1960).

Plato. *Phaedrus*, ed. W. Hamilton (Harmondsworth: Penguin, 1973).

Platt, M. L. *Towards a Speech Act Theory of Literary Discourse* (Bloomington: University of Indiana Press, 1977).

Plett, H. *Rhetorik: Kritische Positionen zum Stand der Forschung* (Munich: Wilhelm Fink, 1977).

Pollmann, L. *Literaturwissenschaft und Methode*, vol. I (Frankfurt am Main: Athenäum-Verlag, 1971).

Popper, K. *Conjectures and Refutations* (London: Routledge and Kegan Paul, 1969).

Popper, K. *Objective Knowledge* (Oxford University Press, 1972).

Popper, K. *The Logic of Scientific Discovery* (London: Hutchinson, 1959).

Puttenham, G. *The Arte of Englishe Poesie* (1958) (bk. III), eds G. Willcock and A. Walker (Cambridge University Press, 1936).

Quintilian *Institutio Oratoria*, trans. H. E. Butler (London and Cambridge, Mass.: Loeb Classical Library, Heinemann, 1920).

Rex, J. *Key Problems in Sociological Theory* (London: Routledge and Kegan Paul, 1961).

Rex, J. 'Typology and Objectivity', in A. Sahay (ed.), *Max Weber and Modern Sociology* (London: Routledge and Kegan Paul, 1971).

Rex, J. and Moore, R. *Race, Community and Conflict* (London: Institute of Race Relations and Oxford University Press, 1967).

Rhetorica ad Herennium, anon.; this edn trans. H. Caplan (London and Cambridge, Mass.: Loeb Classical Library, Heinemann, 1954).

Rivera, J. de. *Kommunikationsstrukturen in den geistlichen Exerzitien des Ignatius von Loyola* (Hamburg: Buske, 1978).

Ryle, G. *Dilemmas* (Cambridge University Press, 1954).

Sacks, H., Schegloff, E., Jefferson, G. 'A Simplest Systematics for the Organization of Turn-Taking for Conversation', *Language*, 50 (1974).

Sanders, R. E. 'Utterances, Actions and Rhetorical Inquiry', *Philosophy and Rhetoric*, 11, 2 (1978).

Sartre, J.-P. *Anti-Semite and Jew* ((1946); New York: Schocken, 1948).

Schutz, A. *Collected Papers*, ed. M. Natanson (The Hague: Nijhoff, this ed. 1973).

Scriven, A. 'Truisms as the Grounds for Historical Explanations', in P. Gardiner (ed.), *Theories of History* (Glencoe: Free Press, 1959).

Searle, J. R. *Speech Acts* (Cambridge University Press, 1969).

Sitwell, O. *Laughter in the Next Room* (London: Macmillan, 1949).

Skinner, B. F. *Verbal Behavior* (New York: Appleton-Century-Crofts, 1957).

Sprat, T. *History of the Royal Society* (1667), ed. Jackson I. Cope and H. Whitmore Jones (St Louis and London, 1959).

Sprute, J. *Die Enthymemtheorie des Aristoteles* (Göttingen: Vandenhoek und Ruprecht, 1983).

Storr, A. *Human Aggression* (Harmondsworth: Penguin, 1968).

Strawson, P. *Logico-Linguistic Papers* (London: Methuen, 1971).

. Toulmin, S. *Human Understanding* (Princeton University Press, 1972).

Toulmin, S. *The Uses of Argument* (Cambridge University Press, 1958).

Ueding, G. (ed.) *Einführung in die Rhetorik* (Stuttgart: J. Metzler Verlag, 1976).

Vatz, R. 'The Myth of the Rhetorical Situation', *Philosophy and Rhetoric*, 6, 3 (1973).

Weber, M. *Economy and Society* (1922), eds Günther Roth and Claus Wittich (New York: Bedminster Press, 1968).

Weber, M. '"Objectivity" in Social Science and Social Policy' (1904), in *The Methodology of the Social Sciences* (New York: Free Press, 1949).

Weber, M. 'Subjectivity and Determinism' (1926), in A. Giddens (ed.), *Positivism and Sociology* (London: Heinemann, 1974).

Weber, M. *The Protestant Ethic and the Spirit of Capitalism* ((1905); London: Allen and Unwin, 1968).

Weimer, W. B. 'Science as a Rhetorical Transaction', *Philosophy and Rhetoric*, 6, 1 (1977).

Weitz, S. (ed.) *Nonverbal Communication* (New York: Oxford University Press, 1974).

Willard, L. A. 'The Conception of the Auditor in Aristotle's Political Theory', unpublished PhD dissertation, 1972 (Ann Arbor microfilms).

Willis, P. *Learning to Labour* (London: Saxon House, 1977).

Woodward, J. 'Industrial Behaviour – Is There a Science?', *New Society* (8 Oct 1964).

Woodward, J. *Industrial Organization: Theory and Practice* (London: Oxford University Press, 1965).

Woodward, J. *Management and Technology*, Problems and Progress in Industry 3 (London: HMSO, 1958).

Wörner, M. H. 'Charakterdarstellung und Redestil' in Kühlwein and Raasch (eds), *Stil: Komponenten, Wirkungen*, vol. II (Tübingen: Gunter Narr Verlag, 1981).

Wörner, M. H. 'Enthymeme – Ein Rückgriff auf Aristoteles in Systematischer Absicht', in O. Ballweg and T.-M. Seibert (eds), *Rhetorische Rechtstheorie* (Freiburg: Alber Verlag, 1982).

Wörner, M. H. ' "Pathos" als Überzeugungsmittel in der Rhetorik des Aristoteles', in I. Craemer-Rügenberg (ed.), *Pathos, Affekt, Gefühl* (Freiburg: Alber Verlag, 1981).

Wörner, M. H. *Performative und sprachliches Handeln* (Hamburg: Buske Verlag, 1978).

Wörner, M. H. 'The Role and Function of Special Topoi Related to Choice in Aristotle's Rhetoric', paper for the International Society for the History of Rhetoric, Florence, 1983.

Worsley, P. *The Trumpet Shall Sound* ((1957); London: Granada, revised edn, 1968).

Ziman, J. *Public Knowledge: The Social Dimension of Science* (Cambridge University Press, 1968).

Index